MINDFUL ETHNOGRAPHY

Ethnography, with all its limitations, has as its strongest impulse the quest to see and understand "others" on their own terms and to step out of our own viewpoints in order to do so. Conjoining ethnography with mindfulness, this book aims to support the best aspects of ethnography by enhancing the capacity to listen more deeply, see more expansively, keep a check on our biases and connect more compassionately with others.

Mindful Ethnography addresses a central dilemma of ethnography: the relationship of self and other. It suggests ways of viewing the world from different perspectives, getting beyond the categories of our culture and working with our own thoughts and feelings even as we aim to understand those of our participants. Chapters address various stages of ethnographic research: entering a field and seeing it for the first time, immersing in ongoing participant observation, writing up elaborated fieldnotes, analysis, the re-presentation of results and letting it go. It offers illustrations and activities for researchers to try.

The book is aimed at students and researchers who are stepping into the craft of ethnography or looking for new ways in and through ethnographic research. It is for researchers who want to integrate scholarship, social activism and spiritual pursuits in order to do research that is deeply engaged with and transformative of the world.

Marjorie Elaine Faulstich Orellana is a professor in the Graduate School of Education and Information Studies at UCLA, the associate director of the Center for the Study of International Migration and the director of faculty for the Teacher Education Program. Her ethnographic research centers on the immigrant youth in urban schools and communities.

MINDFUL ETHNOGRAPHY

Mind, Heart and Activity for Transformative Social Research

Marjorie Elaine Faulstich Orellana

Routledge
Taylor & Francis Group

LONDON AND NEW YORK

First published 2020
by Routledge

2 Park Square, Milton Park, Abingdon, Oxon OX14 4RN

and by Routledge

52 Vanderbilt Avenue, New York, NY 10017

Routledge is an imprint of the Taylor & Francis Group, an informa business

© 2020 Marjorie Elaine Faulstich Orellana

British Library Cataloguing-in-Publication Data
A catalogue record for this book is available from the British Library

Library of Congress Cataloging-in-Publication Data
A catalog record has been requested for this book

ISBN: 978-1-138-36102-7 (hbk)
ISBN: 978-1-138-36104-1 (pbk)
ISBN: 978-0-429-43283-5 (ebk)

Typeset in Bembo
by Apex CoVantage LLC.

To life, the greatest teacher

CONTENTS

FIGURES

BOXES

ACKNOWLEDGMENTS

Many people have led me, both directly and indirectly, to the understandings I share in this book: ancestors of body, mind, action and spirit. Values that were passed to me from my parents, grandparents and their parents include an orientation to be of service to others, doing one's share in collective work, humility, and the equitable sharing of resources; these often sit in tension with those that predominate in academia, but I have tried to find my own way of "doing scholarship" that honors this inheritance. I also strive to do well by my academic predecessors: this includes scholars who mentored me closely (with special thanks to Robert Rueda, Nelly Stromquist and Barrie Thorne) and those who have inspired me through their published work, in presentations, workshops and other meeting grounds. People who have walked before me on the various activist and spiritual paths I have stumbled upon and continue to traverse have inspired me with their wisdom, insights and commitments. Throughout the book, I try to acknowledge some of my many teachers in more specific ways. Apologies to anyone whose ideas have touched me that I have neglected to name; I'm sure I have missed many.

Thanks also to future generations whose beings, and imagined being-ness, motivated my writing: my children and grandchildren, and theirs, by academic, activist and spiritual lineage as well as by blood. Even as my ideas are enriched by wisdom that has been handed down to me, they are invigorated by the hope that they will be taken up, passed on and used to transform the world in ways that I cannot yet imagine by those yet to come.

Particular spaces and places on this beautiful planet inspired my writing and nurtured my soul; I offer my appreciation as well as my recognition that much of this was on unceded indigenous-heritage land. I began and finished the book in Costa Rica (unceded Chibchense/MesoAmerican land): first with the luxury of a three-month sabbatical in the fall of 2017 and then over the next two summer breaks. I hid away in my brother's home in an ecological community outside of the city, far from the distractions of daily life in California. Much of the manuscript was written – or rather, dictated into a voice recorder and later typed out – as I walked through rain forests, marveling at the many shades of green that filled my senses, punctuated here and there by a flash of bright red, yellow or orange. My recordings are accompanied by a symphony of sounds: crickets, birds, howler monkeys, drizzle, thunder and a few sudden downpours. Other segments were drafted on brief writing retreats in the deserts, mountains and beaches of California, sitting in UCLA's Botanical Garden or perched on the rooftop of my urban condominium, surrounded by city but with glimpses of the Santa Monica mountains in the distance (in unceded Gabrielina/Tongva land). My gratitude to the forests, mountains, ocean, sky and deserts, for grounding me on the earth even as I sought the intellectual and creative elevation I needed to write. Experiencing this connection in the process of writing this book was an unexpected gift.

I'm indebted to my brother Robert and sister-in-law Maria for opening their homes in Costa Rica to me for writing retreats, and for other things as well: to Maria for introducing me to mindfulness practices in the first place and continuously stretching me; to Robert for his keen, self-schooled intelligence and critical atheist's mind, asking hard questions about truth, epistemology, politics and empirical reality. The yin-yang of Robert and Maria's relationship to knowledge claims and the ways they have fused them in their lives is a lived example of non-duality: the harmony of opposing forces within a larger whole. Thanks also to Emily Gassenheimer de Friedlander for connection to the ocean, seashore and tropical storms.

Lisa O'Connell introduced me to depth psychology and neo-Jungian approaches to dream analysis, which for me have gone hand in hand with mindfulness. Teachers and peers in several creative writing and depth psychology workshops over the years (at UCLA Extension, Pacifica Graduate Institute and Esalen Retreat Center) helped me loosen the tight hold on my rational mind, enliven my academic voice and unleash more intuitive, unconscious processes as fuel for the work.

Many people read or listened to drafts of this book along the way. The eyes of these thoughtful, considerate and brilliant colleagues and students made me nervous, and none should be held accountable for the choices I made – but they helped me be more conscious of those choices. One found the work "brave," a word that startled me into remembering how hostile a place academia can be, especially for those who choose to color outside its lines, as I most certainly do here. Thanks to Sophia Ángeles, Michelle Bellino, Krystle Cobian, Lisa Dorner, Robert Faulstich, Ariana Mangual Figueroa, Janelle Franco, Tonia Guida, Maria Hon, Sarah Jean Johnson, Krissia Martínez, Andréa C. Minkoff, Laura Chávez-Moreno, Terri McCarty, Elisa Noemí, Gabrielle Oliveira, Chris Patti, Abhik Roy, Jess Schnitka, Ericka Verba and the anonymous reviewers contracted by Routledge. Special thanks to Ericka, for forty years of friendship and for helping me find my clearest, most compassionate academic voice, and to Abhik, for ten years of the same. In various places in the text or notes, I have included commentary from some of these readers, to illustrate the collaborative dialogue that happens behind the scenes but that is rarely visible in our final texts. Hannah Shakespeare and Matt Bickerton, from Routledge, were most supportive editors who waited patiently as I missed deadlines to take the time I felt this book needed. Amanda Quezada provided gracious and skillful assistance hunting up pesky details for the endnotes and helping me address some last-minute formatting nightmares. Thanks to MaryAnne and Jim Paradise for other 11th hour support. Elisa Noemí's stunning artwork graces the cover, bringing mind, heart and activity together in an evocative image. (Be sure to peek inside the third eye.)

I am indebted to the funding agencies that have supported my research throughout the years; what I learned from the projects these funders enabled filters in and through this text in countless, albeit indirect ways. Thanks to UCLA (Academic Senate, Community Partnership program, Transdisciplinary Seed grant program and Faculty Resource Account), Northwestern University, UC-Links, the International Reading Association, the Linguistic Minority Research Institute, the Center for New Racial Studies, the National Institute of Child Health and Human Development, William T. Grant Foundation and the Spencer Foundation.

Countless young people have been my teachers even as I have had the honor of guiding them. Thanks to these students, some of whose words appear in this book. My children, Andrés Gabriel and Elisa Noemí, have truly been two of my greatest teachers, with many times the wisdom that I had at their age. Young people like my children and students give me hope for the future of the planet. Considering that the words in this book will live on in some small way, even after I die, I invoke an epigraph I read on a tombstone in Guanajuato, México: "I seek to act in a way so that my conscience will not reproach me and my children and students will not denounce me." Going one step further, I'd say that I seek to act, and write, in a way that will be both *true* and *invigorating* to my own conscience as well as to my children and my students.

INTRODUCTION

We are living in a time of tremendous polarization. Walls are being erected at political borders and in our hearts. We spend much of our time talking with people who think like us, identify with us or believe the things we have chosen to believe. There are few safe spaces for engaging with people who think differently or whom we presume to *be* different in some fundamental ways – much less for building coalitions across those differences, in order to address the social problems that are threatening us all.

Ethnography, with all its limitations – made evident in its formation through the initial colonialist encounters of the Western and non-Western world – has as its strongest impulse the quest to see and understand "others" on their own terms and to step out of our own viewpoints in order to do so.[1] Contemplative practices – what is popularly called "mindfulness" – can enhance the capacity to do these things: helping us to listen more deeply, see more expansively and connect more compassionately with others as we become more aware of our own thoughts and feelings *as* thoughts and feelings. We can better notice how these arise and change as we engage in relationships and activity in the world and learn to hold our views more lightly, rather than believing everything that we think or letting our perceptions impulsively drive our actions. In conjoining ethnography with mindfulness, I suggest ways of enhancing the best aspects of ethnography and expanding our capacity to understand the lives of others with both clarity and compassion – and with compassion for ourselves, as well, as we navigate both academia and the world. This may be just what we need to nurture in all people, if we are to have any chance of addressing the planetary-level problems that confront us.

This book is aimed at people who are stepping into the craft of *ethnography* or looking for new ways in and through ethnographic research and who want to do research that is deeply engaged with and transformative of the world. I integrate my own experiences as an ethnographer and teacher of ethnographic methods; therefore, some might consider it an auto-ethnography[2] of ethnography as well as a guidebook on the craft. In this sense it differs from a more general guide to mindful inquiry, such as the lucid and comprehensive overview of various research traditions laid out by Valerie Malhotra Bentz and Jeremy J. Shapiro in their book, *Mindful Inquiry in Social Research*.[3] My focus is on practices and processes specific to ethnography.

Like Bentz and Shapiro, my commitments are to *transformative* social research in the tradition of critical scholarship and engaged Buddhism. I am inspired as well by the transformative activist stance that neo-Vygotskian scholar Anna Stetsensko calls on educational researchers to take up, making activism central to scholarship.[4] My aim in this book is to bring together these and other rather distinct perspectives – ones that are not only rarely conjoined but often actively held apart – in order to inform contemplative yet fully engaged, mindful, heart-centered, transformative, ethnographic research.

While I speak to the particular demands of ethnography, I hope the book may be useful to other kinds of methodologists. Grappling with the relationship between ourselves and our participants – the people who live, work and move in the places where we do research – and adopting practices to keep a check on our biases, open our hearts and see more deeply will benefit all researchers, not just those who trek off to spend a year or more in some kind of "field." Social science researchers and social activists who already have some experience with meditation and contemplative practices but who have kept those practices separate from their academic or political work may want to consider how the unification of heart, mind and activity can enhance the quality of our work and our sense of purpose, meaning and well-being as we do it. As well, I hope the ideas I develop in this book are useful for researchers who also view themselves as I do: as students of life.[5]

Mindfulness and social science research

Across disciplines, fields and activities, there is a growing buzz about the promise of presence, with claims about how mindfulness can be used to manage stress, center ourselves, live more fully, connect more deeply and treat ourselves and others with greater loving kindness. These treatises attempt to put into words what has been learned from thousands of years of contemplative practice from many traditions around the world and apply it to contemporary life. But only recently have these perspectives begun to percolate in social science research. And here, their focus is limited. Searches using the key words "mindfulness" and "research" bring up a slew of research studies, but mostly about the effects of mindfulness training on various aspects of human behavior.[6]

The newfound attention to mindfulness in the Western world was the starting point and impetus for this book. Adopting meditation and mindfulness practices in my own life about ten years ago – after a cancer diagnosis and other personal challenges led me to reflect deeply on my own life's meaning and purpose (or what I wanted its meaning and purpose to be) – I slowly began to integrate these perspectives into my research and scholarship. (See Box 0.1.) My motivation for writing this book was simply to share some of the insights I gained from these explorations, in ways that might be useful for ethnographers.

Some have critiqued the mindfulness movement as the co-optation of ancient spiritual practices for a neoliberal agenda in ways that draw away from addressing social injustices in the world.[7] My argument is the opposite: that conscious engagement of both heart and mind can support social science researchers who want to contribute to much-needed, uncharted paths toward social transformation. I write for those of us who want to do more than write thoughtfully about the world as it is (or as we see it) or just to critique it more mindfully but to imagine how it could be and to engage in activity that is informed by both our hearts and our minds, in order to collectively bring into being a better one.

BOX 0.1 MY JOURNEY TOWARD AWAREFULNESS

I discovered the "mindfulness movement" during the most challenging period of my life. In the summer of 2007, I received a diagnosis of breast cancer just three weeks after announcing that my twenty-four-year marriage was ending. My world seemed to be falling apart. The one thing I clung to was my academic work: my ethnographic research with immigrant children and my writing. During a year in which I went to countless medical consultations to get first, second and third opinions for what one doctor said was "the most unusual case he had ever seen" and then underwent five surgeries and a battery of other interventions, I completed my first book, reporting on the results of nearly ten years of working with immigrant youth who translated and interpreted with regularity for others.[8] Poring through field notes, listening to tape-recorded voices and looking at children's drawings and images helped at a time when I needed grounding.

At the same time, I wanted elevation. Facing my own mortality head on for the first time, I sought to tap into something larger than myself. I realized that practices I could count on when life was predictable – planning continuously into the future, assuming I had control over what would unfold – didn't serve me so well anymore. Nor did academic pursuits and values. I began grappling with larger existential questions. What did I want to do with whatever time I had left in this one precious life?[9] What really mattered to me? And what could help me live more purposefully, peacefully and powerfully?

My sister-in-law, Maria Hon, had introduced me to meditation practices when I had spent six weeks in Costa Rica working on a draft of that first book. I had initially been skeptical of Maria's interest in spiritual pursuits. My academic's mind dismissed it as New-Agey pseudo-mysticism. The critical-scholar/activist in me questioned it as cultural appropriation and a distortion of ancient traditions. Maybe it was okay for María to talk about Buddhist notions of compassion, because her ancestors may have been authentic Chinese Buddhists;[10] but me? I was a white woman of European origin; what claim could I lay on loving kindness?[11] At the time, I saw meditation as a practice for those who had the luxury of escaping from the problems of the world. I imagine there will be some readers – if you are still reading – who will view me through that lens, especially after reading the description of my sabbatical retreats to the Costa Rican rain forest.

Academia, rather than offering the benefits of a life of contemplation, may arguably have slowed my grasp of mindfulness or gotten in its way. First, academia privileges the analytical mind over the contemplative one. Even more, most disciplines actively distance themselves from anything remotely "spiritual," except as an object of study. Those scholars who engage in spiritual pursuits usually keep them quite separate from their academic work. Simultaneously, academia calls for a dispassionate, emotionless and "objective" relationship to the world. It rewards individual self-aggrandizement, competition and ego-fulfillment rather than caring, compassionate, community connections. It is also increasingly a place of frenzy: most of the scholars I know are overwhelmed by work. We spend our waking hours in front of either a computer or a classroom, just trying to keep up. And while we are privileged in economic terms relative to most people on the planet, I don't know many academics who feel they have the luxury of time to participate in long retreats and meditation classes.

For many reasons, and especially because I identified as both a scholar and an activist, skepticism kept my mind closed for many years. I clung to the beliefs of my culture, imbricated through more than sixteen years of Western schooling, disparaging what seemed like "soft," nonscientific, nonrational touchy-feely-ness. I elevated and privileged the rational mind, wearing a "critical" mind-set like armor, which kept me firmly rooted in and tethered to what I believed to be true. And I kept very busy, with exhaustion padding my armor, blocking me from other ways of experiencing the world.

But facing mortality is humbling. Moving past my resistance, I began considering a vast new arena of understanding. Through some combination of experience (trying on different forms of meditation and of being in the world) and reading (engaging with the theories that undergird these practices, from diverse spiritual and intellectual traditions), while going through and healing from the biggest crises of my life, I began to change. This is not a journey that can easily be described in words, and I do not pretend to prescribe it for you. Instead, I invite readers to contemplate your own struggles, curiosities and motivations and see where this reflection takes you. Our ideas will most certainly change and continue to unfold throughout life if we let them or don't try to stop this unfolding in its tracks.

Contemplative practices became part of my healing process, offering me things that academic work could not. I was trying to escape my own "mind chatter": what Jon Kabat-Zinn refers to as "the incessant stream of thoughts flowing through our minds (that) leaves us very little respite for inner quiet."[12] I tried on different approaches to meditation: accompanied by music, chants, mantras (Sikh-inspired kundalini yoga and meditation), the calming words of a guide, tape-recorded sounds of waterfalls and rivers, ocean waves or guitar strumming or just sitting silently, alone, or with others. To sit with whatever thoughts that came up, without trying to control or direct them, was a new practice for me. In these retreats away from my logocentric mind, I began to discover deep reservoirs of understanding and ways of knowing that had gotten lost from my own view through twenty years of Western schooling.

Until this point in my life, I had lived largely in my head. I had made endless mental lists, often externalizing them on paper. I had drawn up plans for each hour, day, week, year, projecting my life into the future and trying to anticipate every possible eventuality – except, perhaps, those eventualities that most of us seek to ignore, such as the fact that we all will someday die. My cancer diagnosis taught me that the best laid plans can turn on a dime and that illusions of control are just that: illusions. And we all, in the end, do die.[13] Slowly I began to wonder, by living continuously in a projected future, what was I missing in the here and now?

At the time, I didn't realize how important these questions would become for my work as an ethnographer, a writer and a social justice activist. This contemplative journey has been a long, slow, deep and transformative one, one that continues and takes new forms. But now that I am on this path, it shapes every aspect of my life, including my scholarly work. I still write lists, but I am more aware of myself making them. I still critique the world, but am a little more conscious of the bases for my judgments and kinder toward the objects of my critique. I am still committed to being both a serious scholar and an active social change agent, but I do so with more compassion for myself and for others and a heavier dose of humility. It is my aim to share how this has changed my approach to research and suggest ways that you may use these perspectives to guide your own ethnographic and socially transformative research, as well as your own life journeys.

The limits of labels and the dangers of co-optation

Words are important insofar as they index particular meanings and/or offer alternative ones. But labels can fix meanings, which may keep us from more fully seeing the things we have named. We may presume that we know what the labels point toward and stop trying to see with fresh eyes. When you picked up this book and saw the word "mindful" in the title, did you assume you knew what I meant or what this book would be about? Did you find yourself either aligning with or distancing yourself from the ideas you presumed you would find here?

All language is fraught with contradiction; there are no perfect words that allow us to escape our histories or the systems of oppression that shaped them. Labels can both unite and empower, and separate and divide, keeping us alienated from each other. I encourage you to notice when you have a reaction to particular words as you read. What does "mindfulness" index for you? Does "awarefulness" have less baggage attached to it? How does "mindheartedness" resonate?

Contemporary, popular uses (some would say mis-uses) of the term "mindfulness" most certainly do not align directly with the original meanings of the term in ancient Sanskrit, which connects the mind with the heart,[14] nor with those that emerge from direct experience with meditative and contemplative practices. (See Box 0.2.) In a meta-analysis of how the term has been used in academic and the popular press, Daniel Stolfeth and Valerie Manusov[15] show that academic articles tend to associate the word with attention/awareness (as properties of mind) and conflate mindfulness with meditation. This obscures its spiritual/heart-centered roots.

In this book, I use a constellation of terms that aim to connect dominant, modern, Western cultural notions of mind with the heart and also with activity or action/experience in the world. Most often, I opt for "mindfulness," because that is the term that is likely to be most familiar to contemporary readers, even as it is fraught with contradiction, given the ways it has been co-opted and commodified. Sometimes I opt for "awarefulness" – a term that shifts away from the mind and into the awareness we may gather from all our senses, as well as from our "guts," hearts or other seats of intuition. I use "mindheartedness" as a way of reminding readers that in many cultural contexts the mind and heart really cannot be separated at all. By deploying more than one term, I hope to keep the meaning of these concepts a bit more contingent, dynamic and alive. I also invite readers not just to *think* about these things but to sit with them, *feel* them, put them into action, notice your own reactions and connect them to lived experience.

In the next section, I further problematize and complexify – and then let sit – the terms that appear prominently in the title of this book: "mind," "heart" and "activity." I explain my efforts to conjoin them in the service of research, as best as I can manage to put such elusive constructs into words. I hope these will suffice as starting definitions; but they should not be taken as rigid, final or totalizing ones. May the constructs be generative as you take them into activity in your own life.

BOX 0.2 DEFINING MINDFULNESS

It is not easy to define mindfulness. I offer here a few starting definitions from other writers and teachers.

Tara Brach: Brach, a clinical psychologist who blends Western psychology with Eastern spiritual practices and who maintains an active webpage where she posts regular Dharma talks and guided meditations,[16] suggests,

> In the simplest terms, mindfulness is the intentional process of paying attention, without judgment, to the unfolding of moment-to-moment experience. It is the opposite of trance, a word I use to describe all the ways in which we – therapists and clients alike – live inside a limiting story about life. . . . Mindfulness recognizes and allows, without any resistance, all these thoughts, sensations, and feelings as they come and go.[17]

Pema Chödron: For Chodrön, a Buddhist nun and author of many books about confronting life challenges, mindfulness is about relaxing into rather than avoiding discomfort: "diving into your real issues and fearlessly befriending the difficult and blocked areas and deep-seated habitual patterns that keep us stuck in ignorance and confusion."[18]

Sam Harris: Harris, a neuroscientist and public intellectual whose work is dedicated to "spreading scientific knowledge and secular values in society," does not hesitate in offering a definition. For Harris, mindfulness is "simply a state of clear, nonjudgmental, and undistracted attention to the contents of consciousness, whether pleasant or unpleasant." He equates it with the term "clear awareness"[19] and shows its neurological correlates as well as how it can be cultivated.

Thich Naht Hahn: The Vietnamese monk Thich Naht Hahn, who is credited with bringing a form of "engaged" or activist Buddhism to the West, offers illustrations of what mindfulness looks like in everyday life, rather than pinning mindfulness down in words. He provides guidance for mindful sitting, standing, eating, walking, driving, talking on the phone, reading e-mail, washing dishes and much more. Being mindful is being full of wonder, gratitude and joy:

> We can smile, breathe, walk, and eat our meals in a way that allows us to be in touch with the abundance of happiness that is available. We are very good at preparing to live, but not very good at living. We know how to sacrifice ten years for a diploma, and we are willing to work very hard to get a job, a car, a house, and so on. But we have difficulty remembering that we are alive in the present moment, the only moment there is for us to be alive. Every breath we take, every step we make, can be filled with peace, joy, and serenity. We need only to be awake, alive in the present moment.[20]

Jon Kabat Zinn: Jon Kabat-Zinn, the founding director of the Center for Mindfulness in Medicine, Health Care, and Society at the University of

Massachusetts Medical School, is most known for his clinical applications of mindfulness to stress reduction. He tackles directly the question, "What is mindfulness?" in the opening to his bestselling book, *Wherever you go, there you are: Mindful meditation in everyday life*:

Fundamentally, mindfulness is a simple concept. Its power lies in its practice and its applications. Mindfulness means paying attention in a particular way: on purpose, in the present moment, and nonjudgmentally. This kind of attention nurtures greater awareness, clarity, and acceptance of present-moment reality.[21]

He notes that mindfulness is "simple, but not easy."[22]

Karen Neff: A developmental psychologist at the University of Texas, Austin, who studies the effects of compassion on human development, Karen Neff sees mindfulness as the starting point for self-compassion, a portal to a reality unobscured by denial or the repression of unwanted feelings:

Mindfulness refers to the clear seeing and nonjudgmental acceptance of what's occurring in the present moment. Facing up to reality, in other words. The idea that we need to see things as they are, no more, no less, in order to respond to our current situation in the most compassionate – and therefore – effective manner.[23]

Donald Rothberg: For Rothberg, the author of *The engaged spiritual life: A Buddhist approach to transforming ourselves and the world*, mindfulness is ". . . a way of being attentive to whatever is predominant in the present moment of experience, whether of our inner experiences of body sensations, emotions, thoughts, and so on, or of our outer experiences of external objects and other beings." It is characterized by "directness, focus, fullness, and ability to penetrate deeply" and its "nonjudgmental, non-preferential, and nonreactive quality." Mindfulness is about being "aware and present to what is happening, responding compassionately to suffering, understanding our interdependence, and acting with grace, equanimity, and passion in difficult circumstances."[24]

Clinical researchers: Finally, I offer a group of academics' attempt to define the term, in relation to clinical research on mindfulness. Ronald D. Siegel, Christopher K. Germer, and Andrew Olendzski write, in a chapter titled "Mindfulness: What is it? Where did it come from?" in Fabrizio Didonna's *Clinical handbook of mindfulness*.[25]

Mindfulness is an elusive, yet central, aspect of the 2,500-year-old tradition of Buddhist psychology. We can talk about mindfulness or write at length about it, but to truly understand mindfulness, we have to experience it directly. This is because mindfulness points to something intuitive and pre-conceptual. With committed practice, every person can gradually figure out how to become more and more mindful in life, even in the face of significant suffering. Cultivating mindfulness is, and has always been, a deeply personal journey of discovery.

Mind, heart and activity

I start with the assumption that for most readers, the terms "mind," "heart" and "activity" evoke very different ideas and are associated with different ways of understanding and being in the world. The Western world links the mind with the *brain*, divorcing it from the body, spirit, heart and sensory/emotional perceptions. Mind is generally associated with rational, logical, logo-centric thinking processes. It is presumed to have some kind of physical locus in our brains and neurological constraints.[26]

Hearts are assumed to be the center of our emotions, the seat of understandings that are distinct from those cultivated in the mind. Colloquially, we refer to what we "know in our hearts," as we attune to wonder, awe, mystery and the intuitive, wordless ways of knowing that contemplative practices point us toward. In this book, I cluster heart with intuition and "spirit," hoping to excavate the notion from religious overtones, while retaining its connection to long-standing traditions that move "beyond reason."

I chose "activity" as a third anchoring term, rather than the seemingly more neutral term "experience." Activity is agentic, while still leaving open-ended just what the activity is directed toward or what will emerge from it. We experience the world by *doing* and participating in activities, whether sitting quietly attempting to suspend thinking or actively moving, talking, thinking, struggling, doing. Experience – including sitting on a cushion with eyes closed – is never neutral. We bring intention to everything we do, whether we know it or not. Mindfulness helps us to become more conscious of those intentions and to better align our actions with both our minds and our hearts, as we engage in activities in the world. We can apply mindfulness to the ethnographic activities of observing, participating in field work, writing up our notes, analyzing our data and presenting the results.

Of course, not all readers may compartmentalize mind, heart and activity quite so rigidly as I have suggested here. Mind and heart may already be a fused construct for those who are steeped in contemplative traditions. Mind and activity may be entwined for others, who have been shaped, as I have, by sociocultural and sociohistorical activity theory, which treats mind as emergent from human activity though the use of historically evolved tools and cultural practices.[27] These fusions challenge normative ways of thinking about mind and heart. But they are dyadic at best. Uniting mind and heart, we leave out activity. Linking mind and activity backgrounds the workings of the heart. What if we saw mind, heart and

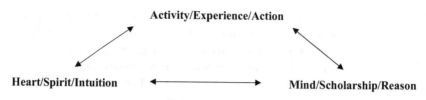

FIGURE 0.1 Triad of mind, heart and activity

activity not as two sets of dyads, or two separate fusions (mind/heart and mind/ activity), but as three points in a triad? The tensions along each side become *generative*, because they can't so easily pull apart. They are held together by opposing forces on three dimensions. If each side is kept in balance, this makes the whole tension-filled, energetic and alive, with each point retaining its own integrity. (See Figure 0.1. See also Figure 5.3 in Chapter 5.)

Scholarship, activism and spirituality: identity tensions

I am a white woman who lives with considerable privilege calling for mindful reflection and dialogue across differences, in a time of divisiveness and growing inequities in the United States (and in many other parts of the world). I understand why some might dismiss this message out of hand. Can we ever really see and hear others across intersecting lines of privilege and power? Can we unify in ways that don't simply re-create hierarchies in some new way? I want to believe that we can, and that we have to, despite the dismal history of our species,[28] if we are to get past the planetary-level challenges that could destroy us all. Hence this book.

I bring to this project more than twenty years of ethnographic and educational research in diverse settings, ten years of trying on and thinking about contemplative practice of different kinds, and thirty years of working in various ways to promote social change. I will speak briefly to my scholarly, activist and spiritual identities (ones that I now try to hold lightly, continuously wondering just who the "I" is that I assume I am)[29] here, as well as to the tensions that I experience among them, and explore them more throughout the book.

Scholarship

As a researcher, I identify principally as an ethnographer and a socioculturalist. Many people assume I'm an anthropologist, though I'm not. My undergraduate degree was in psychology, my doctorate in education; I was a postdoctoral researcher on an interdisciplinary research project, working closely with a sociologist (Barrie Thorne) and developmental psychologists.[30] My first academic position was in the Learning Sciences and Human Development and Social Policy programs at Northwestern University. Now I am anchored in the Urban Schooling and Teacher Education programs at UCLA and participate as well in an interdisciplinary program on Migration Studies.[31] Thus I have enjoyed many opportunities to experience and move across academic borders; I resist being disciplined by disciplines or assuming any fixed identity. Most of my research has been focused on language, literacy, learning and development, set in contexts of dynamic cultural change – work that is inherently interdisciplinary and that is best understood using multiple methodologies as well.

Activism

My activist identity was forged through community organizing with low-wage workers while a college student, a brief albeit intensive introduction to a variety of U.S.-based leftist parties in my twenties, and active engagement with the Central American Solidarity Movement in the 1980s. (These provided many lessons on the challenges and possibilities of coalition-building: how to work toward common goals despite distinct positionalities and ideological differences.) I also identified principally as a teacher in those years, working in an elementary school classroom that served many children of families who were fleeing war in Central America. My activism extended to work with the local teachers' union and teachers' groups that worked in solidarity with Central America. It was at the end of the 1980s that I returned to graduate school and began to assume a different identity as a scholar-activist. My scholar-activism is now centered in engaged community research in educational settings and new immigrant communities. I enact it by participating in public actions and campaigns to support human rights; environmental justice; and the rights of workers, immigrants and members of non-dominant cultural groups and by writing about these matters, including in public blogposts.[32]

Spiritual pathways

And just how do I identify in terms of spiritual pathways? Here, too, I resist assuming any label. I have tried to read widely and experience different approaches to getting out of my thinking mind, including ones associated with a variety of religious traditions as well as with secular ones. I echo many people in saying I am "spiritual but not religious," rejecting rigid religious ideologies along with political ones by trying to peel off layers of dogma while embracing core commitments. I am aware of the dangers of cultural appropriation and have sought to reconcile these beliefs with "my own" lineage (Roman Catholicism, as well as perhaps Christian Mysticism, pre-Christian paganism and German philosophers and social theorists whose ideas diverged from dominant perspectives). See Box 0.1.

Generative tensions

Participating in activist groups, in academia and in contemplative practice communities of different kinds has led me to experience tensions among the stances that are sometimes expected of scholars, activists and those who consider themselves on "the spiritual path." First, these identities are often set in opposition to each other, posed as dichotomies between mind and heart, mind and action, action and spirit. Like all strong forms of identification, these polarizations tend to divide and separate. Activists sometimes look askance upon both scholarship and spiritual pursuits, seeing these as removed from action in the world. Scholars may dismiss activism and spiritualism, believing these to lack the "objectivity" or "rigor" presumed necessary for scholarly inquiry. Those who consider themselves "enlightened" may reject both the life of the mind and the world of action, viewing these as different ways of living in a state of illusion or "maya."[33] I recognize myself in these characterizations of scholars, activists and spiritual seekers; I have felt and wondered similar things myself. And of course, there is tension within each of these groupings, as people affiliate with different lines, platforms, positions, lineages, disciplines, traditions and racialized/ethnic/gendered/sexualized identities within them. I have witnessed much splintering and faction-formation within all three spheres.

I have highlighted my identities as a researcher, scholar and spiritual seeker, but like all of us, I have many other identities as well, which intersect in complex ways. I'm a heterosexual woman of lower middle-class, German-American origins now living with considerable economic and social privilege; a student of life and a product of Western schooling; a middle-aged woman who realizes she is growing older, entering the last phase of her life; a mother, mentor, sister, auntie, neighbor, colleague, friend; a divorcee, cancer survivor, marathon runner, recovering Catholic, quasi-Buddhist, sometimes-artist, scrabble player, lapsed flautist and more. I wonder, as you read this long list of identities, which ones made you feel closer and more connected to me? Which pushed you away?

My aims, hopes and intentions

In writing for scholars, who tend to be strongly oriented toward the "mind" point in this triad, I draw on diverse forms of theory: from cognitive psychology, social science research methods, philosophy and metaphysics and from ethnographies lodged within anthropology, sociology, education and more. My hope is to provide enough mind/thought matter to stimulate and ground scholarly readers and to honor and connect with vast bodies of knowledge and wisdom that have been developed and transmitted, not just by academics but in diverse contemplative traditions as well as in social action. I also seek to re-balance "mainstream" scholarship with creative, nonacademic writing, in pursuit of understandings that transcend the boundaries we often build to keep ideas apart.

But I did not want to weigh the book down with too much "heady" theory, which can interfere with the reach for more intuitive, wordless, heart-centered and often unconscious ways of knowing.[34] I wanted to speak as much from my own heart and lived experience as from my submersion in books. Given that I am writing to researchers, or people who are being trained in the craft of social science research, who are likely equipped with strong analytical mind-sets, and good at reading, citing, analyzing and critiquing texts, my aim is not to disparage those ways but also not to reify them; instead, I seek to balance book knowledge with understandings derived from activity in the world and the intuitive understandings that emerge from them.[35]

Epistemological concerns about what can be known, how, in what ways and by whom ride as a continual subtext to unsettle what may at times seem like a deceptively simple "how to" book on ethnography. I do not pretend to resolve these issues,[36] just to remind readers, and myself, that there are limits of what we can know for certain with our rational, analytical, logocentric, disembodied minds, and it is important to remember those limitations even as we harness our minds' power. Loosening our tethering to the narrative, verbal, rational, analytical, positivist, dispassionate, ego-driven processes that dominate scientific study; enhancing our intuitive, heart-centered capacities; and valuing our own lived experiences, we can *expand* our epistemological, methodological, scholarly and social activist toolkits, combining ways of thinking that are so often forced apart. New understandings emerge when we attune our minds with our hearts and take our commitments from the page to the stage of the world, and vice versa. When we connect deeply with wellsprings of compassion and mobilize the information our minds have gathered, what might we propelled not just to understand but to *do* with that understanding?

Activity and direct experience

Mindful awareness is not something that can be imparted in a text, preached, or taught. It can really only be directly *experienced*. Words may sometimes mediate our experiences or guide us toward ways of experiencing directly. But they can also get in the way. They are poor substitutes for experiences themselves. Each chapter in this book therefore includes a few suggestions for practice that are designed to connect readers with your own lived experiences and to "metabolize" the ideas: to move from intellectualism into fuller, more experiential understandings. I offer examples from my own research and life even as I reflect on how I might have been *more* mindful, more heart-centered and more compassionate with myself and others as a researcher and scholar. I consider how my journey toward awarefulness and mindheartedness has changed – and undoubtedly will continue to change – the ways I do ethnography and act and live in the world.

The activities are intended to help researchers who have different degrees and kinds of experience with ethnographic research, as well as those who are working at different stages of the research process: from entering a field site to writing up the results. They are designed both for those who novices in the craft of ethnography and for experienced ethnographers who want to enliven their approach and perhaps reconsider some assumptions and practices or try on some new ones.

They are aimed for engaged scholars who want to do research that contributes not just to understanding the world as it is but to transforming it through clear and compassionate action.

These exercises should also function for people with varying degrees and types of mindfulness training, as my emphasis here is on *using* such approaches for transformative research. They will introduce contemplative practices that you can continue to explore, pursuing resources from the notes. While it may help to build a mindful ethnographic toolkit, this book is not intended as a "how to" guide. I do not pretend that if you just do *x*, *y* or *z*, you will find enlightenment in your work or write the next great spiritually attuned, heart-centered ethnography. It is my hope, however, that you will find some approaches that will both enhance your research and deepen your commitments, perhaps in surprising ways.

While the practices I describe in this book may contribute to finding harmony among parts of yourself that may have felt irreconcilable, especially within academia, you may experience moments of disjuncture as well. Such tensions can be productive. The aim does not have to be to *resolve those tensions* as much as to *use them in generative ways*. What if we accepted discomfort as it is, and let it settle itself, rather than suppressing, repressing or struggling to resolve paradoxes? In "interludes" between chapters, I share some of the ways I tried to practice what I preach: letting these things settle, not trying to resolve everything or weave it neatly into the narrative, being aware of my own process and sharing that process with readers.

Audience matters

Writers are encouraged to think about who our audiences are. Who is listening to our words? What do we *assume* about those listeners? Considering these things helps us be conscious of our choices of words and the ways we explicate our ideas. As I discuss in Chapter 4, we reveal a great deal about our assumptions through the grammar of our thinking, including through the pronouns we use. I became more aware of this as I wrote this book and caught myself many times in this manuscript referring to readers as "you," and sometimes referencing an uncertain "they, or the abstract category of "readers," only to realize that I really could – and should – include myself in many statements.

You will hear me "thinking aloud" throughout the book, especially in the interludes, as I reflect on my own writing processes, field experiences and decisions I made about this book. I hope you will feel that you can talk back, by writing in the margins, debating points with your friends and colleagues and, if you choose, writing or speaking to me. I would like to imagine I am talking with you while seated around a kitchen table[37] or on cushions on the floor of a meditation hall. (Though I would likely opt for a chair; I'm not really good with those cushions!) I tried to picture readers here with me on this breezy summer day, with sunlight filtering through my window, a cup of tea in hand, rather than meeting me only through printed words in black ink on a white page. I wish we could actually be seated together here and that this could be a plática[38] more than an exposé, not a performance to a silent "audience."

Writers have the challenge of speaking to somewhat unknown audiences and to many different kinds of people, not ones who are of a single mind. In my work with immigrant youth who serve as language brokers for their families, I have seen how young people speak with and for people who bring very different assumptions, background experiences and worldviews to the same conversation. I take inspiration from them as I try to write in ways that will make sense to people who bring different degrees and kinds of understanding about and experiences with ethnography, mindfulness, scholarship, spirituality and activism and different identities to the work as well.

Overview of the book

The book is structured with seven chapters, "interludes" between each chapter, this introduction, a number of "boxes" with information set off from the main text and a hefty amount of notes. Readers may choose their own way through the book, guided by signposts I have placed along the way. For example, those who would like to know more about myself and my motivations may want to start with the first box. Those who like theory might dig into the many notes in Chapter 1, reading them either in conjunction with the main text or independently. Others might prefer to skip that chapter entirely or parse it in small bites, returning as you see where the theory is leading us in practice.

In general, the notes serve to elaborate on ideas introduced in the text. Because I am writing about matters that span disciplines, spiritual traditions and history, there are far more possible resources to cite than I could ever list. I point readers to some of the texts that have been most influential for me and to others that may be considered foundational, classic or representative of particular traditions. I hope that readers will continue the conversation by identifying additional related material and/or writing their own.

The interludes, like the boxed material, are intended to stand on their own, as illustrations of the issues I explore. Some readers may welcome a break as they move through the main substance of the book. These were opportunities for me to "practice what I preach" and try on the things I am advocating. They loosely relate to the material in the preceding chapters but do not depend on sequential reading and could be skipped.

I encourage you to read mindfully,[39] noticing your reactions to the text. What thought-feelings bubble up for you? Where do you find yourself nodding in agreement, scowling in disdain or scratching your head in perplexity? What resonates? Where do you feel resistant? Where does that resonance, or resistance, sit in your body? What aspects of your identity get activated as you read? (Your "critical" self? Activist? Scholarly persona?) Pause wherever you like, or move around through the text as you choose.

Chapter 1 – Conceptual framings: ethnography, epistemology, mindfulness and non-duality

The first chapter is the "headiest" one in the book, and I reflect on the challenges I faced in developing it in the interludes that both precede and follow it. My aim is to offer readers food for thought as well as ideas you can return to at any point. The chapter centers on both epistemological and axiological questions about the knowledge we claim and the values we infuse in our work. The most challenging idea to unpack in this chapter, as in this book, centers on the notion of non-duality. I attempt to define, explain, problematize this construct . . . and let it be. I consider what we can take from non-dualism for the task of social science research and offer a set of guidelines for ethnographers.

Chapter 2 – Entering the field with open hearts and minds

This chapter takes us to the first day of a new field enterprise and offers mindful ways of entering a field site and seeing it for the first time. Presenting examples from the first field notes I wrote in a postdoctoral research project – long before I was aware of awarefulness – as well as those written by my students on their first days in the field, I examine what we first noticed as well as the many things that we missed. I consider how prior experiences, worries about the future and our interpretive minds influenced both what we saw and how we understood it. Looking at our leaps to evaluation, summaries, explanation and pattern-seeking, I suggest ways of slowing down those analytical processes, becoming more aware of our thoughts and feelings and creating more room to listen, and see, with our hearts.

Following the lead of "sensory ethnographers" such as Sarah Pink and Paul Stoller,[40] I also direct ethnographers' attention to aspects of the field that may go unnoticed when not fully grounded in the present: smells, sounds, light and sensations. I offer "centering" strategies that ethnographers can deploy both before and during their first site visit. I go a step further by tuning in on things that kindle – or could kindle – compassion and a deep sense of connection to the pain of others: emotions that are easily shut down through the distancing practices of research.

Chapter 3 – Getting in and along: connecting with clarity and compassion

Building on the ideas presented in the previous chapter, I help readers to notice when we leap to comparisons with the past or the future and to categorizing, labeling, and evaluating what we see rather than, or before, trying to experience its "suchness."[41] I suggest strategies that can help us experience contexts in new ways and disrupt old scripts. I also take seriously what ethnographers mean by "getting along"[42] in the field, as we build relationships and engage in ongoing work. What about when we have emotional responses to what we experience? Or when our participants do? I consider ways of handling the strong feelings that can be triggered in the field, as well as becoming more attuned to things that are *not* emotionally loaded, because these things reveal what is normative or taken for granted.

This chapter, like much of the book, dances with a central dilemma of ethnography, and perhaps of all research, as of *life*: the relationship of self and other. I consider approaches we might take to better see more empathically and more clearly, with compassion for others and ourselves, and perhaps, at times, to rethink the relationship of self and other in non-dualistic ways.[43] Just *who* do we create as others, to what aspects of our selves? What "empathy walls" do we put up — what Arlie Hochschild refers to "obstacle(s) to deep understanding of another person, one(s) that can make us feel indifferent or even hostile to those who hold different beliefs or whose childhood is rooted in different circumstances"?[44] Can mind-hearted practices help us surmount them, transcending our own limits on how far we are able or willing to go — or at least better recognizing them? What might we see on the other side, and how might that help us in our efforts to transform the world?

Chapter 4 – Being there again, now: writing up field notes

A mindful approach reminds the ethnographer not just to "be here now" while observing but to "be there, again" when writing up extended or elaborated field notes after a day in the field. Resisting a drive to report "what happened" (which is really only what *we experienced as happening*, or what we remember of what we experienced as happening — not some totalizing truth of events) can help us to see more deeply into particular moments and resist reporting in linear, observer-centric (ego-centric) chronologies. I provide examples of descriptions that resist the press of time and that bring the reader back into those past-present moments with the ethnographer. I also consider ways of finding *pleasure* in the writing of field notes, as we get to "live twice," reexperiencing our moments in the field. (This is not to dismiss the pain we may also feel, when we re-experienced intense emotions generated through our work. Mindfulness helps us to accept it all.)

Chapter 5 – Analysis: let it settle itself

Analysis presents profound dilemmas for mindful ethnographers, ones that only deepen the challenges to truth claims that already haunt the field. For those of us who are concerned with doing good work that also "does good" in the world — that has implications for transformative policy and practice, not just theory, or that, in the Buddhist value system, reduces the suffering of other sentient beings or at least "does no harm" — this dilemma is fraught with politics and moral/ethical dilemmas as well. We may be so deeply invested in our own belief systems and driven by our analytical frameworks that we cannot see outside them.

Citing the Indian philosopher Tilopa – "No thought, no reflection, no analysis, no cultivation, no intention: Let it settle itself"[45] – I ask: What would it mean to let our data settle itself, at least initially? Certainly, I do not claim that ethnography can be conducted without working with more traditional, "rigorous," analytical processes at some point in time. But suspending thought, words and analyses – letting things settle – can open the way for intuitive understandings to emerge, loosen our ties to our own egos and help us ensure that we don't just impose our own preexisting narratives on what we documented. I suggest the power of pausing: *first* letting things settle themselves, before leaping into the work of right-brained (and ego-driven) analyses. This can create more space for unconscious processes to lead the way. It may allow for unexpected findings – the hallmark surprises of good ethnography – to bubble forth. It may also humble us, forcing us to temper any overly bold claims to universal truths – or facile critiques of entrenched social problems – that we might want to make.

Chapter 6 – Re-presentations

The write-up of ethnography raises new concerns, and much has been written about the problems, dilemmas and even "crises" of representation. What happens as we take the rich pastiche of sights, sounds, images and feelings that were evoked in a field setting and represent them in words on paper? How do we interweave our interpretations with our descriptions, leading readers not just to "see" with us but to grasp the meanings we made from what we saw? Can we do that in ways that do not impose our visions on others, as much as *invite* readers to contemplate what we offer, based on our immersion in the field? Can we do this in honest, fair and *kind* ways? This raises particular questions for activist-scholars. What moral and ethical stances guide our re-presentations?

The approaches I have detailed in this book can facilitate the capacity to do this work at the writing stage. I consider what it means to write what Nancy Scheper Hughes refers to as "good enough" ethnography:[46] the most insightful, respectful and truthful account that we can, checking our own biases and offering something of both usefulness and beauty to the world. We can be honest about our process, recognizing our limitations, taking responsibility for where we may fall short but letting ourselves off of the impossible hook of perfectionism.[47] To hold back on what we have to offer out of our own insecurities surely is a disservice. And words really can contribute to the transformation of the world.

Chapter 7 – Letting go

At some point our work will involve endings. We will have to leave the field, walk away from our computers, put a period on the last sentence of our texts and hit "send" to deliver the file to our committee members, editors or publishers. This chapter addresses what may come up as we complete our work and offers ways of letting go of expectations, fears and of the force that drives both expectations and fears: ego.

Buddhist and other contemplative practices emphasize the importance of being compassionate with all beings on the planet. That includes being compassionate with ourselves. We should do our best to live up to our own highest standards and those of the field. We should honor our commitments to the communities we have worked in, taking great care to re-present them with integrity and kindness. We should present our best offerings to the world but not proclaim what we have to say as absolute, totalizing, and irrefutable truths. Detaching our ego a bit from our projects may help us to accept the critiques that others may levy toward us, without defensiveness. Working with our material with both our hearts and our minds, we will likely reach a point when we feel that what we have written is ready to be released to the world. We can consider it as a gift and hope that it will be received as one but accept that some may not appreciate, want or need what we have to give.

BOX 0.3 ACTIVITY: LET YOUR MIND SETTLE

At this point in your journey into reading this book, I invite you to stop. Find a comfortable seating position, and take a few long, deep breaths. Watch your breath rise and fall, and let the words you have just read settle themselves. What do you notice in your body? Are there particular points of tension in your stomach, chest, throat or head? Where do you feel at ease, or tight? What thoughts bubble up in your mind? Sit with these thoughts and feelings without trying to control or constrict them as long as you can. Just notice, and become aware that you are noticing.

If you choose, you can move from this into a deeper state of relaxation. Sit as long as you like, watching your thoughts come and go. See how they arise on the screen of your mind. Watch them fade away. Breathe. Relax.

After letting things settle in this way, you may choose to turn on your analytical, questioning, searching mind. Jot down the questions that arise, the things that trouble you about what you have just read and the wonderings you have. See if you can connect the feelings in your body with the concerns in your mind. You don't have to resolve these now. Just notice them. Become aware.

Notes

1 McGrane (1989: 2) summarizes the history of conceptions of difference within anthropological thought between the sixteenth and twentieth centuries, beginning with the Enlightenment, when anthropology as a field did not exist. His is an "attempt not to understand the Other, the alien, the different, but rather, historically to understand our understanding of the Other, the alien, the different."

2 Auto-ethnography is gaining popularity, with more ethnographers turning to their own lives for ethnographic analysis and weaving their experiences more centrally in their ethnographic research. For guidance on the genre, including distinctions between auto- and other-focused ethnography, see Adams et al. (2014) and Bochner and Ellis (2016). See Reed-Donahay (1997) for a collection of examples to illustrate themes central to the genre, especially its politically grounded nature. Denzin (2013) sees auto-ethnography as autobiography, in which the author analyzes her personal experiences in relation to larger histories, following storytelling conventions such as centering the text around turning points. This book is not an autobiography, or an auto-ethnography in that sense. But I turn the lens on my own ethnographic experiences more than I might in a "standard" ethnographic or methodological text.

3 I summarize Bentz and Shapiro's (1998) work in the next chapter and recommend it to readers who are wondering what particular methodological approaches make sense for their own interests and their own emerging researcher identities.

4 Stetsenko (2019).

5 Indeed, as Anna Stetsenko (2019) posits, learning is most powerful and personally mean- ingful when it is "in the service of making sense of 'who I am' and 'who I want to become'" as we make our way through the activity of the human existence that we have the honor and pleasure (and sometimes pain) of experiencing.

6 *Mindfulness*, by Ellen Langer (revised and expanded in 2014), summarizes much of the research – including Langer's own – on the effects of mindfulness on particular behaviors. Langer distinguishes this kind of research from research on the effects of mindfulness *training*, for example, studies of the effects of meditation on attentiveness. See also Endnote #1 in Chapter 2. In this body of work, mindfulness is mostly treated as an *object* of study, not a way of going about research.

7 For a lucid and compassionate critique of mindfulness in relation to neoliberal agendas, see Joanna Cook's (2016) "Mindful in Westminster: The politics of meditation and the limits of neoliberal critique." Cook notes that "the primary academic analysis of the popularity of secular mindfulness practice has been that it is a neoliberal tool: it has been analyzed as reflecting changing frameworks of state responsibility and an increasing emphasis on the 'responsibility' of subjects to self-manage at a time of increasing priva- tization." She cites scholars who see Western Buddhism functioning as an "ideological supplement to the stress of capitalist dynamics." Cook takes this critique even further, sug- gesting that mindfulness not only aligns with neoliberalism but could serve as its motor.

But then, Cook makes an interesting analytical move, using observations of meditative practices in British Parliament to show that this narrative is "not borne out ethno- graphically." She writes: "Recognizing the limits of neoliberalism moves us away from a conceptualization of neoliberalism as a totalizing ideology and allows us to explore the practices of people who recognize collective and structural causes of suffering at the same time as seeking practices of subjectification for improving wellbeing."

A "mindful" approach to ethnographic research seemingly kept Cook from being trapped by her own critical neoliberal framing and enabled her to see *both* constraints and possibilities of these practices from the perspective of participants, rather than imposing a totalizing narrative on her field observations. Cook's theorization and ethnographic unpacking are worth a closer reading by those who dismiss mindfulness as a "mere" tool of neoliberal state interests.

8 Orellana (2009).

9 This intertextual reference is to "The Summer Day" by Mary Oliver (1992), whose poetry also accompanied me on my healing journey.

10 Maria laughed when I shared this with her. She said, "Actually, they weren't."

11 See for example Hegel (2015). See further discussion in Chapter One.

12 Kabat-Zinn (1994).

13 A doctor, when I asked, "And if it comes back?" answered, "You die." He told me that his job was to "help me place my bets on the roulette of life" – as if to suggest that he could

somehow keep me from the fate that will meet us all, some day. I juxtapose this with the words of a Buddhist monk, to a friend who also faced a cancer diagnosis: "Don't worry! You're going to die!" This was said with a gentle smile while looking into her eyes. Really grasping our own mortality may be the greatest gift we can give ourselves, so we can fully live while we are here. For a few books that I found helpful for death as a teacher, see Becker (1997), Frankel (2006), Naht Hahn (2003), Kübler-Ross (2014), Rinpoche et al. (2017), Rinpoche (2012), Ostaseki (2017).

14 According to Rupert Ghetin (2015), in a broad overview of Buddhist conceptualizations of mindfulness from diverse Buddhist traditions, the English word "mindfulness" is connected to the ancient Sanskrit word "smrti," the Pali word "sati," the Chinese word "nian" and the Tibetan "dran pa." See also Davids (1969) and Rothberg (2006) for further discussion of its etymology.

15 Stolfeth and Manusov (2019).

16 www.tarabrach.com/.

17 Brach (2013).

18 Chödrön (2013). See also Chodrön (2013, 2017, 2018).

19 Harris (2014: 35).

20 Naht Hanh (2010).

21 Kabat-Zinn (1994: 4).

22 Kabat-Zinn (1994: 8).

23 Neff (2015: 80).

24 Rothberg (2006).

25 Siegel et al. (2010: 17).

26 Considerable new research aims at *proving* the neuroscientific basis for many of the claims made about the effects of meditation. This work keeps the mind strongly anchored in the brain. See for example *Buddha's Brain: The practical neuroscience of happiness, love and wisdom*, by Rick Hanson (2009) and *Why Buddhism is true: The science and philosophy of meditation and enlightenment* by Robert Wright (2018).

27 See for example Lave and Wenger (1991), Stetsenko (2019), Vygotsky (1978), Wertsch (1998, 2001) and Wertsch et al. (1995).

28 By the "dismal history of our species" I refer to the many ways that humans have divided and created groups of "us" and "them" across history and cultural contexts, often leading to civil war, genocide and political turmoil. Of course, each of these countless conflicts has its own unique political history, and imbalances of power, but the basic practice of creating "others" seems to be something that humans are well skilled in. This is carefully laid out in *Sapiens: A brief history of humankind* by Yuval Noah Harari (2014).

29 See Sam Harris' (2014) discussion of "The riddle of the self" in *Waking up: A guide to spirituality without religion*. See also Sri Nisaragadatta Maharaj's questioning of all that we think we are. Many other spiritually attuned thinkers have questioned just *who* is the thinker we assume is thinking.

30 My postdoctoral funding came from the MacArthur Foundation, as part of a large-scale, interdisciplinary, seven-year study of "successful pathways through middle childhood." The experience was formative for me as a scholar and offered a good model of dialoguing across methodological and disciplinary differences.

31 The Center for the Study of International Migration (www.international.ucla.edu/migration) brings together sociologists, anthropologists, historians, political scientists, educational researchers and many others to study the many, varied, complex issues related to the movement of people around the world – matters that really cannot be fully understood from a single disciplinary perspective.

32 See immigrantyouthlanguage.com or marjoriefaulstichorellan.com for blogposts about immigration, education, youth, language, social justice and human rights.

33 The notion of "maya" or "illusion" was perhaps first explicated in the *Upanishads*. This quote is worth pondering by scholars: "Brahman (wisdom) cannot be realized by those who are subject to the pride of name and fame or to the vanity of scholarship.

Brahman cannot be realized by those who are enmeshed in life's duality" [Upanishads (1949: 284)].

34 In developing the book, and especially Chapter One, I started to go down the rabbit hole of epistemological debates, entering into intellectual arguments that would likely never satisfy anyone, and leave other readers either lost or despairing about academia. Thanks to my colleague and friend Abhik Roy, for helping me to keep this in check.

35 I am reminded of the folk wisdom of my former mother-in-law, who told me, "Don't read so much; you'll go crazy." This is echoed in bell hooks' (2007) autobiography, *Bone black: Memories of girlhood*; she writes of being scolded for reading rather than doing her chores. For hooks' family, as for many people, immersion in social relationships and in the world was more important than book learning. In her later academic writing, hooks (2017) worked to integrate these values, arguing for lived experience as theory along with Theory with a capital T – the kind that is privileged in academia. I, too, very much value the world of books but seek to honor folk wisdom as well: to appreciate theory in its many forms and to balance head, heart and experience. As Eknath Easwaran, in his introduction and translation of *The Upanishads* (2007: 13–14) notes, being "well trained in the world of books" does not necessarily "appease the hunger in (our) heart(s)." And Rumi: "You will learn by reading, but you will understand with love."

36 We can engage in social science research without having fully settled these questions. We can likely do this *better* than we otherwise would, simply by becoming more aware of these tensions as they arise and sitting with them, not letting them paralyze us or believing that we need to resolve them.

37 Rachel Naomi Remen, in *Kitchen table wisdom: Stories that heal* (2006: xxv), writes: "When I was a child, people sat around kitchen tables and told their stories. We don't do that so much anymore. Sitting around the table telling stories is not just a way of passing time. It is the way the wisdom gets passed along."

38 See Cindy Fierros and Delores Delgado Bernal (2016) for use of the Spanish term for everyday conversation (plática) as culturally responsive research methodology for work in Latinx communities.

39 See Berthoud (2019) and Carillo (2017) for guidance on mindful reading.

40 See Pink (2009) and Stoller (1989).

41 Capra (2010: 29) defines "suchness" as "undifferentiated, undivided, indeterminant direct experience." He refers to the "absolute knowledge" that we gather from direct experiences that don't "rely on the abstractions and classifications of the intellect."

42 Lofland and Lofland (1995).

43 A reader of an earlier version of this manuscript asked, "Is the goal of the book to support being more mindful of others and/or the self, or to collapse the me/you distinction through ethnography?" The question made me pause. I am certainly trying to raise big questions about polarities of self/other, us/them thinking and to find more ways of creating an "us" within a larger whole, where distinctions may fall away. But I would suggest that the way to get there is *not* to deny a sense of self and other. Claiming our selves (and all of the identities that are important to having a strong core sense of self) and becoming better at seeing our selves clearly and accurately, with recognition of our positionalities, as we also look out on the world of others, to see them in the same way, we can, perhaps, get to a place where the boundaries we hold tightly start to relax. We can aim to hold it all: a strong sense of self, a clear seeing of others and a recognition that we are all part of something larger than us all – and ultimately, very tiny in the grand scheme of things. I discuss this further in Chapters One and Three.

44 Hochschild (2016: 5).

45 Chos-kyi-blo-gros et al. (1995).

46 Scheper-Hughes (1993). Scheper-Hughes writes of growing wearied of postmodernist critiques. She argued (then) that we live in perilous times, and compromising on perfection may be demanded by the pressing need to speak to matters of importance. (We may be living in even more perilous times now.) She calls for writing "good enough"

ethnographies. Luttrell (2005) also refers to "good enough research" as akin to "good enough mothering" (Winnicot, 1973) – not perfect, but good enough.

47 As my dear friend Ericka Verba (who listened with her generous heart and keen mind as I read to her from this book) likes to say, "Perfection is over-rated." Indeed, we can learn more from examining our mistakes and embracing our imperfections than from living in fear of exposing them.

References

Adams, T. E., Jones, S. H. and Ellis, C. (2014). *Autoethnography: Understanding qualitative research*. New York: Oxford University Press.

Becker, E. (1997). *The denial of death*. New York: Free Press.

Bentz, V. M. and Shapiro, J. J. (1998). *Mindful inquiry in social research*. Thousand Oaks, CA: Sage Publications.

Berthoud, E. (2019). *The art of mindful reading: Embracing the wisdom of words*. UK: The Ivy Press.

Bochner, A. and Ellis, C. (2016). *Evocative ethnography: Writing lives and telling stories*. New York: Routledge.

Brach, T. (2013). *True refuge: Finding peace and freedom in your own awakened heart*. New York: Bantam Books.

Capra, F. (2010). *The Tao of physics: An exploration of the parallels between modern physics and Eastern mysticism*. Boston, MA: Shambhala.

Carillo, E. C. (2017). *A writer's guide to mindful reading: Practice and pedagogy*. Fort Collins, CO: The WAC Clearinghouse and University Press of Colorado.

Chodrön, P. (2013). *Living beautifully with uncertainty and change*. Boston, MA: Shambhala.

Chodrön, P. (2017). *When things fall apart: Heart advice for difficult times*. Boston, MA: Shambhala.

Chodrön, P. (2018). *The places that scare you: A guide to fearlessness in difficult times*. Boston, MA: Shambhala.

Chos-kyi-blo-gros, M., Torricelli, F., San s-rgyas-bstan-dar and Cayley, V. (1995). *The life of the Maha siddha Tilopa*. Dharamsala: Library of Tibetan Works and Archives.

Cook, J. (2016). Mindful in Westminster. *Journal of Ethnographic Theory*, 6 (1), 141–161. doi:10.14318/hau6.1.011.

Davids, T. W. (1969). *Buddhist Suttas*. New York: Dover.

Denzin, N. K. (2013). *Interpretive Auto-ethnography*. Thousand Oaks, CA: Sage.

Didonna, F. (2010). *Clinical handbook of mindfulness*. New York: Springer.

Easwaran, E. (2007). *The Upanishads* (E. Easwaran, Introduced and trans.). Tomales, CA: Nilgiri Press.

Fierros, C. O. and Delgado Bernal, D. (2016). Vamos a platicar: The contours of plática as Chicana/Latina feminist methodology. *Chicana/Latina Studies: The Journal of Mujeres Activas en Letras y Cambio Social*, 15 (2), 98–121.

Frankel, V. (2006). *Man's search for meaning*. New York: Pocket Books.

Ghetin, R. (2015). Buddhist conceptualizations of mindfulness. In Brown, K. W., Creswell, J. D. and Ryan, R. M. (eds.), *Handbook of mindfulness: Theory, research and practice*. New York: The Guilford Press.

Hanson, R. and Mendius, R. (2009). *Buddha's brain: The practical neuroscience of happiness, love and wisdom*. Oakland, CA: New Harbinger Publications.

Harari, Y. N. (2016). *Sapiens: A brief history of humankind*. New York: Harper Perennial.

Harris, S. (2014). *Waking up: A guide to spirituality without religion*. New York: Simon and Schuster.

Hegel, G. W. F. (2015). *Hegel's philosophy of mind.* UK: Andesite Press.

Hochschild, A. R. (2016). *Strangers in their own land.* New York: The New Press.

hooks, b. (2007). *Bone black: Memories of girlhood.* New York: Henry Holt and Company.

hooks, b. (2017). *Teaching to transgress: Education as the practice of freedom.* New York: Routledge.

Kabat-Zinn, J. (1994). *Wherever you go, there you are: Mindfulness meditation in everyday life.* Hachette Books.

Kübler-Ross, E. (2014). *On death and dying: What the dying have to teach doctors, nurses, clergy and their own families.* New York: Scribner.

Langer, E. J. (2014). *Mindfulness.* Reading, MA: Addison-Wesley.

Lave, J. and Wenger, E. (1991). *Situated learning: Legitimate peripheral participation.* New York: Cambridge University Press.

Luttrell, W. (2005). 'Good enough' methods for ethnographic research. *Harvard Educational Review,* 70 (4), 499–523.

McGrane, B. (1989). *Beyond anthropology: Society and the other.* New York: Columbia University Press.

Naht Hahn, T. (2003). *No death, no fear.* New York: Riverhead Press.

Naht Hanh, T. (2010). *Peace is every step: The path of mindfulness in everyday life.* New York: Random House.

Neff, K. (2015). *Self-compassion: The proven power of being kind to yourself.* New York: William Morrow Paperbacks.

Oliver, M. (1992). The summer day. In *New and selected poems* (Vol. 1, pp. 95–96). Boston: Beacon Press.

Orellana, M. F. (2009). *Translating childhoods: Immigrant youth, language, and culture.* New Brunswick, NJ: Rutgers University Press.

Ostaseki, F. (2017). *The five invitations: Discovering what death can teach us about living fully.* New York: Flatiron Books.

Pink, S. (2009). *Doing sensory ethnography.* Thousand Oaks, CA: Sage Publications.

Reed-Donahay, D. E. (1997). *Auto/ethnography: Rewriting the self and the social.* New York: Berg.

Remen, R. N. (2006). *Kitchen table wisdom: Stories that heal.* New York: Riverhead Books.

Rinpoche, S. (2012). *Tibetan book of living and dying: The spiritual classic and international bestseller.* San Francisco: Harper.

Rinpoche, S., Gaffney, P. (Ed.), Harvey, A. (Ed.) (2017). *The Tibetan book of living and dying.* London: Rider Books.

Rothberg, D. (2006). *The engaged spiritual life: A Buddhist approach to transforming ourselves and the world.* Boston: Beacon Press.

Scheper-Hughes, N. (1996). *Death without weeping: The violence of everyday life in Brazil.* Berkeley, CA: University of California Press.

Siegel, R. D., Germer, C. K. and Olendzki, A. (2010). Mindfulness: What is it? Where did it come from? In Didonna, F. (ed.), *Clinical handbook of mindfulness.* New York: Springer.

Stetsenko, A. (2019). *The transformative mind: Expanding Vygotsky's approach to development and education.* New York: Cambridge University Press.

Stolfeth, D. and Manusov, V. (2019). Talk about mindfulness: An ethnography of communication analysis of two speech communities. *Language and Communication,* 67, 45–54.

Stoller, P. (1989). *The taste of ethnographic things: The senses in Anthropology.* Philadelphia, PA: University of Pennsylvania Press.

Upanishads. (1949). *The Upanishads.* New York: Harper.

Vygotsky, L. S. (1978). *Mind in society: The development of higher psychological processes.* Cambridge, MA: Harvard University Press.

Wertsch, J. (1998). *Mind as action*. Oxford, UK: Oxford University Press.

Wertsch, J. (2001). *Vygotsky and the social formation of mind*. Cambridge, MA: Harvard University Press.

Wertsch, J., del Rio, P. and Alvarez, A. (1995). *Sociocultural studies of mind*. New York: Cambridge University Press.

Winnicott, D. W. (1973). *The child, the family, and the outside world*. New York: Penguin.

Wright, R. (2018). *Why Buddhism is true: The science and philosophy*. New York: Simon and Schuster.

1

CONCEPTUAL FRAMINGS

Ethnography, epistemology, mindfulness and non-duality

The intellect cannot reveal the self beyond the duality of subject and object. . . . The unitive state cannot be attained through words, thoughts, or through the eye.[1]

(The Upanishads)

This chapter raises epistemological and axiological concerns that will serve as a foundation for the chapters that follow. What do contemplative traditions offer to the particular challenges and dilemmas of ethnography? This takes us into epistemological and axiological questions: How do our beliefs about what can be known (by whom, in what ways) shape our work? What are the limits on our knowledge claims? And what moral and ethical responsibilities follow from this? My aim is not necessarily to answer all these questions but to consider how the unification of mind, heart and activity might lead us to new ways of understanding them and facilitate the doing of mindful and transformative social research.

Moving beyond limiting perspectives

How do we know what we know? This question has been debated with countless words throughout the ages. It will not be settled by anything I have to say about mindful ethnography. What a mindful perspective may offer, however, is more awareness of *how* we all can easily become attached to our own ways of seeing the world and dismiss the truths that other people hold dear. It may help us to *expand* ways of thinking, moving beyond the limits that are imposed by disciplines, fields, ideologies and identities or that we have set for ourselves and opening up new possibilities – with greater *discernment*, reflectiveness, clarity, non-defensiveness and consciousness.

Truth in an era of "alternative facts"

At the time I write this, the world seems to have moved into a strange direction. We are in an era of alternative facts, with competing news sources and information wars.[2] People circulate ideas that back our own pre-established beliefs like sharing a bottle of wine at a dinner party: intoxicating ourselves as we build camaraderie with those we assume are "like us" and forget the world outside our little circles.[3]

On the one hand, a search for truth – and a belief that there *is* a truth that can be separated from the knower – strongly persists, permeating both popular culture and the research world. On the other hand, we may dismiss ideas on the basis of their sources, on the belief that some people or groups have access to "truth" that others do not and on the thought that some are deliberately spreading "fake news." Many people – both in the larger culture and in academia – readily accept claims made by people or groups that we already agree with, and align or affiliate with, and reject those made by people who operate with different frameworks, values and worldviews, without really examining either closely. Often, we don't have direct access to primary evidence, so we may *have* to base our trust on what we know about the sources. But whom do we trust, and distrust? There is a growing body of cognitive science research that confirms that beliefs are shaped by our emotions: that we are not the rational beings we might like to think we are.[4]

Some have blamed the "post-truth" crisis on postmodernists and critical realists, seeing this as the logical extension of the recognition that frameworks matter for how we interpret any facts and that the same data can be interpreted to mean different things. Eduardo Kohn, in a fascinating project to imagine an "anthropology beyond the human," argues that the "fundamental belief that social science's greatest contributions – the recognition and delimitation of a separate domain of socially constructed reality – is also its greatest curse" and that "finding ways to move beyond this problem is one of the most important challenges facing critical thought today.[5]

What would it take to move beyond perspectives that keep us divided, separated and, perhaps, trapped – yet without discarding all criteria for knowing, and for taking principled stances in the world? I explore this by examining key epistemological and axiological questions that have been addressed in discussions of ethnography and suggest how contemplative practices – and the non-dualistic thrust that undergirds these ancient traditions – might offer a different way through epistemological impasses.

The relationship between the knower and the known

Joel Sprague,[6] in a comprehensive edited volume on reflexive methodology in social science research edited by Wendy Luttrell,[7] posits that there are three elements of epistemology: the knower, the known and the process of knowing. Various research approaches have addressed the relationship between these elements in different ways. Some forms push to maximize the distance between the knower and the known; others dissolve the barrier. Still others call for recognizing the influence of the knower on the known, raising critical questions about how knowledge production is shaped by the subject positions of researchers.

Positivist approaches to research, which arose and assumed power during the period of Western European history known, perhaps ironically, as the Enlightenment,[8] dichotomize the knower and the known most sharply and tend to overlook or minimize the critical dimension of the processes of knowing. These ideas are premised on the notion that such a separation is both possible and necessary in order to get at "objective" truth: knowledge about the world that is independent of knowing subjects (and their processes of knowing). Arguably, this belief is deeply entrenched in the modern research world, even in approaches that recognize the permeability of the objective/subjective divide and even as the world has moved from modernity into postmodernism, and toward the current, strange "post-truth" era. Indeed, Valerie Malhoutra Bentz and Jeremy Shapiro[9] refer to the lingering "after-life" of positivism in postmodern thinking.

Radical social constructivism (using Joel Sprague's label), or postmodernism/post-structuralism, moves far from the presumption that it is possible to separate the knower from the known but lands us on the opposite side of the binaries. In these views, all knowledge is socially constructed. The objectivity/subjectivity divide is impossible to surmount, and there are no totalizing narratives or universal truth claims that can be separated from the one who makes the claims. As Michel Foucault argued,[10] science creates official standards for what can be known, how and by whom, and we discipline ourselves into those ways of knowing. Thus, even our own subjectivities are a social construction.

The self-other relationship in ethnography

In ethnographic research, the relationship between the knower and the known takes on a particular shape, and questions of who can know what loom large. Ethnography, after all, is centrally bound up in the study of "the other." Even auto-ethnographers and "insiders" studying "their own" cultural experiences[11] strive to make the familiar strange in order to see in new ways.

The most offensive approaches to the self-other distinction can be found in anthropology's sordid colonialist history, in which mostly white, male anthropologists descended upon distant villages and non-Westernized communities, attempting to understand and then explain the practices of "exotic" groups to Western audiences.[12] The original anthropologists didn't try to explain themselves to the "others" they studied; nor did they seem to consider how their own values, beliefs, epistemological stances and assumptions shaped their understanding of what they saw. Arguably, they didn't really even recognize that they had a standpoint or that their search for "truth" was shaped by their own values and beliefs.[13]

How this relationship is addressed in methodology texts varies. Some scholars suggest that it is possible to achieve some kind of insider-outsider integration. For example, Ray Madden,[14] in his book *Being ethnographic*, calls on ethnographers to "manage the tension between objectivity and subjectivity in order to produce better portraits of the human condition." Madden calls for "synthesis" rather than a balance between insider and outsider perspectives. He implores researchers to get "close but not too close" to their subjects and research contexts, by engaging in "step-in, step-out" ethnography: immersing in the field, then stepping away. He emphasizes a dance-like quality of "being ethnographic," even as he, like many other guides, calls for systematicity and rigor as ways of securing the validity of our knowledge claims.

Others go further in recognizing that it is not at all easy to arrive at such syntheses and that rigor and systematicity may not be enough to check one's own biases or challenge one's own assumptions or even to be aware of the assumptions one makes. Wendy Luttrell,[15] for example, presents ethnography as an approach to research that "bridges art and science, spontaneity and discipline, emotional engagement and detached analysis." She argues that reflexivity demands more than just self-conscious awareness of ourselves as researchers but a willingness to make our own process and decision-making visible at multiple levels: being aware and sharing that awareness with others. By becoming more conscious of how we are interpreting what we see, we may avoid the most egregious errors. This is nicely aligned with contemplative practices. It is in cultivating such awareness that a mindful approach can be of support.

Insider/outsider positionalities

Given the colonialist history of anthropology, ethnographers have grappled actively with ways of studying "others." How can we understand "insider" perspectives when we are not insiders ourselves? This is a challenge even for those studying communities that researchers identify with or originate in, because being researchers almost invariably means that the person is differently positioned on important dimensions of power than those we study.

Feminist standpoint theorists such as Nancy Hartsock and Sandra Harding[16] go beyond arguing that our experiences shape what and how we see; they claim that some subject positions allow for a greater grasp of reality, or truth, than do others. This is because we all tend to see the world in ways that do not threaten our own values, beliefs, choices and positions. People who are in positions of power and privilege don't have the same incentive for seeing the world as do people who suffer from its inequities. Thus, social processes can be more clearly apprehended by those who do not stand to benefit from them.

In her most recent formulation of standpoint theory, Sandra Harding[17] modifies the claim that any singular subject position can necessarily make stronger claims on "truth" than others, suggesting instead that *all* subject positions offer some better angles of vision but also some blinders. Hers is a call for diversity in research endeavors, in order to tap into more complete understandings of the world. This has a certain resonance with the Buddhist supposition that we are all metaphorically in different parts of the forest, seeing what we see, or we are like the blind men who touch different parts of an elephant, experiencing each part as truth, but never "seeing" the whole. Perhaps, working together, we can experience – and to some degree, grasp – the elephant more completely. The trick, I think, is to recognize the limitations of our own viewpoints and genuinely value the viewpoints of others.

To address these issues, ethnography calls for closely examining one's own positionality vis-á-vis the people we study. Whether or not this facilitates *better* seeing is a subject of debate; some argue that focusing on one's own positionality can be merely a performative, confessional or even fundamentally narcissistic move: a form of "naval gazing,"[18] in which researchers turn their attention to themselves but then go on to make the same claims about "others" that they would have made anyway. Most scholars argue that acknowledging one's subjectivity is foundational, however, if for no other reason than this allows readers to better evaluate the claims researchers make, because readers will know more about who writers are, what we bring to the task, how we may be experienced by others in the world and how reflective we are about our own positioning. I unpack this notion, expanding it with a "mindful" approach to *reflectivity* as well, in the next chapter and return to these issues throughout the book.

Dualistic and non-dualistic thinking

At the core of debates about subjectivity and objectivity that reign in social science research is the notion that there *is* an objective reality that *can* be separated from our subjective views of it, and thus that we can know. The entire enterprise of modern, Western scientific research is, arguably, premised on this assumption. This is a *dualistic* perspective, one that dichotomizes subjectivity and objectivity, self and other, the knower and the known. Most of us have deeply internalized the idea that these things are or can be separated, even if we sometimes entertain the idea that the division is illusory.

Under modernity and the rise of European dominance over the intellectual world, many other dualisms became marked and entrenched in our thinking, and naturalized: the separation of humans from animals, living creatures from the earth, mind from heart, intellect from emotions, body from brain. The Cartesian divide – the distinction between mind and body, intellect and spirit, or head and heart that was reinforced and developed in the European Enlightenment – did not just split the mind from the body; it *elevated* rational, linear and logocentric mind processes and *denigrated* intuitive, left-brained, nonrational and emotional dimensions of human understanding. Transcending this divide does not mean abandoning "scientific" (masculinist, rational and mind-driven) ways of knowing and replacing them with intuition – but rather, re-balancing binaries that have gone awry. This book is an attempt to do just that; I join with others who also seek a new way forward.

Academic disciplines arose out of those dualisms, arguably in efforts to control, regiment, categorize, regulate, dominate, master and contain the social and natural world. Such order has its place. It also reigns us in. Working thoughtfully *both* with differentiation/categorization *and* with unification/interrelationships requires the kind of "both/and" thinking that Patricia Hill Collins calls for in her approach to black feminist epistemology.[19] De-colonizing our minds is not easy. But acting mindfully, we can get better at it.

BOX 1.1 NON-DUALISTIC EPISTEMOLOGIES: "POST" PERSPECTIVES

Pre-, post- and de-colonialist perspectives

Post- and de-colonialist perspectives ask what scholarship might look like if non-Western ways had been allowed to develop and flourish and what questions we might ask if we were not *reacting* to neocolonialist agendas. What might be discovered through ways of knowing that are distinct from the modes of reasoning that emerged in Europe's "Enlightenment" era and that are not framed by the encounter between West and non-West, north and south, modern and traditional or *any* "othering" dichotomy? Post-colonialists and Indigenous scholars point to a long history of epistemological traditions that are not grounded in the Cartesian divide, shored up by ideologies of patriarchy, white supremacy and Judeo-Christian beliefs in man's right to dominion over nature and that honor interrelationships between beings in both the social and natural worlds – or, rather, in a world that is not divided into "social" and "natural," a deeply species-centric viewpoint.

There were also non-dualistic, Western perspectives that lost power in the rise of Cartesian thinking. For example, Hegel's notion of dialectics is non-dual in nature.[20] Hegel argues that ideas develop from the resolution of opposing forces; with each resolution, new (dualistic) contradictions emerge that then seek resolution into a non-dualistic whole. This was the basis for Marx's notions of the social evolution and thus offers a Westernized, non-dualistic philosophy to support both comprehending and transforming the world (or at least, understanding how it may be transformed). (It may be helpful to consider the dialectical tensions that seem heightened in the current political moment and hold out the hope for their resolution into something transformative that we can't quite envision yet.)

While we cannot return to the past, we can consider what older, now-non-dominant epistemologies offer to a re-imagining of the world. Deloria and colleagues reframe dichotomies of Western/Indigenous, modern/traditional by positing as follows:

> The point is not so much that Indigenous perspectives need to be included in the general politics of knowledge (though that is true); rather it is that the Indigenous itself is generative of that knowledge,

not peripheral to it. Indigenous studies is not just about Indigenous people. It's also about ways of seeing and investigating the world that have proven central.[21]

Post-colonialist and Indigenous scholars point to ways of writing not *against* colonialist thinking but *from* contemporary Indigenous and de-colonized ways of knowing. This is not easy, because dominant cultural knowledge forms and processes are deeply imbricated in academia. They are cultivated and internalized through Western schooling and academic institutions and thus at least partly shape the subjectivities of all of us, even as we try to escape them. The call is to see through profoundly different frameworks, rather than just to react to or push against dominant ones (which, arguably, may reinforce those very frames).

Post-humanism

Post-humanism is the latest "post" perspective to come on the theoretical scene, attempting to offer a paradigm shift that facilitates a new way of viewing the world. I began reading about post-humanism with some heavy skepticism, which I examine in the interlude that follows. (Examining my assumptions offered an opportunity for me to walk the talk I am advocating in this book.)

Post-humanists are calling for a shift that does not only shake the foundations of modern Western thought; it unsettles *reactions* to that thought, including critical ones. Like Indigenous scholars, post-humanists are not suggesting that we deny humans their place in the world but, rather, just that we *put* us in our place, seeing ourselves as part of the world, not apart from it. They question the tenets of modernism that set "Man" apart, making him (and indeed he was male, and white) distinct from animals, separate from the earth and standing in "dominion" over it. In this sense, these ideas resonate with Indigenous epistemologies.

Post-humanists suggest that this fundamental division between man and animals – elevating humans over other species and seeing them as fundamentally different – provided the foundation for judging some people or groups of people as sub-human. They suggest that calls for "humanizing" those who have been dehumanized in this system may, ironically, actually *reinforce* the basic tenets that created that dehumanization in the first place. The post-humanist paradigm shift involves eliding or erasing the initial claim (that humans are elevated over or fundamentally distinct from animals or the natural world). This conceptual move helps to ensure that we don't *re-inscribe* the structural mechanisms that undergird that elevation. Post-humanism involves a deconstruction of "the common sense, taken for granted naturalness of humanism, not from an anti-humanist perspective, but as a movement beyond the limits and contradictions of the humanist project while still maintaining the modernist and humanist projects of rights, justice, equity and freedom."[22]

Rejecting the premise of human exceptionalism and the fundamental distinction between humans and animals undermines the basis for ranking both within and across species on any scale of development. Further, it eliminates the logic that allowed "man" to feel he had the right to dominate and control all others: animals, women, those dubbed sub-human and the earth itself. Fundamental to post-humanism is a recognition that anthropocentrism and specism have shaped contemporary thought in profound and pervasive ways and in so doing have shored up all kinds of other "isms" as well. In questioning these tenets, dichotomies begin to fall away: between humans and animals, plants and animals, man and machine, conscious and presumably unconscious life, human and subhuman . . . and perhaps, even between self and other – the fundamental line of separation with which ethnographers, like all humans, contend.

Further destabilizing the distinction between self and other, post-humanists call for recognition of the profound ways in which humans are integrated with and connected through technology. In this, post-humanists move beyond what could be critiqued as a mere repackaging of Indigenous epistemologies. Carrie Wolf[23] argues that humans are "fundamentally a prosthetic creature that has coevolved with various forms of technicity and materiality" using language as "the most fundamental prostheticity of all" and a host of "peripheral devices" to store, process and represent information. This allows for "theoretically enhanced" imaginations that "destabilize(s) the boundaries between our thoughts and those of others." Perhaps technology will allow us to capture "emic" perspectives in new ways, by quite literally seeing and hearing through the eyes and ears of others.

Non-dualism

The oldest, enduring, philosophical and spiritual belief systems, including Taoism, Buddhism, Hinduism, Sufism, Indigenous epistemologies and Christian Mysticism, all point toward ways of moving beyond the limiting perspectives of dualism. So, too, do some traditions within Western philosophy, such as Hegelian notions of the dialectical evolution of consciousness.[24] Emerging research in contemporary science joins the chorus, with considerable popular attention going to the idea proffered by quantum physicists that the observer and the observed are fundamentally entwined.[25] Advances in artificial intelligence further interrogate the very meaning of consciousness. These voices join with a growing number of scientists who are calling not for a simplistic return to *religious* interpretations of the world but for an integration of spiritual and scientific knowledge.[26]

Dualisms are anchored in socially constructed ways of understanding the world devised by humans; they are not inherent in the world itself. They are sustained through their relationship to each other. To every yin there is a yang. There is no up without a down. Lao Tzu, the father of Chinese Taoism, wrote poetically of how opposites depend on and therefore construct each other, in these verses from the Tao Te Ching:

> When people see some things as beautiful,
> other things become ugly.
> When people see some things as good,
> other things become bad.
> Being and non-being create each other.
> Difficult and easy support each other.
> Long and short define each other.
> High and low depend on each other.
> Before and after follow each other.[27]

It is not easy to grasp the notion of non-duality with our dualistically oriented minds. Meditation – especially deep, mind-altering states – seems to facilitate this. So, too, do psychedelic drugs, as Michael Pollan explores in his latest book, *How to change your mind: What the new science of psychedelics teaches us about consciousness, dying, addiction, depression and transcendence*.[28] I am not suggesting that readers go out and try Ayuhuasca or other hallucinogenic drugs. But even small moments of wonder and awe that all of us have surely experienced provide hints of non-duality. In *The great conversation: Nature and care of the soul*, Belden C. Lane, who self-describes as a "scholar-in-recovery," suggests that spending time in nature "invites a gradual abandonment of words, an unnerving entry into what the desert saints call the 'via negative.' What's most worth saying, they argued, can't be put into language."[29] The classic text of Hinduism known as the Upanishads offers: "No one can understand the sounds of a drum without understanding both drum and drummer."[30] This is reminiscent of the classic Buddhist zen koan (a statement designed to unsettle taken-for-granted beliefs and prompt paradigmatic shifts in thinking): Does a tree falling in a forest makes a sound, if no one is there to hear it? (What is a sound, if it is not heard? Isn't the act of hearing necessary for something to be a sound?) Non-dualism calls for an apprehension of reality that surpasses verbal understanding and that can really only be experienced or pointed toward in paradoxes, poetry, images and koans.

This is not just an epistemological or philosophical point. Dualistic thinking arguably is at the root of much suffering in the world. It is the *belief* that there *is* a separation between ourselves and others, between ourselves and the world, that alienates us from the world and from each other and sets us into continual wars between those we view as "us" and those we view as "them." The compulsion to name these differences may keep us from seeing how differences are sustained by the push-pull of dualistic thinking and the larger wholes of which they are part. This, in turn, may get in the way of more profoundly de-colonizing our minds (and hearts) – and the social worlds that we construct.

What does this suggest for ethnography?

A fully non-dualist approach may undermine the pursuit of social analysis. It might lead us to remove ourselves from the world, sit in bliss and contemplate our "one-ness." If we can never know anything, except, perhaps, our own consciousness, why should we try to understand the world outside our minds? Our attempts to illuminate, narrate or tame social life in ethnographic texts could, arguably, only contribute to obscuring more profound levels of reality – ones that transcend the categories that ethnography aims to identify and analyze.

But we live and move in a dualistic world. Within that world, there is much injustice and tremendous suffering. What is our responsibility in the face of inequity? As researchers concerned with social transformation, how can we contribute to understanding both the causes and the consequences of that suffering and how to work toward its alleviation?

Socially transformative research of a mindful bent may require sitting with paradoxes. The differences that exist within this world are socially constructed, but they are lived as real, with tremendous impact. We can study the world as it is, identifying differences that make a difference and showing how they operate in the world, even as we imagine how these differences could be made to matter differently, or not at all, in a different setting, place or time.

Anchoring ourselves in the triad of mind, heart and activity (rather than spinning off into the ethosphere of the heart/spirit dimension, and letting the triangle evaporate), I want to suggest how the idea of non-duality can inform our thinking and our actions as ethnographers and scholar-activists, whose work is to study the world and change it – not elevate about it. In what follows, I offer a few guidelines for ethnographers who aim for their work to be both mindful and socially transformative. I then give some flesh to this discussion in the next chapter, as I consider how we see and form categories in our fieldwork.

See categories as relational

First, we can remind ourselves that *all* categories and labels are relational and mostly built on dualisms. Long, short, up, down, high, low, good, bad . . . children, adults, women, men, people, animals . . . old, young, gifted, disabled, right, wrong all depend on what we are comparing things to or what we presume as normative. When we place a label on something, we define it not just by what we presume it to be but in relation to what it is *not*. We can become more conscious of the labels we use to describe what we see in the field and consider what they reveal about our own ways of viewing the world, the dominant categories of our culture and the relationships between entities.

Examine categories within their local systems

Dualities of good/bad, right/wrong, smart/dumb, beautiful/ugly, easy/hard and so on assume their meaning within particular social systems, contexts or demarcated terrains. What is difficult in one area (or for any given person) might be different from what is difficult in another (or for a different person). The meanings of "difficult" are determined by their contrast with what is considered "easy" within that system. We can consider cross-cultural variation in these constructs. What is beautiful in one culture might be ugly in another. We can see how the categories sustain each other within the local systems and consider how they might be shifted within that system and re-defined entirely within different ones.

Imagine how these could be otherwise

Ethnography helps us to see how meanings are locally defined. Non-dualistic perspectives ask us to further consider how *all* such distinctions can sometimes become *meaningless*. There is, for example, no up or down, east or west, or right or left, in outer space. When we step out of the systems that bind particular dualities together in particular ways, their meanings shift and may fall away. Could we imagine a world in which categories of power lose all meaning? I beg to differ with John Lennon, who thought that "it isn't hard to do." Imagining possibilities that do not yet exist is not so easy at all. But sometimes imagining them is the first step to bringing them into being.

See into, through and beyond labels

Labels point to things in the world, but they can never grasp the full meaning of those things. Moreover, the act of fixing things with labels may keep us from seeing them more fully or looking more deeply into their essence. Sometimes we perseverate in trying to get the labels "just right" – ones that will not offend anyone and that will speak some kind of enduring truth. But this is impossible: labels change over time, across contexts, and people prefer different things, for different reasons. All labels are fraught within systems of oppression and histories of power relations. Perhaps we can set "emic" (locally meaningful) terms in dialogue with "etic" ones and use them in conjunction with more contingency to identify not what they *are* – in fixed, essentialized ways – but the meanings or essences they point toward or the ways they are *used* to make meaning in the world. We can be more explicit about our decisions to use one label or another.

Be aware of comparisons

If we want to understand cultural practices as they are, in an integrated and meaningful whole, we have to transcend the press to compare them with something else. Or, when we do, we should be aware that that is what we are doing. When we call something "loud" or "bright" or "smart" or "beautiful," what are we comparing it to? There *is* an up only because there is a down. We cannot exist in a space of non-up-nor-down-ness. But up can become down, simply by changing our orientation to the world. There is no inherent "up-ness"; up is what we have decided it to be.

BOX 1.2 COGNITIVE SCIENCE PERSPECTIVES ON MINDFULNESS

When I first searched the literature using the terms "mindfulness" and "research," a few years ago, Ellen Langer's name popped up. First published in 1989 – well ahead of its time in terms of cognitive science research – and then reprinted in expanded and updated form in a twenty-fifth-anniversary edition in 2014 – Langer's book (simply titled *Mindfulness*)[31] examines the many ways in which being aware of what we are doing, rather than acting in routinized ways, can help us be more open to surprises, less vulnerable to making assumptions, more flexible, inspired and creative. Drawing on numerous experimental design studies conducted by herself and others, anchored within the field of cognitive psychology, Langer makes a case for the power of mindfulness for learning, creativity, business and health, as well as general quality life experiences. She argues that three key capacities are enhanced through mindfulness practices: (1) the capacity to create new categories (rather than rely on predetermined ones); (2) an openness to new information, attending to changed signals in the environment rather than blocking them out through habituation and routinization; and (3) an awareness of multiple perspectives – including the awareness that there *are* other perspectives and that other people have reasons for the perspectives that they hold.

Langer's research on mindfulness began with an interest in the effects of mind*less*ness on human activity, health and well-being. In her introduction to the twenty-fifth edition, Langer goes so far as to suggest that mindlessness is the root of all problems, both personal and social, physical and emotional. This "mindlessness" entails reacting to the world on the basis of emotional triggers rather than more considered responses, passively rather than actively responding to environmental cues, and setting mental limits for ourselves based on preconceived ideas, past history and assumptions. In doing these things, we reinforce and perpetuate stereotypes and constrain our own possibilities in ways that can negatively impact our health, well-being and the quality of our work.

Contrasting "mindless" and "mindful" approaches to engaging in the world (without actually defining mindfulness but rather operationalizing it in contrast with routinized, or unconscious cognitive processing), Langer cites research that shows how mind-sets can quite literally delimit both what and how we see and how alternative framings can facilitate new or enhanced ways of seeing. She reviews experimental work that shows how an orientation to mindfulness resulted in work that was judged by others to be more effective and of higher quality than similar work done without an explicit call for mindfulness.

This decidedly cognitive approach suggests that mindfulness practices can help ethnographers enhance their capacity to do the things that are most valued in their craft. It provides some empirical rationale for the suggestions I will offer for fieldworkers in the chapters that follow: mindful approaches to our work can help us step out of our own perspectives and be more open to surprises.

Examine how differences came to be

By considering differences or categories set within local systems and recognizing them as social constructions, we can then examine how they came to be. How do *these* differences come to *make* particular differences in the social world?[32] This focuses on the *processes* by which dualisms work. How are categories of meaning constructed and reinforced, in everyday lived realities, through specific actions and interactions?

Identify where differences fall away

We might also consider: where, how and why do some differences not make any social difference at all? When do categories assume great power, and when do they fall away? This may help us to conjecture how they might be re-constructed, transformed or refigured. We can almost always find differences if we seek them, and such findings will be more easily received – and published – in the research world than will studies that show "no difference."[33] The differences we find may well be important to name – especially differences that play out in the world as inequities, as most socially constructed differences do. But the danger is that we then come to believe those differences are fixed, solid and enduring, rather than constructed through particular processes, practices and ideologies. We may stop imagining how they could be otherwise or even noticing when they are.

Seek connection and commonality

The research world is strongly oriented toward identifying differences: between groups, cultures, contexts, time periods and more. Bentz and Shapiro[34] suggest that a Buddhist (or non-dualist) approach to research would orient differently:

> Buddhism tells us that our everyday sense of separateness from other beings is illusory and comes from attachments to the illusions of the ego. In the way we experience the other (think here of the other that you are studying, whether it is other people, other cultures, other historical times, other ideas), we may be projecting illusions, fantasies, needs or emotions.[35]

Identifying interconnection is not about ignoring differences that are real in the social world. It is about seeing more clearly what links us (in what Thich Naht Hahn[36] refers to as our "interbeingness" or mutual dependency). We can identify what facilitates us in coming together in supportive, constructive and non-antagonistic ways.

Identify obstacles to connection

Identifying obstacles to interconnectedness can help us understand what blocks us from seeing ourselves in others and others in ourselves. This will take us into important questions about power. We can identify those power relations as obstacles while still holding out a vision of a world in which we could move beyond them.

Nurture the seeds of possibility

It is easy to get lost in critique, seeing only what is wrong, missing, misguided or warped. It is harder, I think, to see potential and possibility. This is true in educational practice: errors and mistakes seem to leap off the page when I put on my teacher's hat. I have to actively and continuously remind myself to direct my attention away from what is "wrong" in order to identify what could be built upon, for the vision I hope to see unfold.[37] The same is true for seeing possibility, not just problems, in the world. We get better at this as we make it a practice, nurturing our own seeds of possibility as well. As Thich Naht Hahn writes: "There are many kinds of seeds in us, both good and bad. . . . Every time we practice mindful living, we plant healthy seeds and strengthen the healthy seeds already in us."[38]

See with compassion

Contemplative spiritual traditions from around the world and throughout history suggest ways of moving beyond all limiting perspectives by asking us to see not just with our heads but with our hearts: to consciously and intentionally activate compassion (for ourselves as well as for others) and cultivate empathy.[39] This provides a foundation for *compassionate* social science research that gets us beyond debates about whose truth is more correct, which we will likely never fully settle. By holding our own egos a little more lightly we may find compassionate points of connection even with people with whom we don't agree.

Listen with our hearts

To cultivate a compassionate stance, we need to actively listen with our hearts, not just our heads: going over as well as under the words people use to contemplate what they are trying to say and why they may feel this way. What may lie underneath their words? Could we give others the benefit of the doubt, listening for the good, as we might wish others to listen to us? This is the kind of listening that our hearts do when we don't get tugged off by our minds.[40]

Attend to our thoughts and feelings

Both are important. Our thoughts and feelings can provide valuable insights into social processes. We can work with them separately *and* together – the "sentipensante" or "thought-feeling" approach detailed by Laura Rendón.[41] I discuss this further in Chapter Three.

Be gentle

The open heart and mind that I am calling for is not easy to sustain and to bring consistently into our work. Contemplative practices encourage us to be gentle with ourselves and others as we fall short of our own ideals. Mindful ethnography asks us to look generously upon others as well. Thich Naht Hahn[42] writes: "To develop understanding, you have to practice looking at all living beings with the eyes of compassion. When you understand, you naturally act in a way that can relieve the suffering of people." This is quite a different approach from what we see in the contemporary "call-out" culture, which operates from the assumption that injustices and imperfections must be named and shamed, with shunning or "cancelling"[43] others seen as the way to bring about justice in the world. But when we focus on others' imperfections, what are we not looking at in ourselves? What changes might we bring into the world if we were kinder with others, and with our selves too?

Axiology and epistemology

The issues I have explored in this chapter are axiological as well as epistemological matters, with morals and ethics entwined with knowledge building. As researchers, we make choices about what we want to study and how we want to study it. The questions we choose to address matter for the kind of knowledge we put into the world, and the cumulative effect of that knowledge building. What direction will we choose to build in? As Anna Stetsensko wrote, "The commitment to transform the world or any of its aspects (including concepts and theories) . . . is the sine qua non for understanding the world around us in its present forms and its history."[44] The visions we hold for the future shape how we act in the present and what we come to learn from that activity. Becoming more aware of what our own visions are and what that means for how we act in the here and now – including what we choose to study, the questions we pursue and why – is a first step.

BOX 1.3 PHENOMENOLOGY MATTERS

The epistemological questions I raise in this chapter are philosophical ones that have been extensively debated and discussed in somewhat different yet related ways within the phenomenological movement, which has a long history that is strongly anchored in Western philosophical thought.[45] This is a check on my own labeling of "Western scientific thinking" as if it's a singular thing; there are the perspectives that assumed dominance in the Enlightenment but there are also divergent and subaltern viewpoints that have persisted and developed along the way in the west.

Valerie Malhoutra Bentz and Jeremy Shapiro[46] offer a different way through the impasses I have intimated in this chapter, one that is anchored in phenomenology, putting up front and center the researcher as a person in the world.

This thought-provoking introduction to "mindful inquiry" invites readers to make active choices, not just about the details of the methods we choose but about how to integrate their research with our ways of being in the world. Bentz and Shapiro address a wide array of methodological approaches (not uniquely ethnography, as I do here) as they put the person at the center and guide novices in finding approaches to research that are consonant with their own values, philosophical assumptions, research interests and inner selves.

Presenting this approach to research as unapologetically *not* value-neutral, Bentz and Shapiro name their own values as oriented to Buddhism, and show how the "Buddhist" turn complements and extends their academic orientations (to critical theory, hermeneutics and phenomenology). They suggest four steps for researchers who want to adopt their mindfully critical and conscious approach: (1) examine historical, political, economic and cultural circumstances; (2) look into your own psychology, psyche and childhood experiences to see how these may distort or shape your perceptions; (3) be sensitive to power in the search for truth; and (3) use your inquiry to reduce suffering.

BOX 1.4 ACTIVITY: PAUSE

Before continuing in your reading journey, take a pause. Do something else. If possible, go out into the world; get out of your head and into your body. Let these ideas metabolize before you go further. In this chapter I have touched on some profound epistemological questions. I have not settled any of them, and I certainly have not pointed to any new, singular, totalizing or revelatory "truth." But I hope I have raised a few things for you to think about.

These epistemological and axiological questions may be unsettling to our work as scholars. They call into question the validity of the work we do, our rationale for the approaches we choose, our trust in our own findings, our *purposes* for engaging in this work. I expect that you have had many reactions to what I have written in this chapter, and especially, perhaps, in the accompanying boxes and endnotes. Where did you have a strong reaction of any kind? When did you feel animated, excited, angry or confused? Where in your body did those feelings sit? Where have they settled now?

Sit with the thoughts and feelings that may be swimming around inside you. It might be helpful to journal some thoughts of your own. Voice-record a verbal response, or pen one. Or try drawing your reactions in some visual art form. Don't "compose" a careful structured analysis. Just attend to the thought-feelings that have surfaced for you, and see where they take you or where they settle.

This is not a journey to be rushed, not a book to be checked off as "read." And as in life, there is no test at the end. I hope that you will find your own path that balances mind, heart and action/experience in a way that feels right for you.

Notes

1 Upanishads (1949: 76).
2 George Saunders (2016) analyzes the "separate ideological countries" that seem to characterize the United States at this point in time: "Not only do our two sub-countries reason differently; they draw on non-intersecting data sets and access entirely different mythological systems." He analyzes facts that he encounters on left- and right-oriented websites, identifying how each side points to truths that are not "complexly" true, seeking facts that serve as ammunition for what we already believe.
3 I take an ironic tone in this section, but I don't mean to dismiss the value of talking with like-minded peers, especially for people from non-dominant communities that are under attack.
4 Jonathan Haidt (2013), in *The righteous mind: Why good people are divided by politics and religion*, argues that human moral decisions are driven principally by the intuitive, not rational, mind and that most people respond to the world more on the basis of emotion than reason. See also Haidt's earlier (2006) book on finding happiness by embracing ancient wisdom from diverse spiritual traditions.
5 Kohn (2013).
6 Sprague (2010).
7 Luttrell (2010).
8 See Apfell-Marglin (2011), Capra (2010), Snaza and Weaver (2015), Stoller (1998), Stokes (1997), Wilber (2017) and Wolf (2009).
9 Bentz and Shapiro (1998).
10 Foucault (1995).
11 See endnote #3 in the Introduction for books on auto-ethnography as a method.
12 "Body Rituals of the Nacirema," by Horace Miner (1956), offers a clever reversal of the anthropological mind-set. (I'll let readers discover for themselves just who the Nacirema are and the meanings of their exotic bathroom rituals.)
13 Such lack of attention to the insider-outsider relationship is deeply enmeshed in the "knowledge" that this kind of anthropology produced; indeed, Paul Stoller (1998: 57) asks, whether "most anthropological theories are based on misconceptions stemming from the inability of the anthropologist to perceive something his or her informant takes for granted."
14 Madden (2010).
15 Luttrell (2010).
16 Hartsock (1983), Harding (1987).
17 Harding (2015).
18 See Luttrell (forthcoming) among others for discussion of this notion of "naval-gazing."
19 Hill Collins (1990).
20 Hegel (2015).
21 Deloria (2018). See also Brayboy et al. (2012), Patel (2015), Smith (2012), Smith et al. (2018), Tuck and Yang (2013) and Villenas (1996). Megan Bang et al. (2015) argue for utilizing Indigenous perspectives on relationships within the natural world as a powerful knowledge-making practice in its own right, one that can stand alongside and in productive tension with contemporary Western scientific approaches. Robin Wall Kimmerer (2013), in her book *Braiding sweetgrass: Indigenous wisdom, scientific knowledge, and the teachings of plants*, illustrates beautifully how we can see the world more fully when we braid together both analysis and aesthetics, "science" and art, and "traditional" and "modern" lenses. (I found Kimmerer's evocative writing and thought-provoking viewpoints to be inspirational, and I will return to her work throughout the book.)
22 Snaza and Weaver (2015: x).
23 Wolf (2009: xxv).
24 See Hegel (2015) for a contemporary reproduction of Hegel's philosophy.
25 See Capra (2010) for a relatively accessible and popular explication of quantum physics.

26 For lively, thought-provoking and cutting-edge discussions between leading scientists as well as metaphysical philosophers and spiritual leaders, and more in-depth discussions of non-duality, see the videos, podcasts and web materials organized by SAND (Science and Non-Duality): www.scienceandnonduality.com/. See also Vrajaprana (1946), Katz (2007). Einstein (in Einstein and Harris, 1949; see also Wilber 2001) wrote about a "cosmic religious feeling" that is articulated across spiritual traditions and felt by "the religious geniuses of all ages." He noted that "it is very difficult to elucidate this feeling to anyone who is entirely without it, especially as there is no anthropomorphic conception of God corresponding to it." See also Revel et al (2000) for a lively debate between a French philosopher and his biochemist-turned-Buddhist son about the nature of knowledge claims.

27 www.goodreads.com/quotes/582339-when-people-see-some-things-as-beautiful-other-things-become.

28 Pollan (2018).

29 Lane (2019: 2).

30 Upanishads (1949: 101).

31 Langer (2014).

32 Duster (2001).

33 Fausto-Sterling (1997), Connell (1987).

34 Bentz and Shapiro (1998: 52).

35 Bentz and Shapiro (1998: 52). Referring to Eduard Said's (1978) critique of Orientalism as a projection of the Western world on Asian cultures, they suggest that "the more ego you have in your inquiry, the more likely that your other is really a projection of your own ego."

36 Thich Naht Hanh (2010: 95) leads the reader to an understanding of interbeingness: "If you are a poet, you will see clearly that there is a cloud floating in this sheet of paper. Without a cloud, there will be no rain; without rain, the trees cannot grow; and without trees, we cannot make paper. The cloud is essential for the paper to exist. If the cloud is not here, the sheet of paper cannot be here either. So we can say that the cloud and the paper *inter-are*." See also his discussion of the interrelationship of difficult and good things, as in "no mud, no lotus" (Naht Hahn, 2001).

37 I unpack this point in Orellana (2016), illustrating ways of disrupting a pedagogical mindset focused on identifying and fixing errors. Tara Brach talks about the "negativity bias" as an evolutionary development in humans and suggests ways of over-riding it: www.tarabrach.com/happiness-is-possible/.

38 Naht Hanh (2010: 74).

39 Jamil Zaki (2019) builds an argument based on social science research that empathy is not a fixed, inborn trait but one that can be fostered and developed. He notes that the *belief* that attitudes can be changed factors in to the change process.

40 Joy Harjo (2015), the 2019 Poet Laureate of the United States, reminds us: "Watch your mind. Without training it may run away and leave your heart for the immense human feast set by the thieves of time." (In "For calling the spirit back from wandering the earth in its human feet.")

41 Rendón (2009). Rendón builds on Eduardo Galeano and colleagues' (1992) use of the term, as "the marriage of thought and feeling", which in turn Galeano borrowed from Uruguayan fishermen.

42 Naht Hanh (2010: 80).

43 "Cancelling" has appeared on the social media scene as a modern form of public shunning. See www.society19.com/uk/what-is-cancel-culture-and-why-should-we-stop-it/. The practice raises many questions, including who gets to "cancel" whom? What are the repercussions of such cancelling both for individuals and for public discourse? Are there other ways to speak up about what we believe, without shunning?

44 Stetsenko (2019).

45 See Luft and Overgaard (2012) for an overview.

46 Bentz and Shapiro (1998).

References

Apfell-Marglin, F. (2011). *Subversive spiritualities: How rituals enact the world.* New York: Oxford University Press.

Bang, M., Marin, A., Medin, D. and Washinawatok, K. (2015). Learning by observing, pitching in, and being in relations in the natural world. In Mejia-Arauz, R., Rogoff, B. and Correa-Chávez (eds.), *Children learn by observing and contributing to family and community endeavors: A cultural paradigm* (pp. 303–313). Cambridge, MA: Academic Press.

Bentz, V. M. and Shapiro, J. J. (1998). *Mindful inquiry in social research.* Thousand Oaks, CA: Publications.

Brayboy, B. M. J., Gough, H. R., Leonard, B., Roehl, R. F., II and Solyom, J. A. (2012). Reclaiming scholarship: Critical indigenous research methodologies. In Lapan, S. D., Quartaroli, M. T. and Riemer, F. J. (eds.), *Qualitative research: An introduction to methods and designs* (pp. 423–450). San Francisco, CA: Jossey-Bass.

Capra, F. (2010). *The Tao of physics: An exploration of the parallels between modern physics and Eastern mysticism.* Boston, MA: Shambhala.

Connell, R. W. (1987). *Gender and power: Society, the person, and sexual politics.* Palo Alto, CA: Stanford University Press.

Deloria, P. J., Lomawaima, K. T., Brayboy, B. M. J., Trahant, M. N., Ghiglione, L., Medin, D. and Blackhawk, N. (2018). Unfolding futures: Indigenous ways of knowing for the twenty-first century. *Daedalus,* 147 (2), 6–16.

Duster, T. (2001). The 'morphing' properties of whiteness. In Rasmusen, B. B., Klinenberg, E., Nexica, I. J. and Wrey, M. (eds.), *The making and understanding of whiteness* (pp. 113–137). Durham, NC: Duke University Press.

Einstein, A. and Harris, A. (1949). *The world as I see it.* New York: Philosophical Library.

Fausto-Sterling, A. (1997). Beyond difference: A biologist's perspective. *Journal of Social Issues,* 53, 233–258.

Foucault, M. (1995). *Discipline and punish.* New York: Random House.

Galeano, E., Belfrage, C. and Schafer, M. (1992). *The book of embraces.* New York: W.W. Norton.

Haidt, J. (2006). *The happiness hypothesis: Finding truth in ancient wisdom.* New York: Basic Books.

Haidt, J. (2013). *The righteous mind: Why good people are divided by politics and religion.* New York: Vintage Books.

Harding, S. G. (ed.). (1987). *Feminism and methodology: Social science issues.* Bloomington, IN: Indiana University Press.

Harding, S. G. (2015). *Objectivity and diversity: Another logic of scientific research.* Chicago, IL: University of Chicago Press.

Harjo, J. (2015). *Conflict resolution for holy beings.* New York: W. W. Norton and Company.

Hartsock, N. C. M. (1983). The feminist standpoint: Developing the ground for a specifically feminist historical materialism. In Harding, S. (ed.), *The feminist standpoint reader: Intellectual and political controversies* (pp. 35–51). New York: Routledge.

Hegel, G. W. F. (2015). *Hegel's philosophy of mind.* UK: Andesite Press.

Hill Collins, P. (1990). *Black feminist thought: Knowledge, consciousness, and the politics of empowerment.* New York: Routledge.

Katz, J. (2007). *One: Essential writings on non-duality.* Boulder, CO: Sentient Publications.

Kimmerer, R. W. (2013). *Braiding sweetgrass: Indigenous wisdom, scientific knowledge and the teachings of plants.* Canada: Milkweed Editions.

Kohn, E. (2013). *How forests think: Toward an anthropology beyond the human.* Berkeley, CA: University of California Press.

Lane, B. C. (2019). *The great conversation: Nature and the care of the soul.* New York: Oxford University Press.

Langer, E. J. (1993). *Mindfulness.* Reading, MA: Addison-Wesley.

Luft, S. and Overgaard, S. (eds.). (2012). *The Routledge companion to phenomenology.* New York: Routledge.

Luttrell, W. (2010). *Qualitative educational research: Readings in reflexive methodology and transformative practice.* New York: Routledge.

Luttrell, W. (forthcoming). Reflexive ethnography. In *Oxford research encyclopedia of education.* Oxford, UK: Oxford University Press.

Madden, P. (2010). *Being ethnographic: A guide to the theory and practice of ethnography.* Thousand Oaks, CA: Sage Publications.

Miner, H. (1956). Body ritual among the Nacirema. *American Anthropologist*, 58, 503–507.

Naht Hahn, T. (2001). *Thich Nhat Hahn: Essential writings.* New York: Orbis Books.

Naht Hanh, T. (2010). *Peace is every step: The path of mindfulness in everyday life.* New York: Random House.

Orellana, M. F. (2016). *Immigrant children in transcultural spaces: Language, learning and Love.* New York: Routledge.

Patel. (2015). *Decolonizing educational research: From ownership to answerability.* New York: Routledge.

Pollan, M. (2018). *How to change your mind: What the new science of psychedelics teaches us about consciousness, dying, addiction, depression, and transcendence.* New York: Penguin Books.

Rendón, L. (2009). *Sentipensante pedagogy: Educating for wholeness, social justice, and liberation.* Sterling, VA: Stylus.

Revel, J. F., Ricard, M. and Canti, J. (2000). *The monk and the philosopher: A father and son discuss the meaning of life.* New York: Schocken Books.

Said, E. W. (1978). *Orientalism.* New York: Pantheon Books.

Saunders, G. (2016, July 11 & 18). Who are all these Trump supporters? *The New Yorker.* Retrieved June 27, 2019. https://www.newyorker.com/magazine/2016/07/11/george-saunders-goes-to-trump-rallies

Smith, L. T. (2012). *Decolonizing methodologies: Research and indigenous peoples.* London: Zed Books.

Smith, L. T., Tuck, E. and Yang, W. (2018). *Indigenous and decolonizing studies in education.* New York: Routledge.

Snaza, N. and Weaver, J. (2015). *Posthumanism and educational research.* New York: Routledge.

Sprague, J. (2010). In Luttrell, W. (ed.), *Qualitative educational research: Readings in reflexive methodology and transformative practice.* New York: Routledge.

Stetsenko, A. (2019). *The transformative mind: Expanding Vygotsky's approach to development and education.* New York: Cambridge University Press.

Stokes. (1997). *Pasteur's quadrant: Basic science and technological innovation.* Washington, DC: Brookings Institution Press.

Stoller, P. (1998). *The taste of ethnographic things: The senses in Anthropology.* Philadelphia, PA: University of Pennsylvania Press.

Tuck, E. and Yang, K. W. (2017). In Paris, D. and Winn, M. (eds.), *Humanizing research: Decolonizing qualitative inquiry with youth and communities.* Thousand Oaks: Sage Publications.

Upanishads. (1949). *The Upanishads.* New York: Harper.

Villenas, S. (1996). The colonizer/colonized Chicana ethnographer: Identity, marginalization, and co-optation in the field. *Harvard Educational Review*, 66 (4), 711–731.

Vrajaprana, P. (1946). *Vedanta: A simple introduction.* Hollywood, CA: Vedanta Press.

Wilber, K. (2001). *Quantum questions: Mystical writings of the world's great physicists.* Boston, MA: Shambhala.

Wilber, K. (2017). *A brief history of everything.* Boston, MA: Shambhala Press.

Wolf, C. (2009). *What is posthumanism?* Minneapolis, MN: University of Minnesota Press.

Zaki, J. (2019). *The war for kindness: Building empathy in a fractured world.* New York: Crown Press.

Interlude I

HOLDING THE WEIGHT OF THE ANALYTICAL MIND LIGHTLY

In developing the last chapter, I felt the weight of the analytical mind. I found myself weighted down by the "mind" side of the triad of mind, heart and activity. My various identities began a tug of war. The scholar in me felt I needed to keep reading – just one more book, one more author, one more school of thought. My critical-scholar-self wanted to throw it all out the window: "This is exactly the problem of Western rational thinking: the assumption that we "can" organize the world in just the right way, delineate constructs in a neat taxonomy, know exactly what should come first, second, third . . . or worse, what should be at the top and what at the bottom . . . ." The activist in me screamed, "This is why academic work never makes it into action in the world! Academics get all caught up in "words", fighting turf wars and thinking that we have to say things in just the right way, rather than getting on with the business of transforming the world!" My spiritual-self wanted to say: "Here are a bunch of thought-words. This is what this person or group once said. This is what this other person or group wrote. Make what you will of them. See it as a tapestry; don't read it as a text. Experience its "suchness." Don't try to categorize and separate the ideas. They are all interrelated. Some are reactions to the others but still part of a singular whole. It's all one!"

As scholars we all face challenges in writing literature reviews and conceptual frameworks. We may begin with some understandings of the topics we study but then realize how little we actually know. We delve into reading, and our minds expand. But then we have to present this vast material in a way that guides others and serves the task at hand. Often, the literature speaks to the issues in very different ways: some overlapping, some contradictory – certainly not in a harmonious or neatly sequential dialogue. We are expected to lead readers through a maze of ideas with certainty and confidence, assuming a voice of authority. This requires creating a route through an amorphous set of ideas, for which no map exists. But the world of ideas is more chaotic than we might like. There is an audacity to the presumption that anyone can put ideas into their proper place: fixing, ordering, labeling and properly crediting constructs that really nobody owns.

How could I pretend to capture all of these ideas in one short section of this book? The contradictions seemed so blatant. Contrasting non-duality with duality! Writing about things that I was arguing really can't be expressed in words!

And post-humanism? Initially I found my mind closing, as I made a series of assumptions about this paradigm. Didn't the prefix "post" negate the term that precedes it ("humanism")? Didn't this dichotomize the human and non-human, elevating the non-human and discarding people? I mused at the timing for post-humanism's entry into the theoretical scene, right when people who have been deemed less than fully human – people of color, women, people with disabilities, all those who have been minoritized – are beginning to claim their humanity and be heard on the world stage. I further wondered: wasn't this just a co-optation or repackaging of Indigenous epistemologies? I felt a righteousness about this critique – a stirring of ego and an attachment to ideas.

I realized, however, that this was an opportunity for me to practice what I preach: to keep my mind and heart open, check my assumptions, look for points of connection and examine possibilities rather than leap to build walls of judgment and then stay safely behind them. My aim was to see "others" (in this case, post-humanist scholars) with interest and generosity, not judgment; to look for convergences, not just differences; and wherever possible, to promote constructive and transformative inter-relatedness, not foment divisions.

First, I simply noticed my resistance. How interesting to see how my mind leaped to critique without even knowing just what I was critiquing! How curious that I thought I understood what these scholars might be saying, without having listened to them or read their words. I had immediately slipped into binary thinking: posing animals rights against human rights, and post-humanists against critical scholars. How easy it was for me to create an "other" of this group of people – revealed in the grammar of my thinking, as I referred to "them" as a monolithic block – and not even to realize that I was doing so.

Having noticed this, I decided to investigate further, with curiosity. What might be underneath my response? Perhaps some cynicism about the enterprise of academia and the way it compels scholars to stake new claims, create new terminology, put their names on new ideas and demarcate those ideas from that which has come before? Pre-established ideas about privilege and power within this institution? (I assumed post-humanists were coming from a privileged position. But just why did I assume this?) Could there be traces of jealousy, or academic rivalry (those feelings we don't like to admit that we all sometimes feel)? Perhaps I had some fear that readers would judge "me" for even taking "interest" in these ideas.

I came to see that I was at least partly policing myself based on assumptions about what others might think. (And indeed, they – you - might.) These assumptions and fears made me averse even to try to understand the philosophy of post-humanism. I was choosing what camp I wanted to be affiliated with – without even knowing what the camps believed! This was fundamentally an ego challenge: I was attaching these ideas to presumed characteristics of "people" that I wanted to differentiate myself from. I was not fully seeing those people or hearing their ideas.

So I noticed this aversion, considered where it sat in my psyche, my body and the world . . . and let it be. Then I dug in to the readings anyway.

As I read, many of my assumptions were given pause. I hope I have represented these and other ideas fairly, if incompletely. It would be easy for me to dismiss the ideas of post-humanists as mere repackaging, co-optation or cultural appropriation and to invite others to resound that critique with me. Standing with others "against" something can be comforting. Instead, I considered: why not recognize, underscore and even celebrate the interconnections between ideas that have developed in different cultural groups, historical moments, social contexts and disciplinary and spiritual traditions? This seems to me a more profoundly de-colonizing and non-dualist move, because it presses against the drive to separate, segregate, differentiate, dominate, judge, evaluate and "own." Finding commonalities and intercon-nections may help us better understand what all of these thinkers are trying to point to – an understanding that does not fit easily into words and that cannot be reduced to a label or a brand.

Thinking about scholarship in this way helped me to read generously. I continued to notice my reactions to the texts I read – where I resonated, and where I did not. But instead of engaging defensively (or offensively, looking for points of disagreement, gaps, limitations and problems), I searched for and found "interconnections" with these ways of thinking. I didn't relinquish all discernment, but I tried to hold my evaluations lightly, so they didn't get in my way of understanding what these scholars were trying to say and where their ideas fit within the larger scheme of things. This is the same kind of stance that ethnography demands, as we strive to understand how others see the world, which may be very different from the ways we do. It is also, arguably, what we need in order to work in coalition in the world in order to imagine and bring into being a different one. We will likely not all agree on what that world should look like or how to get there, but suspending judgment is key to identifying points of convergence.

2

ENTERING THE FIELD WITH OPEN HEARTS AND MINDS

There's something exciting about opening a new file and writing my first notes on a new project – one that will undoubtedly consume me for the next several years. There's also something that feels hard about it – knowing that I have to/want to be really disciplined in writing these notes after each encounter with anything/anyone who can enrich my understanding of the community I'm setting out to study, but knowing there will be many times when it will feel oppressive to have to sit and put my experiences into words on paper, and that I will be tempted to think, "Oh, I'll remember. I don't need to write THAT down," only to find out later that that is not true, that I did forget.

(Field notes, MFO, June 16, 1995)

These are my first notes as I prepared to enter the field in a postdoctoral study of children's daily lives and experiences in and around the school where I had taught for the previous ten years.[1] They were written long before I had been introduced to mindfulness and at a time when I was still rather novice in the art of fieldwork. They were warm-up notes, not actual field notes. In them, I did what I now call on my students to do in their first entry to a new field site: I noted my thoughts and feelings, giving room for my emotions on the page.

In this chapter, I scrutinize some of my earliest field notes from this research project, in a sort of auto-ethnography of ethnography: turning the mirror on myself, I make myself both the object and subject of scrutiny. I then examine first notes written by students in a field-based class I have taught for the last ten years, when they entered into this same community for the first time, some twenty years later.[2] Analyzing how we saw this community, and the people in it, in our initial encounters, I identify ways in which we all fell short in meeting the highest standards both of ethnography and of the "mindful" approach I am advocating now. My intention is not to evaluate our efforts, however, as much as to draw lessons for expanding ways of seeing, more fully opening hearts and minds and better recognizing the limits of our ethnographic instruments (our selves). I will use these reflections to consider ways of enhancing a mindful approach to seeing our field sites for the first time.

First field impressions

We only have our first impressions of any field site *once*. First impressions can tell us a great deal, both because we see things with relatively fresh eyes (approaching the Zen "beginner mind"[3]) and because they can reveal to us what *we* first notice and what we miss. This may in turn shape what we continue to attend to, and miss. Our first impressions may give us important clues about our own orientations to the field sites and the people in them, our positionalities and relationships, and the larger "self-other" epistemological questions I addressed in Chapter One. Thus, it is important to document our thoughts – and feelings – at the start of our work. As I noted in my field note entry, we won't remember most of the details, either of what we saw or of what we felt, without writing them down. Our initial thought-feelings will get mashed into an amalgam of observations, perceptions and interpretations as we proceed through the work.

We can never detail everything we see on a single day (or that is available to be seen) in a comprehensive, objective, complete and totalizing narrative. Undoubtedly, we know this (intellectually), but we often forget just how limited our viewpoints are: constrained by the limits of our senses, the angles of our vision, our histories of experiences in the world and our capacity to process the vast array of information that is "out there." We can never describe the fullness of life in words on a page: we are limited by language, by our memories and cognitive processes and by the sheer enormity of the task. Being aware of these limitations and making them transparent to ourselves keeps us from over-reaching in our claims.

Writing down our initial impressions – whatever they are – is mostly just a way for us to get started in settings that may seem overwhelming. As Emerson, Fretz and Shaw put it, in their essential guide for writing field notes: our notes are "inscriptions [that] inevitably reduce the welter and confusion of the social world to words that can be reviewed, studied, and thought about time and time again."[4] By acknowledging the sense of overwhelm, we may be more able to see how paltry our efforts to see it all are – and then *use* our initial impressions to think more about what is salient to us, and why – and open ourselves a little more to other possibilities.

Embracing a new project

Our first entry into any field site, and our start of any new project, is bound to be saturated with feelings such as worry, anxiety, hopes, fears, excitement, uncertainties and discomfort. As we progress more in the work, those initial reactions may fade and be reshaped. Being aware of our emotions may help us to recognize how we are orienting to our work. This awareness can provide insights into why we notice what we notice and what we don't notice. It can also help us to more consciously take on other orientations.

In the opening passage I voiced anxiety. Perhaps voicing that anxiety helped me to contain it. It may have been realistic to start that new project with anticipation of the potentially burdensome nature of the work. I was reminding myself of the need to be disciplined about writing field notes, because I knew how important such notes are and how easy it would be to say, "Oh, but I'll remember." And yet, I knew, I wouldn't.

At the same time, I was worried about a future that hadn't come to pass. I wonder now at the seeming lack of excitement, anticipation and joy that I named. A new field project should bring us alive! What an incredible opportunity to immerse ourselves in the social world, observing and participating, trying to understand how others live and expanding our own visions of the world. This in turn can help us formulate visions of how things *could* be, which we can then offer as informed possibilities for transforming the world.

The writing of field notes does not have to feel burdensome, as it seemed to feel to me. In Chapter Three I will suggest ways you may find pleasure in writing them: in the physical act of putting words on a page, in the creative process of painting richly colorful portraits with words; in the experiential process of living and re-living your own life more fully by documenting these days as they come to pass. We can also enjoy the fieldwork itself, more deeply and consciously, by being more fully present in the field and more actively involved in ongoing relationships and activities. We can focus on contributing something in the here and now, rather than on what we will have to say when we write our notes later on.

Ellen Langer, in her treatise on mindfulness from a cognitive science perspective,[5] cites research that shows how the ideas that we hold about the future can affect us in the present. Eduardo Kohn[6] suggests something similar in his provocative theorizing about semiotic processes, which emerged from ethnographic research in the Amazonian jungle; he uses moments in the field to illustrate that how humans – and other beings – act is largely shaped by our semiotically mediated anticipations of the future, with those anticipations ricocheting back to affect us in the here and now. What we *believe* (or fear) will happen changes what we choose to do right now. Anna Stetsenko[7] argues from a sociohistorical perspective for seeing a *dialectical* relationship between the future and the present, as well as the past: these are coextensive, co-creating each other, as our ideas about where we want to go and where we have come from shape what we do in the present moment.

Did my worries about the future keep me from being fully present in that here and now? Did they make me focus my attention on *the work* of fieldwork – and on the work that happens *after* each day in the field – more than the fieldwork itself? What might I have seen differently if I had entered with interest, curiosity, excitement, even joy, not worry or dread, ready to "participate fully and humanly in another way of life"?[8]

BOX 2.1 REFLEXIVITY AND REFLECTIVITY

In ethnographic research (and arguably in other research approaches as well), we are instruments of data collection. We understand social contexts by immersing ourselves in them, filtering them through our own senses, and through our own accumulated understandings of the world, gathered across our lifetimes. The question is: are we going to use the instruments of our being rather than let *them* use us? How can we better attune these instruments?

The first step toward more productively *using* our selves as tools of the research process is to become aware of what and how our instruments work. What do these human instruments allow us to do? In what ways are we limited? How can we be better aware of both the affordances and the constraints on what and how we see?

Awareness of our own positionality in the social world is critical for understanding how our social experiences delimit our understandings of the world. This includes but is not limited to our racialized, classed and gendered identities. These matter in terms of both who we are seen to be (and thus how others react to and treat us) and the experiences we accumulate, which shape our understanding of the world.

This kind of self-awareness is generally captured by the term "reflexivity." I have sometimes wondered if this is the term we really want to use for contemplative activity, however. I think of reflexes in terms of knee-jerk reactions: we kick violently before returning limply to stasis when triggered by a jolt. Indeed, the first three definitions of the word "reflexive" in Google's online dictionary[9] are as follows:

1. denoting a pronoun that refers back to the subject of the clause in which it is used, e.g., *myself, themselves.*
    *   (of a verb or clause) having a reflexive pronoun as its object, e.g., *wash oneself.*
2. (of an action) performed as a reflex, without conscious thought.
    *   "at concerts like this one, standing ovations have become reflexive."
3. (of a relation) always holding between a term and itself.

These contrast with the more reasoned, thoughtful, *reflective* workings of our more conscious mind. It seems strange that narcissism, knee-jerk reactions, and automatic, unconscious thought (the first three definitions) have been transformed into something of value for research, the fourth definition:

4. (of a method or theory in the social sciences) taking account of itself or of the effect of the personality or presence of the researcher on what is being investigated.

If we follow these meanings of the term, I believe mindful research involves **reflectivity**, which is about *reflecting light onto others*, not **reflexivity**, kicking outward and then settling back on our selves. Reflection happens in the pause between stimulus and response, not in the reflex. Mindfulness helps us to lengthen the pause.

However, rather than getting caught up in labels, I accede to the meanings of the term as used by ethnographers. In this volume I will use reflexivity and reflectivity interchangeably, as a few other scholars, such as Ray Madden,[10] do. We can look both inward and outward, seeing others and seeing ourselves seeing them. We can pause before responding, reflecting on how others may see us. What we see is always a reflection, filtered through the instruments of our being; and reflections always entail some level of distortion. Particularly big distortions likely happen around our gendered, raced and classed identities, because these profoundly shape what we experience in life and how we are treated by others. We should also consider other aspects of our lived experiences that are likely to show up in relation to the questions we are exploring, the populations we are working with and the things we are doing in the field. We can get better at recognizing how our instruments may both distort and illuminate, reflect and deflect, reveal and conceal.

Beyond judgment

As you proceed to read the excerpts I present in this chapter, and my reflections on them, I remind you to notice your own responses: what surprises you or gives you pause, what you notice about what we noticed as well as what we did not, what you assume about who we are and what led us to see things in those ways. You might admit where you feel clever in your analysis of our notes, even, perhaps righteous[11] in your judgments. Do you think you could have done better? Or perhaps you think such writing is a grand waste of time: mental gymnastics by scholars who don't have better things to do? Becoming aware of our judgments is an important first step in using them in *discerning* ways rather than letting them use us.

Consider as well as where your own feelings of inadequacy, uncertainty or confusion arise. I too have often felt uncertain, confused and inadequate myself. As I reviewed my field notes for this book, I also was certain that I could have done better, if I had only been a little more, well, . . . mindful. I sometimes wondered at the amount of time and energy I spent writing about the world. Perhaps I should have used that time for *action*? (This is one way in which my activist mind-set reacted to my scholarly persona: judging the choices I made in terms of where I put my time and energy.)[12] Once again, I encourage you to be aware of yourself as a reader, thinker, researcher, actor, fieldworker and sentient being: to notice your own thoughts, feelings and thought-feelings about everything you encounter. Just remember we don't have to *believe* everything we *think*.

Making our thinking visible

I turn to the next page in my field note binder, one of dozens on a shelf in my office. The pages have slightly yellowed and stick together after almost twenty years of sitting on this bookcase. The world has moved on to a digital age, and my more recent field notes are in electronic files, encrypted on my computer. I have wondered why I keep these thousands of pages of printed work. Will I ever really work with them again?

But I feel a fond attachment to these pages, marked up with highlighting and scribbles in the margins and more than a few coffee stains along the way. They represent many days and years of work – days that have long faded. I wish now that I had realized then that I was not just trying to capture some kind of objective field reality; I was inscribing particular moments in time and in the time-space continuum of the universe, as experienced through the instrument of my consciousness and my being, and memorializing those moments in print.

At the same time, field notes are not really intended to be memorialized. They are *thinking* notes, fodder for development into more considered published pieces. These were never intended to be exposed directly to the light of day. I did not write them with any audience in mind, except possibly that of my mentor in my postdoctoral research project, Barrie Thorne. (Barrie's scribbles in the margin joined mine in conversation, as we delighted in thinking together about this study.[13]) The informal nature of field notes is important to underscore, because the initial descriptions of this community that I examine next never appeared in my published writing. What I eventually published about this community was from a more considered stance, based on views that I built up over time.

This is as it should be for all fieldworkers: your notes are your notes. They shouldn't be scrutinized with the same rigor we give to final representations. You need to feel free to write whatever you think or feel, *in order to make your own thinking visible to yourself.* You can use that awareness to enhance your work. Let the meta-analysis happen *after* you have sketched out your notes. As Emerson, Fretz and Shaw[14] suggest, words should be "dashed upon the page," while your thoughts and impressions of a moment in time are fresh. Write what you remember; what stood out to you; and what memories, emotions and intellectual ideas were stimulated for you. After this, you can step back to consider them. Use a meta-analytical eye not as an editor *as* you write, but afterward: to step back, become more aware and add more.

My first set of actual field notes in this musty old binder present my first official observations of the community as I drove through the streets to visit the school where I had previously worked as a teacher. (At the outset, I should say, from my newly informed mindful perspective, the first egregious error that I made was to assume that I could observe the city while driving. Basic advice to mindful researchers should be rather obvious: do not multi-task in field work!) I was not detailing a scene that was entirely new to me; I had lived in this neighborhood for several years and worked in it for over ten. So not only are these notes from distracted eyes; they are not from fresh ones at all. And because I did not take the kinds of mindful steps that I outline later in this chapter, which might have helped me to see in fresher ways, my notes are very much suffused with my history of experiences in this community. They were also shaped by the focus of my project: I wanted to understand children's daily life experiences in this community. What was it like for children to grow up here? To walk through these streets to school each day? Where could children be found in this community, outside of homes and schools?

Seeing what's there

Let's consider the "scattered impressions" I drew from behind the wheel as I drove into this community:

> My scattered impressions as I drove south down Vernon Avenue. As I went south, the area seemed more thickly and thickly populated – a very real sense of dense living, overcrowded conditions, dirty air filled with the black fumes of city buses.

My very first sentence was not a description of this street at all, but some kind of critical social analysis about this area that I had built up over time. I *knew* that this was a densely populated community; the school I was heading toward (and where I had taught for ten years) served 2,700 children in grades K–5; it was one of the largest schools in the nation, designated as a multi-track, year-round school in which three classes of students shared two classroom spaces.[15] Their families lived within about ten square blocks of the school. I had visited the homes of students who lived with five or more people in studio apartments.[16] All of this informed my thinking. Likely it is important for seeing beneath the surface of the community. However, it may also have blocked me from detailing what I actually saw that day. What would I have seen with more of a beginner's mind, detached from my mental formations?

A critical social analysis is implied in my mention of "dirty air" and "black fumes" emanating from city buses. I think often about the everyday injustices in urban communities: dirty air being one. I imagine I did sense the dirt in the air on that day. But I might have described an actual city bus as it passed by some particular people. Where did the fumes flow? What did they smell like? Taste like? How did the air *feel?* Did pedestrians recoil from the fumes, cover their faces, turn away or continue on? Where was *their* attention directed? How did *they* move through and engage in this space – so different from my drive-through approach?

What if I had stopped the car, gotten out and walked along the sidewalk, inhaling the fumes from the buses along with the people I walked beside? This would take my critical analysis away from theory and into embodied experience. Offering my lungs up to the same poison would likely not have *softened* or neutralized my critique; it might have strengthened it and given me a deeper sense of empathy for the people I described rather dispassionately from behind the wheel of my car.

My notes for this day continue with a tangent about the products that were and weren't available in stores for people living in low-income communities (or that I presumed were or were not available, based on my experiences, but not based on direct perception, for example, by walking into a store and taking note of what exactly was sold or not sold). I spun a brief sociological analysis about consumerism and capitalism. Again, because field notes are thinking notes, it's fair to engage in such analytical diversions. Such ideas can be useful for developing more considered analyses later. Critical analyses of the social world are, well . . . critical, for critical scholars. We need to name the problems in the world if we want to change them. But I see now how quickly my mind leaped to *interpret* what I saw, to categorize and summarize it, rather than describe it in greater detail, *feel* it or experience it in other ways. Nor did I check my assumptions against the details of what I saw in any particular space.

What do we miss when we leap too quickly to interpretation, analysis, judgment and critique? I could have better checked my interpretations by comparing with what other people living in this community think, feel and understand. I could have stepped further out of my mind and into their shoes, walking in their footsteps rather than my own (or driving in my own car).

Seeing a little more

My notes reveal my own thought processes as I went on, as I asked myself, literally: "What else did I see?" For sure, this was an attempt to see more expansively. However, I can see now how impoverished my vision actually was:

> *What else did I see?* Lots and lots of stores and small businesses, increasingly Korean-owned along Vernon Ave . . . [a] cluster of women walking with smaller children. . . . Except for the school kids walking home I did not see any kids just hanging out, only young men.

I ask myself now, "Is that really all I saw?" Clearly, I attempted to consider what I was not seeing, but even the "not-seeing" was delimited by what I had set out to study (the lives of children). Reading these notes now I can list countless other things I did not see. I did not see what people looked like, what they were wearing, what they were carrying or *how* they were walking. I did not see what was on the windows of the stores, what signs were on display.[17] And so much more.

The next segment of these notes followed the flickering of my mind from this scene to my history of experiences in this community, in a kind of "observer comment" – the overtly subjective commentaries that ethnographers are encouraged to make and to mark off through italics or bracketing, in an attempt to distinguish between what is "really" there and what is thought about it.[18] (I discuss observer comments more in Chapter Three.) I leaped to a reflection on the presence of liquor stores in this and other urban neighborhoods, noting that children walk past them on their ways to and from school and are often drawn in by bright displays of Flaming Hot Cheetos and other junk food targeted at them.[19]

But still, these are my thoughts, and they read to me now as coming much more from my head than my heart. I didn't really get in touch with the *feelings* of vulnerability I had felt walking past liquor stores, which might have helped me empathize more deeply with people who walk here every day or children who are sent to run errands in these stores. My analysis also seemed to block me from perceiving the complex and *contradictory* emotions that a liquor store might evoke for children, perhaps: fear of urban dangers, connection to community, the sugary delight of candy, finger-licking goodness of spice and salt, perhaps resentment, anger or jealousy when they see others buying things that they can't.

My "objective," distancing viewpoint may have helped me to critically analyze the world but not to *empathize* with its inhabitants as much as I might. Instead, in a free-association style, my notes retreated into an intellectual critique of capitalism and patriarchy. I questioned what it was like for children to grow up surrounded by liquor stores and bars. These are important questions. There's just no evidence in my notes that I *felt* these injustices. Where did my feelings go?[20]

What I see now is how in that first movement through the community I was not just enclosed in a ton of steel but was encased deeply inside my own head. My thinking-thinking-thinking mind was hard at work. My experiential mind was asleep. My emotional, embodied self was absent. I was *analyzing* the community based on the ideas I had built up over time, rather than trying to see-feel-sense it afresh, or from the eyes of children. There is very little rich description here, no sense that I was really present, seeing, hearing, smelling, tasting and experiencing the suchness of that moment in time. There is plenty of social analysis but very little palpable sense of empathy or compassion. How might social research be different if we didn't try to separate, control and distance ourselves from our emotions and from what we were seeing, but rather if we actively cultivated connection through our hearts, bodies and minds?

Not seeing what's not there

Along with missing many things, it is easy to fall into the trap of focusing on what is *not there* (in this case, children) rather than what *is*. Noting absences can be an important way of keeping check on one's assumptions; this may lead us to notice when the thing we thought was not there appears or to dig deeper and question what it is we thought we should see. But it will only serve us in this way if we engage mindfully and reflectively enough to notice and to question our every assumption – rather than being blinded by what we have already decided is true.

We might consider what my "not-seeing" revealed about what I expected to see, surfacing the dualisms that undergird much of our thought processes. What exactly was I looking for, anyway – "kids just hanging out"? What does it mean to "just hang out"? Did I presume that in other communities, kids did this? What did I take to be normal, natural, correct, good or right? Noting what is not happening involves some kind of judgment of what "normally" happens, or what might happen in some other space, or what I assumed might happen in this one. (It's not always clear just what we are presuming when we note what we don't see, and it's good to probe; but at a minimum, noting what we don't see is certainly very different from noting what we *do*.)

Comparing community views

Two or three times a year for last ten years, I have either taught or led an instructional team in teaching a course at UCLA that introduces undergraduates to the art of writing field notes. The course includes a field experience: weekly participation with elementary-school-aged children in an afterschool program. The program is located in a school about a half mile from the one where I taught in the 1980s, in the same general community that was the site of the field work I introduced above.[21]

On the first or second day of class, my team and I offer an introductory workshop on field noting. After providing some background information on the history of ethnography, its uses, purposes and problems, we ask students to observe a video clip or a live action, jot down what they notice and compare their notes with each other. Students are generally surprised to see how different their notes are, in terms of where their attention was drawn, what they attended to and what they missed, and how they felt or what they thought about what they saw. They see where they glossed over detail and where they made assumptions and interpretations.

After this brief in-class experience, students go out for their first site visit. We ask them to note their initial impressions: what they see, hear, smell, taste and notice, including the physical setting and the people and activities that populate that space. We try not to shape their initial impressions too much, because we are curious about what they will notice and how certain they will be of their descriptions. We encourage them to write whatever they notice about the community and the school. (See guidelines in Box 2.2.)

BOX 2.2 FIELDNOTE GUIDELINES

These fieldnote guidelines have been revised over the years I have taught undergraduates about ethnographic methods. Originally, I placed much more emphasis on observing and describing – focusing *outward* on "the other." I also policed more heavily the boundary between "what you saw" and "what you thought or felt about what you saw." I have come to question the importance of shoring up these distinctions (between self and other, between thoughts and feelings, between "facts" and ways of experiencing the world). I still ask students to try to be aware of the bases of their feelings, opinions and ideas and to ground them in details that they saw, heard, felt or sensed in some other way. But I relax on the assumption that this separation is possible or that we always can, or should, try to divide our very selves. I try to strike this balance in these instructions:

> Your first set of notes should present as much detail on this as you can. Aim for two to three single-spaced pages of detail. "What do you notice about the community as you approach the school? What do you notice about the school as you enter it? How about the club space? The kids? Other participants? What thoughts and feelings are you aware of as you commute to and engage in the field site?" . . . Be as accurate as you can about what happened, focused on "describing" and noticing when your mind leaps to evaluate, compare or judge.
>
> At the same time, it is important that you include your thoughts and feelings about these interactions in your notes. These are ideas, hunches, questions, wonderings and connections to theory. Do your best to recognize them "as" your opinions, thoughts and feelings. You can try to separate these thoughts by calling them "O.C.s" (Observer Comments) and italicizing them. But don't worry if you slip on this separation. It's really hard to separate our ideas about what we see from what we see. You'll have more opportunities to review your notes and to notice times when you do that. Learning to notice your interpretations is the important thing.
>
> Don't approach this as you would a school essay. You do not need to "compose" your thoughts, nor should you edit them except for clarity and accuracy. Just pour the words out on the page in a free-flowing narrative. Don't bring in your editor eye too early in the process, because that can interfere with recalling all the details of the site. And try to enjoy the writing. Use the writing as an opportunity to re-immerse yourself in the site and to create a record of your experience so you won't forget this day in your life, and in the lives of kids at the site!

We then spend some time in class having students read each other's notes. This helps to deepen understanding of the selective nature of our seeing. Students see that each has noticed different things and that no one has captured everything. No one comes even remotely close to describing everything that could be said about the community and the school. Nor, of course, did I, in the notes I shared above. This is a vibrant, dynamic, colorful and densely populated urban community, and a complete description of all the buildings, signs, people, cars and activity on even a single block could fill volumes. The school is also a complex setting, filled with people of many ages and appearances, dressed in many ways, doing many things.

Our notes are *always* selective; we can never paint a full portrait of anything we experience in the field. As Emerson, Fretz and Shaw write, "[D]escriptions differ in what their creators note and write down as 'significant,' and, more implicitly, in what they note but ignore as 'not significant' and in what other possibly significant things they may have missed altogether."[22] But we can become more aware of our own awareness.

Visual intellectualism

With so much to fill the senses, what do students typically focus on? Comparing the multiple "first day" notes that students wrote in this course across the years, a few patterns are evident. For the most part, students started with things they *saw* (or thought they saw). (I did this as well.) Perhaps this privileging of sight is a modernist human orientation, inculcated through schooling. Immanuel Kant's "critique of judgment," written in 1790, denigrated smell, taste and touch as the "lower senses" and elevated sight to a kind of "visual intellectualism" of the Enlightenment era.[23] (With the kinds of mindful approaches I suggest at the end of this chapter, we can bring other stimuli into more conscious awareness, enhancing our capacity for the kind of "sensory ethnography" advocated by Susan Pink.[24])

And what did they see (or remember seeing)? Most commented on traffic, people and buildings. Many described these things as a broad gloss, rather than detailing *particular* buildings, traffic or people. Here are a few fairly typical descriptions:

> "I noticed that the surrounding neighborhood had a rich variety of diversity within it. The signs on the street were in both English, Spanish and Korean as well as the people walking in the street."
>
> "Entering the neighborhood in which the school was in, I noticed that it was fairly crowded with cars as well as people."

In a rare acknowledgment of non-visual stimuli, one student wrote: "This part of Los Angeles is busy with people walking, vehicles driving and muffled noises from a combination of sounds from the community."

Some students – unlike me in my first notes – mentioned the multi-lingual signs that abound in this area, though here, too, they generally made broad claims about signs that were written in "many languages," in "another language" or in "English, Spanish and Korean," without differentiating exactly what was written in what language on what signs. Presumably based on the signage, they (like I) affixed ethnic labels to businesses: "Korean stores" and "Mexican restaurants." We similarly tended to describe the people in generalities, as "adults" or "children," or simply "lots of people." The one descriptor that many used was that of ethnicity: they described the strangers they saw by either pan-ethnic or national labels. "Asian," "Latino," "Hispanic" and "Mexican" were the most common.

Invariably, as in these examples, we all painted the community with rather broad strokes and offered few specifics. We zoomed in on some things we noticed and generalized about what we had seen. What exactly are "copious amounts"? What does it mean to be "fairly crowded with cars as well as people"?

Evaluating and interpreting

As I did as well, many students included their evaluations, interpretations, assessments or judgments of what they saw. The interpretations were also revealed in small ways, in the adjectives we selected or the things we set up for contrast. Many described the community as "crowded," "busy," "bustling" or (in a rare acknowledgment of sounds) "noisy." Is "crowdedness" an objective quality of a place, or does it depend on what we assume is normal, or what we compare it to? Some implied comparisons without being explicit about *what* their point of comparison was, saying, for example, that the area was "trashier" or "more congested" (than what?).

Occasionally these involved personal opinions about what they saw. These seem to get us a little closer to what I was calling for above: a sense of connection, compassion and understanding of lived experiences. María,[25] for example, noticed families sitting on their porches, presumably talking. Ariela, like me, riffed with a sociological analysis of urbanization. But unlike me, she carefully set off her interpretation in italics, signally very clearly that these were *her* thoughts, and she added her feelings about what she saw:

> I saw people walking on the sidewalks, street vendors selling flowers, and groups of people crowding at bus stops. Specifically, getting closer to the school the side streets were dangerously narrow. The building and homes were old and unkept, *comes with poverty. The conditions of the community near the school made me think of White flight. The suburbanization of the suburbs and goal to make the suburbs more rich and white while deplet(ing) what was created to be the urban community. Housing segregation is so saddening specifically because of various labeling/limited outcomes of the community and the people that reside/ born into them.*

Ariela's mention of her feelings – unusual among students – was instructive. In contrast with Ariela's, most students' descriptions, like my own, seem rather flat, emotionless, devoid of connection to the people they were detailing. This was generally even true for students who identified with the community and who saw it as like their own. What is lost in our understandings of people and places when we sever our heads from our hearts – or believe we should do so?

Noticing our feelings does not mean that we should hold our thought-feelings as "truth." Standard ethnographic practice would insist on bracketing these in some way, as Ariela did with italics. (I suggest something a little different at the end of this chapter, and in Chapter Three.) But our aesthetic and affective responses offer important information for us to consider. Making note of our thoughts and feelings gives us material with which to work.

Different responses to the same things

We can also consider how *different* people view and react to any setting. Students in my classes often evaluated the same things quite differently. While most saw the school, or school campus, as "big" (or "huge"), for some it was beautiful; for others it seemed cold and clinical. (See Chapter One on how we generally see through implied or actual comparisons.) For some it seemed "safe"; for others it "felt like a prison." The same features – heavy metal gates and security cameras – may have led to both claims, but most people bypassed the details as they made the claims, and often they did not recognize their opinions as opinions.

Within the school context, most did not spend much time describing the walls, murals or additional physical features; their attention, not surprisingly, went to people. Many noted that the children seemed "friendly" and "happy." In contrast, Marian named a general tone to the school that she felt: "The school seemed very modern and technical (for lack of a better term?). It doesn't seem to have a loving or friendly vibe." (Marian went on to recognize that she was comparing it with her elementary school, "which had many colorful colors on the hallways and murals with vibrant themes." This led her to notice a mural at this school as well, which she thought was "cool, but not exactly friendly.") When she described the room our club met in, she evaluated it: "The room is a little bit plain, which has its pros and cons! Pros – cleaner, enables more unique creativity, less hectic environment. Cons – boring, too plain, not enough color!"

These illustrations make evident what Howard Becker points out, in a thought-provoking book about "tricks of the trade" for ethnographers: that when we write what we think is straight description it is "usually nothing of the kind, but rather a sort of analytic summary of what they have seen, designed to evade the requirement not to sample, but to report it all."[26] We all, invariably, summarize and interpret what we see. This is why writing out details, while also paying attention to the feeling-tones that are evoked for us, matters. This makes everything open for reflection: "the facts" (or what we think are the facts) as well as our aesthetic responses, opinions and feelings.

Categorical thinking

Taking the theoretical discussion of categorical thinking from Chapter One into practice, we might consider how the undergraduate ethnographers-in-training in my classes described the children when they first encountered them in our program. Here are first impressions of kids on the yard, written by students on the same first field visit one quarter:

"I saw a wide diversity of kids from various ethnic backgrounds, such as White, Asian, Black, and Hispanic."

"Once I entered the school I immediately noticed that it had a majority Latino population and then after Latino, the next big population was African American."

"The first thing I notice about the children is that they are a mix of mostly Latino, and African American children. I also see a few Filipino children as well."

These first impressions (and others like them) bear consideration. Almost invariably, students described children on the school yard first and foremost in terms of their presumed racial/ethnic or national categories and labels. They did this with a tone of certainty, making claims about children's ethnic/racial or national affiliations based on a glance at the yard. Certainly, in the race-conscious culture of the contemporary United States, people make assumptions about the race/ethnicity (and gender, age, etc.) of other people. We read, or try to read, race/ethnicity all the time (even as many pretend they do not, claiming "color-blindness.") But just *how*, and on what basis do we read it? Students did not describe the features of the children that led them to categorize them in these ways: no mention of the color or tone of their hair, skin, eyes or what they were wearing or carrying (given that clothes, backpacks, lunchboxes and other accoutrements may offer clues to ethnic identities), saying or doing. Thus, it is not clear how exactly these racialized/ethnic and national origin categories were "seen."

In unpacking this point, I am not arguing for a color-blind approach to fieldwork or endorsing the silences around naming race that abound in the larger culture. I am only wondering at the certitude with which students make claims about these *particular* identity categories, convinced that they *saw* these categories, and not examining what, specifically, they saw, or heard, that led them to name these groupings.[27] They may have been reading a disparate collection of phenotypic and social markers – from hairstyle to skin color to eyebrows to clothing – filtered through and heavily shaped by their ideas about who they *expected* to see in this space.

This is especially important when we use race (or gender, age or any group label) as a category of difference. Eduardo Kohn writes, "The world of living beings is neither just a continuum nor a collection of disparate singularities waiting to be grouped – according to social convention or innate propensity – by the human mind." He goes on to argue that categorization "can lead to a form of conceptual violence in that it erases the uniqueness of those categorized."[28] Referring to his work studying non-human beings in the Amazon Rain Forest, he suggests that "attending to the ways other kinds of selves inhabit and animate the world encourages us to rethink our ideas of relationality built on difference."[29]

We can get better at seeing, not with color-*blind* eyes but with color-*full* ones: recognizing phenotypic features as important parts of kids' racialized identities, in varied, particular, social and locally meaningful ways, and in combination with other expressions of their identities and self-presentations (including gender, age, size, dress, ways of speaking and acting and moving and being), set within particular local and historical contexts, and understood in interaction with a host of other identity markers.[30] We can be more "mindful of race,"[31] using mindfulness practices to see race more fully, understand its construction within particular systems and structures, recognize how it operates and how it is used and imagine other possibilities, rather presuming its meaning to be absolute, fixed and essentialized.[32]

Locally meaningful categories

We might also wonder: what other aspects of kids' identities – group or individual ones – were missed, by so *immediately* seeing kids in terms of dominant cultural notions and socially constructed groups, in such totalizing ways?

One of the most significant, locally meaningful and "emic" differences that distinguished kids at this school site was abundantly available for the eye to see – and yet virtually never mentioned by students. This campus houses four different elementary schools. Students at each school wear a different color school uniform: white, purple, orange or green. Students from all four schools play on the same yard. Thus, a mix of white, purple, orange and green shirts were sprinkled around. Yet not a single student in ten years of fieldwork ever commented on the different colors of these school uniforms – or even on school uniforms at all. This points to how the categories that are salient in the larger culture may absorb our attention and blind us from noticing other categories that are significant to participants in our sites.[33] What else might we be missing that is important to understand, and that might offer fresh ways of seeing the world, from outside our own vantage points?

I and my students all tended to notice and focus on things that we assumed were important or that we brought to the field from our histories of experiences in the world. We operated largely from our own cultural and generational perspectives – and an adult-centric stance. What stood out was usually what either contrasted or resonated with our own experiences. What we missed were things that were not important to us but that may in fact be very important to the participants, and to the shaping of children's daily life experiences. For socially transformative research, things that are not on our own radar screens, that are seemingly invisible to our eyes, might help point to new ways of both understanding and reformulating the world.[34]

Certainly, we shouldn't lose the critical sensibility that helps us to discern differences that matter in the social world as it is today, built from our own engagement in the world. But mindful approaches can help us to *use* that critical sensibility, rather than having *it* use *us*. We can more consciously and deliberately deploy a critical analysis by noticing what we notice, not presuming what we see to be essential or absolute truth, and holding our perceptions at enough of a distance to allow us to see more, as we more consciously consider our own perceptions and imagine new possibilities. In this way we can see more expansively, so that we are not *constrained* by the categories of our culture and by our own histories of experience.[35]

Key to this is asking again and again what leads us to identify the categories we name. Staying mindfully close to our senses will assist. What do we actually *see*, and hear, sense and feel? We can slow the leap from description to interpretation and be more aware when we do make the leap. Because once we interpret reality, our interpretations easily become our own unquestioned truths, and we can lose touch with what led us to those understandings, what may lie underneath them, what they may point toward, what else may be there or how we might otherwise imagine the world.[36]

The triad of heart, mind and activity

When I initially began teaching ethnography, I argued – as is standard practice in ethnography – for the importance of separating our thoughts and feelings from what we "actually see." Now, I wonder what is lost when we enforce this too tightly or when we *believe* that we can do this. We may fool ourselves into believing we can see "just the facts," separated from how we feel.[37]

In a beautiful passage in a quasi-memoire by Tim O'Brien (*The things they carried*), O'Brien plays with and questions the nature of truth, explaining that he wanted his audience to feel what the Vietnam war was like: "I want you to feel what I felt. I want you to know why story-truth is truer sometimes than happening truth."[38] I am not suggesting that ethnographers should spin fictional tales to evoke feelings in readers. I am only noting that our own feelings about what we observe and participate in are important, and leaving them off (in pursuit of "happening truth" or "the facts") may make our work in some ways *less*, not more true. We cut off from conscious awareness things that might help us both understand and better connect with the people in our field sites, with our readers, with our own selves, and with other people we care about. We might consider: how might academia better serve the world, and welcome more people into its ranks (especially those who often do not see themselves represented here), if the price of entry were not to cut off one's spirit, heart, passion, feelings and commitments, the things we care deeply about? Why are our minds so afraid of our hearts?

Rather than trying to enforce a separation of thought and emotion, or fact and feeling, a mindful approach asks us to notice it all, as it arises. We can notice what we see, hear, smell, taste and sense, tuning into both inner processes and the outer world. We can go inward and outward as these sensations arise and fade away. We can pay attention to thoughts that come and go, feelings that arise and what hits our senses. Sometimes, we may fuse our thoughts and feelings, sifting our thoughts through our feelings, and both through our experiences in the world. All of this becomes material for exploration. Such exploration does not have to mean categorizing, splitting off and dichotomizing: putting the "real stuff" on the one side and the "subjective stuff" on the other. It means becoming more aware of it all and using it *all* as data.

And I do not just mean using it to enhance our social research. By uniting our thoughts and feelings, rather than policing their separation, or believing that we can or should do so, we may be more propelled into "right action." Donald Rothenberg writes, "This work is to be aware and present to what is happening, responding compassionately to suffering, understanding our interdependence, and acting with grace, equanimity and passion in difficult circumstances."[39] Rothberg is not speaking to social science researchers, rather to those who seek to unite spiritual convictions and social action. But being aware of and present to what is happening is what ethnographers are called to do. Rather than trying to detach from our emotions, or demarcate thoughts and feelings, a mindfully *compassionate* approach to fieldwork asks us to connect deeply with everything we think and feel. We might also notice when walls go up in our own heads and hearts, keeping us from connecting fully deeply, empathically and kindly with the people we are studying.

I dig further into these ideas in the next chapter.

BOX 2.3 ACTIVITY: DOING THINGS DIFFERENTLY

An awareful approach to ethnography – one that I did not have an inkling about how to adopt when I began the fieldwork I detailed above – begins by recognizing the interpretive nature of the human mind. That recognition itself may allow us to hold our own assumptions at a distance, in order to look more deeply and compassionately at what is in front of us now. We can adopt some practices for *experiencing* the moments we are in, with all of our senses: feeling deeply and slowing or suspending our analytical processes. We can also try things that will deliberately facilitate seeing in more expansive ways – approaches I detail more in the next chapter. And we can work actively at surmounting the "empathy walls"[40] that we put up and guiding ourselves to see over those walls, with greater loving kindness.

Here I describe some centering and entering strategies that I now try to take on during each new day in the field. I suggest how these might enrich and expand on the kinds of notes I, and my students, wrote, as explored in this chapter.

Centering: preparing to enter the field

Before entering your new field site, sit for a moment with your eyes closed. Depending on where you are, how you got there, where the entry point begins or what is expected of you when you arrive, you may need to be creative in locating such space. Perhaps you can sit in your car in a parking lot or garage. Perhaps you can wait in the airport before locating the taxi or bus that will transport you to a new place. This is particularly important for your very first site visit, which can only be had once; why not mark it in a ceremonial way? It can also be good practice to center yourself like this every day.

Sitting quietly might not be possible or appropriate in all field sites, of course. It may mark you as a stranger, which counters the expectation that we get "in" as unobtrusively, and quickly, as we can. If you can't sit in your car in a corner of a dark garage, perhaps you can excuse yourself into a restroom or rest on a public bench. You may be too excited, nervous or defensive in a new, public space. But even a few moments of centering can be helpful.

Find a place with few distractions. Sit as quietly as you can. Take long, deep breaths, perhaps counting from ten to one as you release each one. Notice your own "mind chatter." Say hello to it, if you like, but don't talk back. This is about slowing down your senses, getting centered enough to be as fully present as you can when you walk in. Attend to what you *feel*, not just what you think: Anxiety? Fear? Excitement? Nervousness? Calm? Curiosity? *Where* do you feel these things? Deep in your stomach, or high in your throat? A fluttering around your heart, or a tightness in your head?

What memories swim into your consciousness? What parts of your own past are you bringing into this new context? Who are you as you enter this space? If you have your trusty voice recorder with you, you might want to record these thoughts. On the other hand, you might just notice them and let them go, so that you don't pull yourself into your own logocentric thinking right before entering the field.

You might think that this kind of check-in on your own thoughts and feelings will only serve to heighten or privilege *you* – *your* thoughts, *your* feelings, *your* ways of seeing the world. Isn't this what we are trying to escape from in fieldwork? Aren't we striving to move past the narcissistic gaze in order to see the world from others' perspectives? But we are thinking and feeling all the time, whether we realize it or not. Becoming more aware may help us to detach from ourselves or at least to notice how what we bring into this context shapes our understanding and what may get in the way of more fully seeing and hearing others.

Are you ready to walk into the field site? Take a few more minutes to breathe deeply, to orient yourself to being *here*. What can you let go of? Worries, fears, annoyances, stress, anticipation? Leaving emotional baggage behind – or holding it lightly – may open you to the newness of what you will see.

Entering

When you think you are ready, enter the field slowly. Make a subtle shift from an inner-focused stance to one that is alert to the world around you, while still maintaining the sense of equanimity that you hopefully established through the centering practices. You could try walking meditation: taking slow, deliberate steps as you feel each foot contact the ground. This can help – literally – to ground yourself in the field. If you are like me, walking this way in a crowded urban environment may make you feel very self-conscious. It may make you stand out too much. Perhaps you can only do it for a few steps. But see if you can ground yourself on the land, and remember where you are and why you are there.

Now, using all of your senses, record your first impressions of the site (in your mind, or possibly on that trusty voice recorder). Remember that these first impressions can only be had once, and they may point you to things that will very quickly be covered over or lost from view. The challenge is to *experience* fully without trying to convert the experience into a narrative and without trying to *analyze* what you see. Perhaps you could start with what you smell, taste or feel, rather than what you see, because it is so easy to default to our sense of vision and miss so much else. If you can, pause, close your eyes and *feel* the space you are in before you look at it. Paul Stoller writes, "We tend to allow our senses to penetrate the other's world rather than letting our senses be penetrated by the world of the other,"[41] Instead, could you let sights, sounds, smells, tastes "flow into you" with "epistemological humility"[42]?

Soon after walking into your field site for the first time, try to find a quiet place to sit and record these very first impressions. If you have your voice recorder, you'll be able to capture more than just words; you may later hear emotions in your own voice that you may not even have been aware of at the time. Where do your thoughts flow smoothly? Where do you hesitate, stumble or pause? What emotions seem to ride on the words? Do you feel giddy, tired, ecstatic or scared?

Don't edit your thoughts, and don't try to organize your thinking into categories or chronologies. Do try to include all your senses and your awareness of your own body and mind as well. What did you hear, sense, feel, smell, think and see? What emotions arose, and what bodily sensations? What was the quality of light, the timber and resonance of the sounds, and what did these evoke or awaken in you?

Now close your eyes again, and let the sensations settle. Prepare to step back in with renewed presence.

What do you see/feel/hear/smell or otherwise sense now? This time, see if you can step a little further away from your own thoughts and feelings. You have already attended to them, acknowledged them and made note of what *you* think and feel. Now you may be more able to sense a little more of how other participants in this setting – who bring very different histories of experiences in the world – may think and feel in this context. You may be ready to observe a little more closely, seeing others a little more clearly, a little less refracted through an ego-centric lens.

Repeat as many times as possible, until you stop noticing anything new.

BOX 2.4 ACTIVITY: MAKING THE STRANGE FAMILIAR

Before you take your first trip to your planned new field site, try going to a different place. Pick somewhere that you aren't very familiar with, making it easier to see with new eyes. Choose a place that *contrasts* with the site you plan to study in some kinds of significant ways. For example, if you plan to observe a classroom, try visiting a playground. If you will be focused in a city, spend a few hours in the countryside. If you plan to work with pre-schoolers, hang out with some elderly people. My point is not to emphasize dualities but to use the comparative ways that our analytical minds work to make otherwise "normalized" aspects of a setting more visible.

Follow the steps outlined in this chapter. You might consider going with a friend to a place that *is* familiar to him or her. What do you notice that she does not and vice versa?

You might keep your voice recorder with you to capture thoughts that arise spontaneously when you are doing things. Some of your richest insights into your work may arise when you are not trying to think at all.

Notes

1 The "California Childhoods" project was directed by Catherine Cooper and Barrie Thorne and funded by the MacArthur Foundation Research Network on Successful Pathways through Middle Childhood. For publications based on this work see Cooper et al. (2005a, 2005b), Orellana (2009, 2001), Orellana et al. (2003a, 2003b), Orellana and Hernández (1998), Orellana and Thorne (1998), Thorne et al. (1999), Thorne (2005, 2001).
2 I do this at the risk of falling into what has been called "naval-gazing," a critique levied against ethnographers who become self-absorbed rather than focused on others. We are expected to be self-reflective but not self-possessed. It's a delicate balancing act, even in auto-ethnography.
3 Suzuki (1970). See also McGrane's (1993) application of the notion of "beginner's mind" to sociology.
4 Emerson et al. (1995: 12).
5 Langer (2009).
6 Kohn (2013).
7 Stetsenko (2019).
8 Emerson et al. (1995: 3).
9 http://googledictionary.freecollocation.com/meaning?word=reflexive.
10 Madden (2010).
11 The social psychologist Jonathan Haidt (2012: 3) presents a lucid analysis of the formation of morality in *The righteous mind: Why good people are divided by politics and religion.* Haidt argues that human nature is intrinsically moral, but it's also "intrinsically moralistic, critical, and judgmental."
12 I am not suggesting that we should withhold critique or suppress our own thought-feelings. But we could notice both when we feel critical and when we feel connected, engaged, animated, curious, excited and inspired. Where does that enthusiasm live in our bodies? How is it fueled by, and invigorating of, connections to the world, and to each

other? We could identify what helps us to keep that kind of positive, constructive energy alive as we go about our work, refueling ourselves when we start to feel self-critical, negative or weighed down. See Neff (2015) for research-based advice on cultivating self-compassion and the power of doing so.

We might further notice what energizes others. Words can uplift. How do others react when we appreciate what they think, say and do? This "looking for goodness" (see Lawrence-Lightfoot, 1983) is a stance we can actively take into our research efforts; it's an example of the ways I suggested for moving beyond dualities in Chapter One.

13 Working with Barrie Thorne as a postdoctoral researcher was one of the great thrills and pleasures of my academic career. Barrie delighted in engaging with ideas; her scribbles in the margins were a conversation with me about what I was seeing and learning, and they helped me to see more and differently. She pushed me out of what Matthew Speier (1976) refers to as the "adult ideological viewpoint." Seeing through the eyes of children who have not been as fully formed by the social world can help us all to see in new ways. Striving to see through "the eyes of those not yet born" (a favorite line from the poem *Frente al balance, mañana*, by the Guatemalan poet Otto René Castillo, 1984), can help us to imagine possibilities that are not even on the horizon yet.

14 Emerson et al. (1995).

15 Orellana and Thorne (1998).

16 Orellana (2001).

17 This would have been very relevant for the focus of my study – the lives of children – because children in urban immigrant communities are immersed in a print-rich, multilingual environment; yet the wealth of those community resources invariably goes unseen, with educators instead focusing on the presumed limits of children's literacy experiences in homes rather than seeing the word "wealth" in their local environs. I went on to make this argument based on fieldwork walking *with* kids in their community – arguing for urban print as a literacy resource in urban communities (Orellana and Hernández, 1998) – and speaking back to deficit ideas such as the "word gap" (www. huffpost.com/entry/a-different-kind-of-word_b_10030876). But this realization took time; it was not evident in my first observations of the community. See Adair et al. (2017), Avineri et al. (2015), Baugh (2017), Blum (2014), Miller and Sperry (2012) and Sperry et al. (2019) for informed responses to the supposed gap.

18 Emerson et al. (1995: 82–83) refer to these as "asides and commentaries," seeing both as involving "a shift in attention from events in the field to outside audiences imagined as having an interest in something the fieldworker has observed and written up." Separating these from the description "helps avoid writing up details as evidence for preconceived categories or interpretations."

19 A fact check tells me that there are 8.5 liquor stores per square mile in South Los Angeles, as compared with 1.97 per square mile on the wealthier west side of the city. See Park et al. (2008).

20 In "Space and place in an urban landscape: Learning from children's views of their social worlds" (Orellana, 1999), I compare my ways of seeing with the ways in which kids saw their community, expanding my own vision. Walking with children in the community helped me to see how my attention was drawn to fences, while they noticed the flowers that grew behind the bars. I revisited these ideas to see from kids' perspectives some fifteen years later, in Orellana (2016).

21 The pedagogical principles, theoretical rationale and ways of connecting theory and practice that this class and field experience involves are detailed in Orellana (2016) and Orellana et al. (2019).

22 Emerson et al. (1995: 9).

23 Stoller (1998: 8).

24 Pink (2015).

25 All names from fieldwork projects, except my own, are pseudonyms. Most were selected by the participants. I model this disclaimer on that made by Jean Briggs (1998). The

practice of saying "all names are pseudonyms" neglects that the researcher has a name and is a person in the setting. This is an unconscious way in which we set our research participants up as "others" and mark ourselves as separate from them.

26 Becker (1998: 79) notes that readers expect to be given such interpretations, and social scientists see it as their obligation to provide. But, he suggests, "perhaps these interpretations aren't as necessary as we think. We can get a lot from simpler, less analyzed observations." This is a way of letting the details speak for themselves, letting readers draw their own conclusions by bringing them in close to the field. Becker offers some interesting examples of what straight-up description can look like.

27 Its meanings vary across contexts and history. Troy Duster (2001) suggests that we need to understand just where and how the many kinds of racialized differences are used to *make* a difference in the social world.

28 Kohn (2013: 100).

29 Kohn (2013: 100).

30 Roger Sanjek (2014: 287) offers: "The point is not to be, or pretend to be, 'color blind.' Racial categories, after all, are something we learn to see from childhood, and they are in constant use around us. Our goals, rather, should be to see racial identity as one among the many aspects of every person and to acknowledge and value the full range of human physical and cultural diversity in what always has been and is now an increasingly interconnected, color-full world. Thinking consciously, not 'blindly,' about race in order to work toward representative and proportional inclusiveness is not racist. And it can be politically empowering when it results in color-*full* ranks of local leadership and supporters."

31 In a book titled *Mindful of race: Transforming racism from the inside out*, Ruth King's (2018) approach to helping people manage the discomfort and confusion that can arise in talking about race and racism is informed both by Buddhist philosophy and many years of practice on diversity awareness.

32 The mix of racialized, pan-ethnic and national origin categories that are found in undergraduates' descriptions of kids at the school suggests that the particular racial/ethnic categories that are used in U.S. schools and the larger society have become naturalized as ways of seeing by these eighteen- to twenty-two-year-olds. Kay's comment that she saw people "such as *White, Asian, Black, and Hispanic*" (emphasis added) shows the power of the categories. Did Kay really *see* members of each of these groups, presumably in some kind of equal balance? (Note that this is different from the second and third reports, who attempted to quantify the balance of ethnicities they believed they saw.) School records indicated less than 1 percent of the student population identifies as White, and only 2 percent as African American. Or did she translate whatever she "saw" in the sea of children's faces on the playground into the four standard major categories that signify ethnic diversity in the United States today? Would these students have "seen" diversity – or read these same bodies in the same way – if they lived somewhere else – say in Brazil, South Africa, Germany or Korea, where people are racialized in different ways? This is not to say that they would not have seen *race*, only that the racialized categories they named, and presumed to be real, would likely be different.

33 One reason why it is problematic to immediately and only see kids in terms of ethnic groups is that categorical thinking can lead to false or incomplete interpretations of social processes. At B-Club one year, a group of girls came to be referred to as "the Filipina girls" in many undergraduate fieldnotes. This group consisted of three or four girls who did identify as Filipina but also one who did not. These kids also happened to be the older girls in the program at the time; they were all fourth or fifth graders, and in the same classrooms at school. Referring to them as "the Filipina girls" rather than "the older girls" suggested that it was their "Filipina-ness" that bonded them, when it is at least as likely that they hung out together based on their shared age-grades, interests and classroom experiences.

34 Livia Jiménez-Sedano (2012: 375–376) suggests three ways in which ethnicity can (but does not always) shape children's social lives: in terms of belonging, political struggle and structuring. She argues that "children (a) shape some of their belongings ethnically and (b) try to empower themselves in some situations through ethnic symbolization, but (c) do not structure their peer groups following ethnic criteria." She suggests that "when we start our studies about children by classifying them into ethnic groups, we are reproducing the bureaucratic discourse but we are not taking the children's perspective into account." Children *do* use ethnicity to express relationships among themselves, she argued, "but it is not the criterion for deciding whether they will socialize with each other or not. Behind the apparent distribution of children into ethnic groups there is something else going on." That something, she suggests, are shared codes of communication.

35 Maria Kromidas' (2016) ethnography of fifth graders in one of New York's most diverse public schools reveals how kids both take up and *challenge* dominant cultural stereotypes about race and racialized differences. Listening deeply to kids, and avoiding the imposition of an adult-centric interpretation of their words, Kromidas examines how power is shaped in kids' worlds while also seeing possibilities for re-shaping it.

36 Michelle Bellino (personal communication, June 2019) pointed out: "I often find that students first do not document race at all, then they overemphasize race and other categories, and then eventually arrive at adopting some kind of system they are comfortable with – but it always leads to really interesting questions – what it reveals about how we process one another and the assumptions we operate with."

37 Haidt (2012).

38 O'Brien (2009: 171).

39 Rothberg (2006).

40 Hochschild (2016).

41 Stoller (1998: 39).

42 Stoller (1998: 5).

References

Adair, K. J., Colegrove, K. S.-S. and McManus, M. E. (2017). How the word gap argument negatively impacts young children of Latinx immigrants' conceptualizations of learning. *Harvard Educational Review*, 87 (3), 309–334.

Avineri, N., Johnson, E. J., Brice-Heath, S., McCarty, T., Ochs, E., Kremer-Sadlik, B. S., Zentella, A. C., Rosa, J. D., Flores, N., Alim, H. S. and Paris, D. (2015). Invited forum: Bridging the 'language gap'. *Journal of Linguistic Anthropology*, 25 (1), 66–86.

Baugh, J. (2017). Meaning-less differences: Exposing fallacies and flaws in 'the word sgap' hypothesis that conceal a dangerous 'language trap' for low-income American families and their children. *International Multilingual Research Journal*, 11 (1), 39–51.

Becker, H. S. (1998). *Tricks of the trade: How to think about your research while you're doing it.* Chicago, IL: University of Chicago Press.

Blum, S. D. (2014, June 30). The language gap. *Liberal Guilt Creates Another Not-So-Magic Bullet.* Retrieved from www.huffingtonpost.com/susan-d-blum/language-gap-liberal-guilt-creates-ano_b_5233638.html.

Briggs, J. (1998). *Inuit morality play: The emotional education of a three-year-old.* New Haven, CT: Yale University Press.

Castillo, O. R. (1984). Frente al balance: Mañana. In Castillo, O. R., Fernandez, M. and Volpendesta, D. (eds.), *Tomorrow triumphant: Selected poems of Otto René Castillo.* San Francisco, CA: Night Horn Books.

Cooper, C. R., Garcia Coll, C. T., Bartko, T. W., Davis, H. M. and Chatman, C. (2005a). *Hills of gold: Rethinking diversity and contexts as resources for children's developmental pathways* (pp. 241–262). Chicago, IL: University of Chicago Press.

Cooper, C. R., García Coll, C. T., Thorne, B. and Orellana, M. F. (2005b). Beyond demographic categories: How immigration, ethnicity, and 'race' matter for children's identities and pathways through school. In Cooper, C. R., Garcia Coll, C. T., Bartko, T. W., Davis, H. M. and Chatman, C. (eds.), *Hills of gold: Rethinking diversity and contexts as resources for children's developmental pathways* (pp. 241–262). Chicago, IL: University of Chicago Press.

Duster, T. (2001). The 'morphing' properties of whiteness. In Rasmusen, B. B., Klinenberg, E., Nexica, I. J. and Wrey, M. (eds.), *The making and understanding of whiteness* (pp. 113–137). Durham, NC: Duke University Press.

Emerson, R. M., Fretz, R. I. and Shaw, L. L. (1995). *Writing ethnographic fieldnotes*. Chicago, IL: Chicago University Press.

Haidt, J. (2012). *The righteous mind: Why good people are divided by politics and religion*. New York: Random House.

Hochschild, A. (2016). *Strangers in their own land: Anger and mourning on the American right*. New York: The New Press.

Jimenez-Sedano, L. (2012). On the irrelevance of ethnicity in children's organization of their social world. *Childhood*, 19, 375–387.

King, R. (2018). *Mindful of race: Transforming racism from the inside out*. Boulder, CO: Sounds True.

Kohn, E. (2013). *How forests think: Toward an anthropology beyond the human*. Berkeley, CA: University of California Press.

Kromidas, M. (2016). *City kids: Transforming racial baggage*. New Brunswick, NJ: Rutgers University Press.

Langer, E. J. (2009). *Counterclockwise: Mindful health and the power of possibility*. New York: Ballantine Books.

Lawrence-Lightfoot, S. (1983). *The good high school: Portraits of character and culture*. New York: Basic Books.

Madden, P. (2010). *Being ethnographic: A guide to the theory and practice of ethnography*. Thousand Oaks, CA: Sage Publications.

McGrane, B. (1993). Zen sociology: Don't just do something, stand there! *Teaching Sociology*, 21 (1), 79–84. Washington, DC: American Sociological Association.

Miller, P. J. and Sperry, D. E. (2012). Deja Vu: The continuing misrecognition of low-income children's verbal abilities. In Fiske, S. T. and Markus, H. R. (eds.), *Facing social class: How societal rank influences interaction* (pp. 109–130). New York: Russell Sage Foundation.

Neff, K. (2015). *Self-compassion: The proven power of being kind to yourself*. New York: William Morrow Paperbacks.

O'Brien, T. (2009). *The things they carried*. Boston, MA: Houghton Mifflin Harcourt.

Orellana, M. F. (1999). Space and place in an urban landscape: Learning from children's views of their social worlds. *Visual Sociology*, 14, 73–89.

Orellana, M. F. (2001). The work kids do: Mexican and Central American immigrant children's contributions to households and schools in California. *Harvard Educational Review*, 71 (3), 366–389.

Orellana, M. F. (2009). *Translating childhoods: Immigrant youth, language, and culture*. New Brunswick, NJ: Rutgers University Press.

Orellana, M. F. (2016). *Immigrant children in transcultural spaces: Language, learning and Love*. New York: Routledge.

Orellana, M. F., Dorner, L. and Pulido, L. (2003a). Accessing assets: Immigrant youth as family interpreters. *Social Problems*, 50 (5), 505–524.

Orellana, M. F., Franco, J., Johnson, S. J., Rodríguez, G. B., Rodríguez, L. and Rodríguez-Minkoff, A. (2019). A transcultural pedagogy of heart and mind: Core principles. In Pacheco, M. and Morales, P. Z. (eds.), *Transforming schooling for second language learners: Policies, pedagogies and practices*. Charlotte, NC: Information Age Publishing.

Orellana, M. F. and Hernández, A. (1998). Talking the walk: Children reading urban environmental print. *The Reading Teacher*, 52 (6), 612–619.

Orellana, M. F., Reynolds, J., Dorner, L. and Meza, M. (2003b). In other words: Translating or 'para-phrasing' as a family literacy practice in immigrant households. *The Reading Research Quarterly*, 38 (1), 12–34.

Orellana, M. F. and Thorne, B. (1998). Year-round schools and the politics of time. *Anthropology and Education Quarterly*, 29 (4), 1–27.

Park, A., Watson, N. and Galloway-Gillman, L. (2008). *South Los Angeles health equity scorecard*. Los Angeles, CA: Community Health Councils.

Pink, S. (2015). *Doing sensory ethnography*. Thousand Oaks, CA: Sage Publications.

Rothberg, D. (2006). *The engaged spiritual life: A Buddhist approach to transforming ourselves and the world*. Boston, MA: Beacon Press.

Sanjek, R. (2014). *Ethnography in today's world: Color full before color blind*. Philadelphia, PA: University of Pennsylvania Press.

Speier, M. (1976). The adult ideological viewpoint in studies of childhood. *Rethinking Childhood Perspectives on Development and Society*, 168–186.

Sperry, D. E., Sperry, L. L. and Miller, P. J. (2019). Re-examining the verbal environments of children from different socioeconomic backgrounds. *Child Development*, 90 (4).

Stetsenko, A. (2019). *The transformative mind: Expanding Vygotsky's approach to development and education*. New York: Cambridge University Press.

Stoller, P. (1998). *The taste of ethnographic things: The senses in Anthropology*. Philadelphia, PA: University of Pennsylvania Press.

Suzuki, S. (1970). *Zen mind, beginner's mind*. New York: Weatherhill.

Thorne, B. (2001). Pick up time at Oakdale Elementary School: Work and family from the vantage point of children. In Hertz, R. and Marshall, N. L. (eds.), *Working families: The transformation of the American home*. Berkeley, CA: University of California Press.

Thorne, B. (2005). Unpacking school lunch time: Structure, practice and the negotiation of differences. In Cooper, C. R., Garcia Coll, C. T., Bartko, T. W., Davis, H. M. and Chatman, C. (eds.), *Developmental pathways through middle childhood*. Oxford Shire, England: Psychology Press.

Thorne, B., Orellana, M. F., Lam, W. S. E. and Chee, A. (1999). Raising children: And growing up-in transnational contexts: Comparative perspectives on generation and gender. In Hondagneu-Sotelo, P. (ed.), *Gender and U.S. immigration: Contemporary trends* (pp. 241–262). Berkeley, CA: University of California Press.

Interlude II
FEELING THE "SUCHNESS" OF A SPACE

I tried following the advice I gave in the last chapter while writing this book in Costa Rica. This was not actually a "field site"; I was here on a writing retreat, not a new research project. I had no driving questions. I chose a quiet spot devoid of human activity near a river in a rain forest. This felt like a place where I could easily render a "still life portrait," because nothing seemed to be changing (though, of course, there was much more happening than I could grasp). This made it easier to enact this exercise and to make the familiar strange. It felt relatively easy to attune to all my senses, because the sounds, smells and feelings in the air were so distinct from my city life, and I was so unused to sitting, listening and smelling rain forests.

I started by closing my eyes. With visual input cut off, my attention went first to what I heard: a steady stream of water babbling over rocks in the river. I recalled Robin Wall Kimmerer's description of listening to a river during a rainfall: "The sound of individual raindrops is lost in the foaming white rush and smooth glide over rock."[1] Like Kimmerer, I couldn't follow the sound of particular water drops rushing over any particular rock: it all added up to a waterfall symphony of sounds.

The river muffled other noises, but they were there if I listened hard: the bark of a dog in the distance. Bird calls: many different chirps and warbles that I don't have the language to describe. I glossed over variation and described things in vague, categorical terms, as "bird calls," using the label as a shortcut instead of trying to describe them.

How about my sense of touch? Tuning in, I noticed where the water and air touched my skin. Writing these notes after returning to my desk, I found that just as it was hard to describe the bird calls, I couldn't find adjectives to describe the feel of the wind and water. I could feel it in my mind's eye, but all the words I found felt impoverished and imprecise. They did not capture the "suchness" of the sensation. Cool? Silky? I wanted to say the water felt peaceful, or calm: both calming to me, and perhaps, evincing a sense of calm itself. That's the kind of descriptive word I sometimes questioned in my students' writing; I might say: "Show what made you think it was peaceful; don't tell us what you felt." But the problem was: I didn't know how to show it. I just felt it.

Something in the water tickled me, and I startled, worried that it was a fish or a snake. Fear drove my mind toward a "what if" future. What would I do if I were bitten? At the same time, my mind was beckoned into the past. I recalled days of childhood, wandering with delight in the woods near my home.

How quickly my thoughts danced between the future and the past, imposing a whole series of meanings on the canvas of my experiences, as I tried to look at this forest, this river, this moment. What interesting instruments our minds are! And how ego-centric of me to see this particular rain forest through my own memories and preoccupations. I tried to recognize this without judgment; just noticing all that tugged me away from the present, and that shaped what I thought-felt-sensed right then, as well as right now as these words leap onto my screen, and in a later-present as I edit them, tinkering with the wording with delight.

Back in the river, after noticing some of my thought-feeling-sensations, I opened my eyes. What met my eye-mind first was "green": a green that both looked and felt damp, lush, packed with water, brimming with life. Again, I couldn't − then or now − really conjure the right words to describe the combination of color, texture, shape and feel that I saw-felt. My analytical mind jumped in, wanting to understand and explain it, but I tried just to notice the feeling of moisture all around. How did it feel on my skin?

I closed my eyes and re-centered myself before looking once again. Now I realized that there were many shades of green: many combinations of color, shape and texture. It would take hours (or days, weeks, months, years) for me to detail in words the shapes of the leaves, the curves of the branches; the texture and feel of the bark; the girth and breadth and reach of their roots; the way they were dressed with vines and moss . . . how they clustered together as they formed the forest, the whole being much more than the sum of their parts. . . .

I can imagine some readers thinking, "Alright, already. Why all this detail about a forest? I'm a social scientist. I'm interested in people, actions, social processes and social justice − not the look and feel and texture of a rain forest. How can this help me to do critical scholarship? What does this have to do with doing transformative, engaged and activist research to change oppressive conditions in the social world?

Immersing myself in a rain forest in this way led me to some realizations. First, I saw that both literally and metaphorically, I was (relatively) good at seeing forests, but not trees, or the leaves on the trees, or the ways these unique trees came together. I realized how much I rely on labels as short cuts and just how much those labels obscure. I experienced how hard it was to describe the world when I didn't have the words (e.g., names for the bird calls, or labels for the trees).

I was also jolted out of my usual human-centric stance. Here, I couldn't focus on human activity, and I didn't really know how to see the activities of other life forms. I didn't have categories to group them into, beyond the most rudimentary ones (rocks, trees and water); not a single label for a tree type came to mind. I couldn't interpret movements in this setting as I might those of people: I had no idea how to elicit the meanings of the dance of butterflies fluttering from flower to flower.

This helped me to recognize my own lack of understanding, the species-centric frameworks that shape my understandings of the world. It also facilitated "experiencing" something beyond my own consciousness. As Kimmerer wrote:

I suppose that's the way we humans are, thinking too much and listening too little. Paying attention acknowledges that we have something to learn from intelligences other than our own. Listening, standing witness, creates an openness to the world in which the boundaries between us can dissolve in a raindrop.[2]

Invoking Martin Buber, Belden C. Lane[3] suggests that to really see trees we have to treat them not as objects, but enter into relationships with them. He details the way he built a relationship with one tree over time.[4]

Why does this matter for social transformation? This small experience offered me a window into what it means to step out of our driving frameworks and to adopt a beginner's mind. It made more visible the ego-centric, ethno-centric and human-centric ways I usually go about viewing the world. We are all a bit narcissistic, seeing the reflections of ourselves in the world that we gaze onto, and when we can't, we are given pause. This experience humbled me. It pointed out the limitations of this human instrument that I am. But it also gave me practice in embracing rather than bracketing, repressing or dismissing diverse ways of experiencing the world. I got a small taste of non-duality, experiencing just being part of, not master of, that landscape, in that moment in time.

Reading my write-up here is not a good way for readers to understand what I sensed-understood in that space. Don't take my word for it. Instead, try something similar yourself. Go out into a space that feels different from your routinized life and distinct from your field sites. Sit in it. Feel it. Sense it. See what bubbles up for you. Try to put it into words. I suspect you will see how the words pale in comparison with what the "suchness" of the experience that you felt-thought-sensed. This a good reminder that the words we write in our ethnographies will always be partial. They will never, ever do justice to our field sites.

In the next chapter, I will show how students experienced something similar while looking at a single tree.

Notes

1 Kimmerer (2015: 297).
2 Kimmerer (2015: 300).
3 Lane (2019).
4 See also Wohlleben (2016) for insights into the ways trees live, grow and communicate.

References

Kimmerer, R. W. (2015). *Braiding sweetgrass: Indigenous wisdom, scientific knowledge, and the teachings of plants.* Minneapolis, MN: Milkweed Editions.

Lane, B. C. (2019). *The great conversation: Nature and the care of the soul.* New York: Oxford University Press.

Wohlleben, P. (2016). *The hidden life of trees: What they feel, how they communicate – Discoveries from a secret world.* British Columbia, CA: Greystone Books.

3

GETTING IN AND ALONG

Connecting with clarity and compassion

'When we want to really understand something, we cannot just stand outside and observe it. We have to enter deeply into it and be one with it to really understand.'
                                                                    Thich Naht Hahn[1]

In Chapter Two, I began to consider some of the greatest challenges that ethnographers face: to "make the familiar strange"[2] and to observe without distorting what we see too drastically based on our history of experiences in the world. I focused on the first impressions we make of our field sites because these give us the best opportunity to see with "beginner eyes." My "think-aloud" notes in the interlude revealed how much my mind filled with chatter and shaped both what and how I saw, when I thought I was "just" observing.

This retreat into mental formations, shaped by past experiences, generally happens even more as we move into our fieldwork process, beyond the first day. We contrast new events with what we saw the day before or the previous week, as well as with our own pasts and our anticipations of the future. A student in my class wrote in her notes for her second observation: "The school was exactly as how I remembered it as it was when I attended orientation last week," and in the room where we gathered "everything looked the same." In responding, I tried to push gently: "Everything?"

Alternatively, our attention may be drawn to what seems new or different from what we have quickly established as familiar in that setting: in *contrast* or *opposition* to what we observed previously. This still keeps us tethered to our own starting points. This is our dualistic mind at work, seeing the things we expect to see, and their opposites, or absences.

In this chapter, I take mindfulness practices into the ongoing work of fieldwork and the *participation* phase of participant observation. I continue to address some common tendencies of the human analytical mind as it operates in the field, suggesting strategies not for silencing but for suspending and holding them in check and balancing them with other ways of experiencing. This allows us to harness the power of our analytical minds for our own purposes, rather than handing over tight control of the process from the beginning. I consider ways of staying centered and fully present even as we participate in the buzz of ongoing human activity and how to balance thinking, feeling and sensing as we listen intently, observe keenly, think-feel deeply and participate actively in our field sites.

I further ask: how can we connect *compassionately* and empathically with our field participants and with ourselves in this research process? When we stay connected with our hearts as well as our heads, as we immerse in activity in the field, what might we understand and then do with what we learn?

Presence and participation

Over the last twenty years, I have participated in many field settings. I have observed in classrooms that were structured different ways and that served children of different grades and ages. I have worked in homes, parks, playgrounds, community centers and afterschool programs. I have interacted with hundreds of children and dozens of parents and teachers, building relationships that were sustained over time, and that felt *real*. I have been a *participant*, not just an observer, in each of these settings.

Looking back on these many days of fieldwork, I wonder now: just how *present* was I? Did my aim of analyzing social processes keep me from connecting more deeply than I might have? My memories give me clues: I have very detailed and rich recollections of some spaces, moments, activities, interactions and events, but many others are a blur. The ones I most recall involve moments not unlike my hour in the Costa Rican rain forest, when I was aware of all my senses, fully immersed in that space and time, not trying to think consciously about anything at all, but soaking it all in. I also remember when I felt deeply connected and attuned with the people I was engaged with – truly being a *participant* observer, not an observing participant.

Interestingly, these are *not* the moments I have most closely analyzed or written about. I have developed many detailed analyses of verbal interactions, such as when I observed young people translating in parent-teacher conferences. I can remember many of the words I transcribed, but I can't recall many sensorial details of the original events: the weather, quality of light or air, what was on the walls or in the environment, what was expressed in the faces and bodies of participants or what I thought and felt. I recollect more about my *thoughts* about what I witnessed, my worries (about my presence, about how I was capturing the events), and the interpretations I was already beginning to make.

BOX 3.1 MAKING THE FAMILIAR (MORE) STRANGE: SEEING TREES

Last week (at the time that I drafted these words) in my undergraduate class-room, I tried an activity that had been suggested by Maria José Botelho and Ellen Prader at the Contemplative Mind in Higher Education conference[3] held at the University of Massachusetts, Amherst, in 2018. I asked the group of twenty-three budding ethnographers: "Did you see a tree on your way in to class?" Most of my students nodded and said yes. "Of course!" A few looked perplexed. Later, Shirona (a pseudonym) wrote in a class reflection: "When the first question prompted to us by Dr. O. was, 'Did you see a tree today?' I immediately began to wonder if there was some popular fallen tree that I'd missed while walking to class – what tree was she talking about? Around me, my classmates had similar looks of confusion."

Bemused by students' expressions, I probed: "I mean, did you really see one? Or do you know that there are trees out there, and you walked by them, so you believe you saw them?" I went on. "And did you see *a* tree? What particular tree did you see? Did you really 'see' it? Or did you pass by some things that you know to be trees? Could you describe one you really saw?"

Karina later wrote: "When she asked if we had really seen a tree and asked to describe it, I could not think of a single tree. I had different types of trees and what they looked like came to my mind, but I still could not think of a single tree." Britta noted: "Many students believed that they saw a tree, but very few were able to describe their tree specifically. This question helped me to recognize how easy it is to assume we have seen something in our every-day encounters, because it is so common, but it takes more intentionality for someone to take time to observe objects that seem so mundane."

At a break in our class, I asked students to go outside and see (and hear, smell, touch and sense) a particular tree and to come back in and try to describe it. Students attempted to do this in many different ways. Some started with colors or shapes of the leaves, branches, trunk or flowers. Others described the overall height, girth and shape, sometimes in comparison with other trees. Three named the specific location of the tree or described their tree within its local context. A few noted things they *couldn't* see, such as their tree's roots. Manuel explained: "I felt I couldn't grasp its essence completely. I could see its phenotypical attributes, but I cannot observe its history or insides." Most relied on visual descriptors, but one mentioned a "woodsy" aroma," another a "spiky" texture. One student tried looking at her tree from different angles: sitting in the grass, lying down and standing looking up through the canopy. Another tried to envision her tree at a different time of year, when it would be full of leaves and flowering. Only one named the *type* of tree it was; Carla knew hers was an "Aleppo Pine." (I wasn't sure if it didn't occur to the others to type the trees in this way, if they thought it was "cheating" or wrong to do so, or if they, like me, didn't *know* their scientific nomenclature.)

For many, this task felt very difficult. Katrina wrote: "All trees seemed the same to me so I thought it was pointless to have to look and describe a single tree; I did not see anything special in any tree. Even when focusing all my attention on a single tree, I did not know how to describe it." Katrina noted that she tried to do this by describing the leaves, the branches and the flowers, but she felt this simply didn't really capture the essence of the tree. This honest reflection reminded me, once again, how very hard it is to describe in close detail things that we take for granted or to reduce to words what we experience holistically using all of our senses. It also helped me to appreciate what students were trying to convey when they said things like "It portrays a positive vibe." Perhaps describing the "vibe" of a tree captured its essence better than a long list of attributes.

A number of students anthropomorphized their trees, describing them in peculiarly human terms. Karla, for example, saw hers as a "bully" ("because it was leaning toward this other tree that looked completely dead, so it looked like this tree was slowly killing that other tree"). Marlon saw his leafless tree as "a little sad," because "people tend to lay under trees with leaves." Vincent similarly noted, "It doesn't seem like anyone has ever played with it." Carola and Anna observed together and took their tree as a metaphor for Anna's life: "how the curved trunks and branches represent a wild child like her sisters while a straight tree is a child raised with strict parents, like Anna." Bianca and her partner – students of color – observed a tree with dull and cracked bark that covered over a dark-brown center. Bianca wrote: "We felt ourselves in this tree. We saw ourselves trying to pass in society as something we are not in order to succeed, yet deeper inside we show our truer selves." Denise similarly projected onto her tree: "I would like to take this further and elaborate on how hard I try to become like others . . . but sometimes forget my true inside colors. The very crackly areas remind me of how it is to be chipped off but it just needs more acceptance." Britta saw her tree "lively, elegant and beautiful":

> My tree was a medium sized palm tree that had a "necklace" of dead leaves, something about this tree seemed very noble, like it was royalty. Although there were many green leaves coming from the top, the dead leaves that hung around the trunk was very thick as well. I had no idea how old the tree was, but there was something very elegant and beautiful about the way it possessed the old and the new. The tree was lively, yet carried a lot of wisdom, and probably has seen a lot of things.

When I first read these notes, with my scholarly researcher-training eyes, I felt I should challenge students to "show" rather than tell me about the trees' supposed liveliness, elegance or loneliness. I thought I should caution them against projecting their thoughts, feelings, emotions and perceptions onto other beings. How do you know what the tree thinks or feels? Can you see, touch, hear or taste its wisdom? To see children's worlds, we need to try to stop seeing like adults; shouldn't we try to understand humans from a non-humancentric stance?

But then I stopped myself in my tracks. What is gained, or lost, when we try to repress or cut off our own unique ways of seeing, the things we sense or intuit that go beyond words? What if instead I encouraged these budding fieldworkers to notice, embrace and celebrate their own unique ways of seeing the world and of seeing themselves through that seeing – and just bring in a little more awareness of themselves as the seers? What new insights might we all garner from honoring diverse ways of seeing, feeling, sensing, knowing, experiencing, understanding and being – not defining one way as the "right" way?

In our debriefing conversation, Marlon shared that he had chosen a tree that he thought was dead. He explained that he made that assumption because the bark was dry and shriveled, and it had no leaves. But when he looked closely, he saw tiny buds poking through the bark: new branches, new life emerging. He likened it to resurrection. Marlon's insights reminded me of a beautiful passage I had just read Robin Wall Kimmerer's beautiful book, *Braiding Sweetgrass: Indigenous wisdom, scientific knowledge, and the teachings of plants.*[4] In it, Kimmerer writes of learning the Anishinaabe word for "the force which causes mushrooms to push up from the earth overnight" – a word for a sense of life emerging in "a world of being, full of unseen energies that animate everything" that has no equivalence in Western scientific vocabulary. She notes that Western science is a language "of careful observation, an intimate vocabulary that names each little part. To name and describe you must first see, and science polishes the gift of seeing."[5] But this can lead us to see certain things, in certain ways, and to miss so much more. Science is a language of objects: naming things in the world and then dissecting them into their component parts, to catalogue, taxonomize and organize. In naming the world, we think we control it. As Kimmerer notes, "[O]ur terminology is used to define the boundaries of our knowing. What lies beyond our grasp remains unnamed."[6]

Marlon's view of the resurrection of this tree, enhanced by a borrowing of the Ashinaabe notion of emergence, has become a metaphor for my ways of thinking about ethnography. There is new life emerging in all kinds of ways, all around us, if we can only see it. Seeing requires letting go of our assumptions and observing closely. When we do that, new possibilities burst forth. Some may be impossible to capture in words, however, and we may need to play with how to capture what we *sense*, such as the elegance and wisdom of a tree.

In our conversation, Britta said that she would never look at trees in the same way anymore. Now that she had seen this one in this way, she couldn't go back to her old ways of seeing trees as a categorical thing. I can't either. I came to see that there are many ways to see and to describe a living being such as a tree, or a girl, or a man, or an insect. Who is to say what is the "right" way to capture its essence? There may be many things we can notice, intuit and understand, and that will move us beyond static, superficial, limiting or essentializing categories if we use all our senses, feelings, memories and histories of experiences in the world, in the service of more fully and completely seeing others.

We can also become more aware of our own intuiting processes, and ourselves as the intuiters. We can *use* our intuition to garner insights into the world, while remembering that we are filtering that world through *our* thoughts, feelings, memories and imaginations. We can consider how our views align with those of others and continually stretch ourselves to better intuit from other beings' perspectives.[7]

Looking from different perspectives

What lessons can we learn from observations of the more-than-human world – my views of the rain forest in Interlude III, and my students' observations of trees, in Box 3.1 – that can be usefully applied to the study of social processes within human-centric spaces? Some lessons follow from my suggestions for seeing beyond categories, as detailed in Chapter One. Here, I consider ways we can expand our ways of seeing social contexts. My focus will be on classrooms and schools, as these have been a central site for my own research, and they are prime contexts for researchers concerned with social transformation. Thus this section may be especially useful for educational ethnographers, but the points I make should be adaptable to other social and human-centric contexts as well.

In shifting from "natural" and more-than-human-life contexts to designed institutions of modern life, I don't mean to suggest that schools are more complicated ecosystems than are forests. What is most challenging about studying schools is not their greater complexity than any other setting; it is that virtually all educational ethnographers bring long and deeply internalized histories of prior experiences into school. So too does nearly every reader of our ethnographies. (Ethnographers in other settings may be able to escape the force that such institutional contexts may have on our ways of seeing, but seeing anew is still a challenge.) Thus, it is difficult to avoid comparing any given classroom with others we have seen.[8]

A search for "classroom" on Google images reveals many versions of the same basic structure: groups of young people seated in rows at individual desks, looking toward an adult, usually a woman standing presumably at the "front" of the room. Often, she towers over the kids, with a pencil, ruler or pointer in her hand. More often than not there is a chalkboard – or sometimes a white board – behind her, with words or numbers written on it. An apple may sit on her desk.

Such archetypes likely influenced how I saw classrooms. Generally, I assumed there was a "front" and "back" of the room and that the teacher's prerogative was to be in the "front." I usually stood or sat in the "back." This led me to see the teacher and the backs of most students' heads. If I brought a video camera, I had to make choices: should I set it up at the back, focusing on the teacher? Or at the front, to gaze on the class? (Of course, there are other options; I now use Go-Pro cameras, worn by participants, to capture more directly how *they* orient to the world.[9])

Since adopting more of a mindful approach to fieldwork, I've asked myself, "What do I *not* see about teaching and learning when I assume this teacher-centric stance? How else might I see?" Asking this question opens up new possibilities – from the sublime to the ridiculous. For example, what would I see from the perspective of an ant on the floor? Surely all kinds of things that are not visible up above: bits of trash and pencil shavings, dust, cobwebs, spider webs, bugs. I'd also see a lot of *shoes*. And chair rungs.

The goal of fieldwork isn't necessarily to see from *all* possible angles, however, and unless I am trying to make arguments about bug life and its relationship to schooling, an ant's eye perspective may not be the most useful new position to adopt. I'm interested in teaching and learning and in the experiences that human beings have in these spaces we call school. But I could try to see from the perspective of students, disrupting a teacher-centric gaze. What is at students' eye level on the classroom walls? What does the student in the front row experience in this space? How about the one in the corner? Small- or large-for-their-age students, in these one-size–fits-all seats?

Attuning to all our senses

And what do I not sense, feel, hear, taste and smell when I attune only through my eyes? Besides the visual stimulus of a classroom, what affects the experiences that teachers and students have in the many hours and days they spend in such rooms? There is the quality of light, both the natural light that filters through windows and the artificial light inside the room. There are odors: the smell of pencil shavings, rubber erasers, whiteboard markers, sweat, scraps of food, school lunch wafting up from the cafeteria or released into the air through burps or breath after lunch . . . and whatever filters in through the windows. How about the feel of the chairs and desks? What is it like to sit for hours each day on hard wooden or plastic chairs? How long do I endure in such seats myself, before asserting my adult privilege of getting up, moving around or walking out the door, and going to the bathroom whenever I please?

As well, there are sounds. Many sounds, besides the teacher's voice. Most of us have been well trained to listen to teachers. Through many years of schooling, we have learned to block out sounds that might compete with their voices.

But other noises may be more audible to kids whose hearing has not been as "disciplined" as ours: the ticking of a clock, the hum of an air conditioner, voices on the school yard outside the window, the rustling of papers and, of course, the voices, and movement, of peers (which may be far more interesting than anything the teacher has to say). If you were a first grader, what might you *hear* in your classroom?

Relationships and emotions

Thus far I have focused on describing field settings as if they were still life portraits. Of course, they are not. They are filled with actions, movement, animation and life. They don't hold still long enough for us to paint them. Even if they did, our aim is not to paint portraits but to understand dynamic social actions. How can we bring a mindful mind-set to bear when all is not calm around us?

One of the challenges – and joys – in the "getting along" stage of the research process is that we will be involved in the action. We will interact with many people, enmeshing ourselves in activities and relationships. These will be real relationships, with all their complexity, even if they are "field" ones.

There is much that has been written about fieldwork relationships: how to "get in" and "get along."[10] Often these are framed in pragmatic terms for advancing the research agenda: what to do or not do to blend in, to balance viewing and participating and to retain some distance while integrating into the ongoing activities. While the "reflexive turn" in ethnography has led to greater self-awareness of the effects of the ethnographer in any setting and greater consideration of moral and ethical matters as well,[11] the advice that is typically given to ethnographers on finding ways to blend in unobtrusively to their field sites suggests that they believe those effects can be controlled.[12] I am suggesting something a little different: to be as conscious as we can about *how* our presence influences ongoing activities, starting with an awareness of ourselves.

Being aware of ourselves can facilitate us in diminishing the most egregious effects of our presence and in stepping out of our own standpoints to see from different angles. Barrie Thorne writes about her awareness of her adult self when observing children in classrooms and on the schoolyard, from the physical size of her body to the roles she got tugged into playing. This awareness led her to strategies for minimizing her adult status[13] when working with children, such as sitting where they sit, rather than in a larger chair in the back of the room, or with the teacher. Thorne also makes a move that is rarer in ethnography: she acknowledges her own emotional reactions to things she experienced in the field: moments of repulsion as well as delight.

Why be aware of our feelings?

I want to suggest that becoming more aware of our emotional responses to fieldwork can enhance the doing of transformative social research for two, somewhat contradictory, reasons. On the one hand, this allows us to put some distance between our feelings and the conclusions we draw. This does not mean bracketing our feelings, dismissing their importance, or treating them as "interference" to objectivity. It's about inserting a *pause*, so we can better contemplate what our feelings indicate. This can help us better recognize associations we make between our feeling-senses and our thoughts.

We will surely feel many things in our field sites: warmth, connection, love, joy, peacefulness, anger, confusion, delight. These feelings may lead us to many thoughts. Sunlight shining through an open window in a hot and stuffy classroom may evoke memories of childhood longings to escape from school. A teacher's sharp tone may startle us. A teasing comment by one child to another may kindle our own memories of being bullied or bullying. These feelings may be subtle, sitting more in our unconscious than conscious minds. Pausing to notice can help us to avoid imposing *our* feeling-thoughts on others, opening up space to consider how others experience these things.

On the other hand, attending to our feelings may bring us *closer* to our participants. Given the press in academia to separate mind and heart, such closeness may be viewed with suspicion.[14] But what channels of understanding have we cut off if we engage closely with other humans for an extended time *without* having strong feelings arise? Nancy Scheper-Hughes was one of the first ethnographers to proclaim as a strength the practice of listening empathically and compassionately: "Seeing, listening, touching, recording, can be, if done with care and sensitivity, acts of fraternity and sisterhood, acts of solidarity. Above all, they are the work of recognition. Not to look, not to touch, not to record, can be the hostile act, the act of indifference and of turning away."[15]

When strong feelings are triggered

Reynaldo Rosaldo's classic essay "Grief and the head hunter's rage"[16] describes the intense anger Rosaldo felt as part of his own grieving process when his wife, Michelle Zimbalist Rosaldo, died in a fieldwork accident. Rosaldo uses his anger to grasp the deep connection between rage and grief and to better understand the cultural practice of "head-hunting" engaged by the Ilongot people of the Philippines during times of devastating loss.

Lyall Crawford, in a more explicitly auto-ethnographic approach, similarly worked with the emotions that were evoked for him from a traumatic and tragic event: witnessing the death-by-crocodile of a friend while the two were serving in the Peace Corps. Crawford uses this incident to suggest that even singular experiences can "supply a very long train of thought" that can be elaborated and developed over the course of the ethnographer's life. He notes: "It was a personal struggle with the imminence of death and physical mortality that brought about taking the ethnographic turn and living the ethnographic life," and that this intense personal experience helped him to "more deeply appreciate the experience of others."[17]

Other researchers as well have worked actively with their own emotions even as they also attended to the emotions expressed by participants in the field.[18] There is certainly precedence for ethnography that is infused with feeling – and that works actively with those emotions, utilizing them to cross the self-other divide[19] and connect more empathically with others, as well as to theorize. While we should take care not to project our feelings onto the participants in our studies, tuning in to our own feelings may help us attune to others, facilitating more empathic, compassionate and ethical research.

But working with our own emotions in relation to fieldwork is not for the faint of heart. Ruth Behar, who, along with Rosaldo, was part of the initial "reflexive turn" in anthropology and who has also entwined her own emotion-filled personal experiences with those of the people and issues she studies, reflected on the "cruelty" that the mainstream anthropological world unleashed in critiques of this vulnerable approach to research.[20] To do such work, we have to be willing to confront or withstand the forces of academia that can try to shame us into staying safely on the "mind" side of this work.

If you are lucky, nothing as terrible as the death of someone you are close to will happen while you are in the field. And you may choose to avoid writing publicly about emotionally intense contexts and issues that arise in your field settings or in your own psyche. You may not want to expose your own psyche to the harsh eyes of academia. But whether or not you work actively with your own intense emotions in order to understand social and cultural processes, a mindful approach to research involves being *aware* when, where and why strong feelings arise and when, where and why they do not.

BOX 3.2 SEEING OTHERS AS OURSELVES

I don't have any real experience studying groups of people with whom I am ideologically opposed or that I dislike. I've never "studied up" across established lines of power, peering into the lives of people I might resent.[21] But I have observed some interactions that have distressed me in the field. More than a few times, for example, I have heard teachers shame children for moving their bodies, expressing their opinions or resisting their efforts to control. I've witnessed similar situations in everyday life, when adults assert their power over children in ways that seem to be violent, destructive and wrong.

I've tried to connect with the feelings these incidents evoked for me and to pause in my interpretations of them. The strength of my reactions seemed partly shaped by my own experiences as a child, feeling judged or shamed by teachers or other adults. This may or may not be a feeling commonly shared by children, given that adults do often assume – or abuse – power in this way. Recognizing this attunes me empathically to what children may feel (though

I can never be sure that they experience things as I did). It makes me want to speak up on behalf of children, perhaps calling teachers out.

It would be easy for me to blame teachers. I could assert my *own* power to call them out, shame or shun them. But would that likely bring about the changes that I hoped for? It might have the opposite effect: entrenching people in defensive positions, causing them to react rather than respond, and pull away, shut down, disengage or pass the shunning on to others. And it wouldn't really help me to *understand* what might lie underneath the teachers' actions, or how to promote deeply transformative change.

Slowing down my reactive thoughts, if I am very honest with myself, I can recall various moments when *I* was the adult who got angry at children: at my own children at home or the ones I taught in school. Most often this anger arose when children resisted, ignored or rejected me in some ways: when I felt disrespected or disempowered. Or when children simply declared themselves, through their words or actions, to be separate, different – not me. When distance between me and them was exaggerated.

I'm not proud of those moments. Even more: I feel a deep sense of *shame* for times when I have lost my cool with children and other living beings. I don't want to look at that part of me or even acknowledge that she could exist. I'd like to believe I am not invested in my adult power, or need to feel in control, and that I can take anything that life throws at me with equanimity and grace.

But by pausing long enough to see myself in these "other" moments, I gained a little more compassion for, and insight into, the teacher who lost her cool, the principal who asserted his power and maybe even the bully on the school yard who acts out his or her own pain, passing it on to others. Seeing myself in these ways doesn't mean I condone the practices or stop questioning the underlying power dynamics. It doesn't mean I won't try to find helpful, kind and effective ways to intervene (rather than more directly and self-righteously calling people out – a move that would surely heighten their defensiveness). It does help me to understand and connect with all participants, not just the ones I *want* to identify with. I can see myself in both the "victim" and the "perpetrator." This helps me better understand the *dynamics* that underlie these power relations and how they might be reshaped.

When they are not

Noticing when strong feelings are evoked can reveal our own interpretive processes, the ways our own histories of experiences shape what we see and how we understand it. They may illuminate something about what others may feel. But it's also important to notice when we *don't* feel much of anything about what we see. This may suggest what we have normalized and taken for granted. Or, it may point to ways we have *shut down* our own feelings. What are we not allowing ourselves to feel? What would it mean, for example, not just to study the suffering of migrants and refugees in contemporary migration crises but to *feel* the pain that mothers experience when they are separated from their children at the border?

Sometimes the academy seems *overly* focused on documenting pain, damage and oppression in marginalized communities, as Eve Tuck and K. Wayne Yang (2017) note in their approach to "humanizing pedagogy." Documenting pain, however, is not the same as *feeling* that pain, and much research reveals little empathic connection with the suffering of people from non-dominant groups, even when it documents horrific conditions of social injustice. To have no feelings could mean that we have retreated too much into our minds, bracketed our own emotions, diminished the humanity of those we are observing and/or heavily policed the line between self and other.

When strong feelings are triggered in others

One day I entered our after-school program and saw a young boy, whom I'll call Joaquín, sobbing loudly in a corner of the room. An undergraduate student, Jolene, was with the boy. Jolene seemed to be listening empathically, and Joaquín was slowly calming down. Apparently, another undergrad had tried to keep an art project that Joaquín had made. She wanted it to display as part of her final project for our class.

One of the most offensive errors for which researchers have earned some infamy for is that of "take the data and run" approach. When we focus on getting what we "need," we may not realize how others experience our presence. In this case, Joaquín let his feelings be known quite clearly, at least to Jolene. Often, however, participants may not let you know what they are feeling. Learning to read other people's feelings – especially those evoked *by the research project* – is an ethical imperative of research. Invariably, in any encounter there is an emotional subtext. Being awareful, we may notice subtle body cues: the tightening of face muscles, the furrowing of brows, shoulders pulling back, bodies turning away: body language that we intuitively read but may never have brought to our conscious awareness.

We can learn to recognize resistance in these kinds of subtle body cues, in the words people choose and the ways they put their words together with body language. Someone may be saying yes with their words but no with their bodies. Tuning in to your intuition, you may sense this and give the person a way out of what you are asking or a way to express what they are really feeling. In our fieldwork, we should do our best not to increase suffering in the world. Perhaps we can even reduce it and aim the products of our labor toward that end as well.

Seeing others

As I have discussed in other chapters, ethnography purports to be about seeing, and writing, the "other" into existence on the page. Nancy Scheper-Hughes writes, "If theology entails a 'leap of faith' of oneself toward an invisible, unknowable

Divine Other, anthropology implies an 'outside-of-myself' leap toward an equally unknown and opaque other-than-myself, and a similar sort of reverential awe before the unknown one is called for. . . . Anthropology involves, at base, the working out of an ethical orientation to the other-than-oneself."[22]

Doing this requires that we try to see the world from the perspective of whatever group or community we set out to study – from "emic" rather than "etic" perspectives. But even before we can try to see the world as others see it, we have to first *see those others in the world*. Who do we see, and do we really *see them*? Who do we *not* see, or not see fully or see briefly, but ignore?

Here, I think, is where the best impulses of ethnography meet up with what is most needed in the world, if we are ever to get past the seemingly basic human orientation to divide into groups of "us" and "them," and to see the people we have "othered" in flat, one-dimensional, "unreal" ways.[23] Here, too, is where a mindful approach to ethnography might help us stretch and grow as humans, not just as researchers. I am not just talking about seeing the big "Others," as marked by the most salient lines of difference in our culture - race, gender and social class – though that is important. I am referring to the many ways we form ideas about some kind of (presumed) group: teachers, doctors, lawyers, middle-school students, the homeless, Red State residents, private school principals . . . you name it. This can lead us to make assumptions without investigating to see if our ideas about these people are correct; glossing over within-group experiences; and presenting them in flat, unidimensional, non-nuanced ways.

There is a Nahuatl saying: "Tú eres mi otro yo" (*"You are my other self"*).[24] As ethnographers, are we willing to try to see ourselves in others and us in them? In *all* others, even those we consider quite different from – and oppositional to – ourselves? Ones who hold very different beliefs about the world? Are we willing to try to understand both the views of those with whom we feel some affinity and the views of those we might want to distance ourselves from, or who seem to want to separate from us?

I recognize that for some readers, the answer may be "No." Histories of racism, sexism and other oppressions may lead us to not want to connect with people that we see as oppressors. As one student told me, years ago, "If you're the enemy, I don't want to listen to you." This was an honest response based on his history of experiences with betrayals and power plays in the world. And perhaps he felt there was no need to listen to dominant viewpoints, because they abound all around. Recognizing the limits on how far we are willing to go in seeing others as our "other me" may be all we can do.

Noticing the feelings that others evoke

Working mindfully and attending closely to our own feelings, we can notice who we feel drawn toward and repelled by (both subtly and overtly, consciously and unconsciously) in our field sites, as well as those for whom we feel nothing at all. We might consider: have we spent more time with the people that we like than with those we dislike? Listened to them more? Given more credence to their perspectives? How might this have shaped what we have learned?

And how about those we feel some kind of active repulsion toward? What are the interactions that keep us awake at night or that we find ourselves venting about? What could we learn from examining the roots of those feelings? Barrie Thorne writes about the school girls she was drawn to (the popular ones) and repelled by (the ones who evoked her own fears of being repellent to others).[25] When we notice our own empathy walls[26] going up, could we perhaps just pause to consider what we may be missing by not climbing over them?

Noticing who we are drawn toward

In the afterschool program I direct, undergraduate students interact with K–5 participants in an informal, play-based, free-flowing setting. The youth choose what they want to do, from within a variety of activities. Undergraduates can also choose how they integrate into this setting: with whom they talk and what they do. We ask UGs (a pet name for undergrads) to try to notice which youth might benefit from some mentoring and mediation, but we don't prescribe a buddy system or any formal way of matching kids and UGs.

Invariably, some UGs create closer relationships with some kids than others, and vice versa. Some kids are immediately drawn to particular UGs. Some UGs stay rather far away from particular kids. I have done this myself. Sometimes, I have found myself drawn more toward the "tough" girls – the kind of girls who scared me when I was their age but whose feistiness I secretly admired. I have also found myself drawn to the "good girls," or the studious students, who remind me of my younger self.

Noticing who is drawn to us

Beyond these categorical differences, UGs seem drawn to kids who *like them* – who approach them with interest and curiosity, seemingly open to connecting. UGs have reflected in their field notes, many times, about how good it feels when kids remember their names, invite them to play, write them a note, give them a handmade gift or just remember them. Some kids do these things more than others, and those kids have shown up much more often in field notes than do the kids who, for whatever reason, choose to retain some distance. The other kind of kids who shows up often in field notes are the ones who are perceived as resistant to our efforts to connect: those who are described as "difficult," non-compliant, "troubled" or "tough."

But ethnographers have the task of trying to understand their field sites not just from the perspective of the people they most resonate with or connect to and not just in contrast with those they set up as "problematic," or resistant to their agendas. We need to understand "emic" perspectives whether or not we agree with them. We need to attend to views that may initially be invisible to us. The trick, I think, is to really notice our own emotional responses to what we see and experience in the field, including the absence of responses. We need to own these feelings, not suppress or repress them, and work with them, even as we consider how others experience these things – and how others experience *us*. Mindfulness practices help us to get better at doing this.

Listening, and really hearing

If seeing "the other" – and others that we create – is difficult, hearing them may be even more difficult. Hearing involves more than just turning our ears in the direction of the sound. Tara Brach[27] says this:

> To listen well we must become aware of the mental state that runs interference: aware of our emotional reactivity; aware of all the ways we interpret (and misinterpret) each other; aware of our haste to prepare a response; aware of how we armor ourselves with judgement. Learning to listen involves stepping out of our incessant inner dialogue.

Brach refers to deep listening as a form of breathing in, with compassion. She also suggests the reward: "if we really pay attention to another person, if we really listen and try to enter his or her experience, we may begin to discover who he or she is beyond any preconceived notions."[28]

Natalie Goldberg,[29] in a book about writing that I will reference extensively in Chapter 6, offers: "Listening is receptivity. The deeper you can listen, the better you can write. You take in the way things are without judgement, and the next day you can write the truth about the way things are." Carolyn Ellis and Chris Patti[30] describe their own shift from "traditional oral history interviews to "compassionate listening" with Holocaust survivors. Rather than one-time interviews, they provided multiple opportunities for interviewees – and interviewers – to "re-story" their experiences, bringing the past into the present and using the present to discover new insights about the past. In much research, interviews are mono-directional events that don't really require deep listening, because the aim is to secure the "data" and process it later. What if our aim were not to "get something" from the experience but to really see and hear the person we are with, entering into communion with the person? What did it require of Ellis and Patti to listen repeatedly to the pain that surfaced anew in each re-telling of the loss of family members in the Holocaust?

Meditative practices can help us clear space in our own heads in order to really hear: to listen with our full attention, not focused on what we plan to say next, and not with an ear to what we agree or disagree with, like or dislike. We can listen to what people are saying and what they might be trying to say. Mindful ethnography builds on the best of ethnography by assuming people make sense in their own cultural and social worlds and that it is our job to understand what that sense is.

Listening over and under the words

Listening to more than the words themselves, we can wonder: What is *not* being said? What do people seem to *want* to say that they are not quite saying? What may be actively repressed, or simply overlooked or ignored?

I watched Ann Phoenix, a social psychologist, conduct very mindful life history interviews: allowing participants to share their stories with an inviting, open-ended prompt and then listening carefully without interruption. She might later return to an earlier point, inviting more discussion, but she didn't try to interrupt the flow of the interviewee's thoughts. She offered an empathic presence but did not try to express that empathy overtly with words (which would have diverted from the interviewees and focused attention on her instead).

In reviewing the transcripts with Ann, we listened again, carefully. We noted pauses, hesitations and places where speakers seemed to stumble. These often pointed to places where they weren't telling "well worn" stories – the kinds of stories they have built up over time. These might also be cues to things they were sorting out, signaling something troubling or unclear that was arising from more unconscious motivations.[31] (I discuss Ann's approach to analysis further in Chapter Five.)

Just as we can read others' uncertainties, confusions and hesitations, we can get better at recognizing our own. The first step to listening with open hearts is to notice when our hearts start to close. When do we become defensive about our own ideas and opinions, rather than hearing what others are saying, or trying to say? When we are tugged into ego defensiveness (as we all sometimes are), we may notice a tightening in our throat or chest, the rush of blood to our face, a tendency to clench our fists or jaw. Closed hearts are accompanied by a physical sense of constriction.

Noticing those changes, we can slow our responses down. A mindful approach asks us to consciously "look" (and listen) for the good, especially in people that we may be predisposed to judge more negatively. The Sanskrit term "Namaste" – now integrated into everyday English vocabulary through yoga classes – means something like "The sacred in me recognizes the sacred in you."[32] Substituting "goodness" for god helps me to remember that we all have goodness within us and that we can honor that goodness and help draw it out.

BOX 3.3 THE PARADOX OF ACCEPTING THINGS AS THEY ARE WHILE ACTING TO CHANGE THE WORLD

Is it a contradiction to accept things as they are and simultaneously act to change the world? The perspective I offer here will not surprise people who have fully embraced Buddhism; these are not contradictions at all within that worldview. But the current political moment makes this feel more challenging to argue to activists (including to my own activist self).

In the 1980s, I identified primarily as a teacher and an activist. I worked in a new immigrant community, teaching by day and organizing for solidarity with the people of Central America by night. My focus was on making *change*, in the classroom, in my students' lives and futures, in the community and in the world. During those years I had some minimal exposure to Buddhism or to "Zen-like" philosophies of life. But I rejected these out of hand. I saw them as a way of ignoring social injustice: religious institutions conspiring to pacify the masses, keeping people content with their lot. We need to be upset about injustices if we want to change them! We must critically examine the world and *refuse* to accept it as it is!

Through the years I have not let go of my commitment to social change, but I have changed my perspective about the role of critical analysis in effecting change or ways to go about it. I no longer reflexively reject the idea of accepting things as they are or see this as paradoxical to acting in ways that may bring about changes. How so?

First, accepting things as they are requires that we really *see things*. We have to open our hearts and minds to look and feel and see what is going on in the world – without pre-determining what *we* think or feel. We have to really hear what is being said and see what is being done. This includes acknowledging things that make us uncomfortable or that may not fit with our assumptions about the world. We have to accept our own discomfort and sit with it. (This is hard for me. It's hard for all of us. The natural human tendency is to try to push that discomfort out by rejecting – not accepting – these things.)

We see, we acknowledge and we accept what is as it is.

And then, we act from where we are in ways that accord with what we want to see in the world. We take action based on what we hope to bring into being, rather than on the basis of what we reject. We *be* the changes we hope to see.

Critical analyses may help us see through facades and imagine things in new ways. But there is a danger of getting invested in the critique itself, identified with it and inflated by it. That can result in reinforcing the very things we hope to change. As martial arts practitioners know, what we go directly up against we make stronger.

Accepting what is does *not* mean that we passively absorb it. Not going up against something directly doesn't mean that we can't dance around it. We can still think about how we want to channel our own energy as we move through "what is" to something that we can't quite imagine yet. Accepting what is, as it is right now, just means that we act in the here and now in ways that are consistent with the changes we hope to bring about in the world. We are ready to respond to whatever comes up from a clear, focused and centered place.

Re-centering

When you feel overstimulated in the field, see if you can step away from the activities to re-center yourself. The centering practices I detailed in the last chapter may help you to maintain equanimity. When we find our thoughts racing forward or backward, or overstimulated in the present, we can do what meditators do: return to the breath. Breathing slowly and deeply, we can remind ourselves that the past is not here with us in this moment (except insofar as we bring it in through our minds). The future has not yet come to pass.

But we are human, and we will be interacting with many other humans. All kinds of things may come up in the relationships we build. Could we allow room for ourselves when we are not our best selves? Could we accord that same grace to others?

Meditative centering strategies can help us maintain equanimity when our fieldwork is overstimulating, relationships are difficult or we are triggered emotionally. They can help to anchor ourselves in what we see, feel, hear and sense, rather than in mental formations about those things. An ongoing practice of daily meditation may have effects that play out long after the meditation session ends. (There are many approaches to meditation; I have listed some resources in the endnotes.[33])

When we let go of fears and worries (or hold them lightly, recognizing them with a gentle nod), we can engage more thoughtfully in present relationships in our field sites. As I have been suggesting throughout this book, mindfulness practices help us become more aware, and aware of our own awareness. We can notice our thought-feelings as they arise and as they pass. We can *use* them, along with theory, for analytical and socially transformative purposes, rather than letting them use us.

BOX 3.4 ACTIVITY: "METTA" MEDITATION FOR ETHNOGRAPHERS

"Metta" is a Pali term meaning "loving kindness," derived from Buddhism.[34] I have adapted this form of meditation from my practice within the Vipassana tradition at Insight LA: https://insightla.org/ for ethnographers:

> Sit for a minute quietly, taking up whatever approach to meditation is most comfortable to you. You can pay attention to your breath, listen to the sounds around you, attend to your physical body and notice your mind. After you have centered yourself as best as you can in the present moment, let your mind wander deliberately to your field site. Who are the people that first surface for you in your mind's eyes? What emotional responses are evoked for you? Are these people that you like? Do you feel a sense of connection, warmth and resonance? Or are these

people with whom you feel some dissonance, disconnection, tension or separation from? Perhaps your feelings are entirely neutral, but often there is some emotional loading connected with the people who first come to mind. And we may not know why.

Pick one of these people, starting with someone you feel warmly toward and that you feel warmth from. See if you can see them in your mind's eye and through your heart-mind: Imagine you are looking into their eyes. Sense their subtle bodies. Watch how they move. Hear their voices. Imagine what is in their hearts. Feel their "suchness." What do you wonder about them and about how they are living in and experiencing the world?

Now try this with someone you feel less strongly aligned or connected with – someone neutral, or someone you simply haven't thought much about. What thought-feelings bubble up for you? What sensations arise in your body? What do you wonder about this person?

Continue with other participants from your field setting, moving toward those you feel least connected with or perhaps even antagonistic toward. Do this slowly, gradually, noticing subtle changes in your body and the thoughts that arise as well. If you start going off into story – analyzing *why* you feel as you do, or why you think they act as they do, or theorizing about your relationship with these people – just notice that. Come back to the people. Try to connect with them in your mind/heart's eye, not your ideas about them.

What would it take to lean in a little more, get a little closer, climb over the empathy walls? What might you need to tend to in yourself before you are ready to do so?

Return slowly to the room. You might take some time to journal about the thought-feelings that arose. At some point you might bring in your theorizing/analytical mind, to investigate what lies underneath the thoughts and feelings that arose. Investigate with curiosity, as best you can.

You might notice how you feel when you next interact with each of these people out into the field.

Notes

1 Naht Hahn (2010: 100).
2 Kohn (2013), who models making the familiar strange by "attending to the ways other kinds of selves inhabit and animate the world" so as to "rethink our ideas about relationality built on difference" (p. 60), suggests that ethnography involves the opposite as well; we come to see "the strange as familiar, so that the familiar feels strange" (p. 22). He takes this argument beyond the human, and beyond culture, to consider the kind of anthropology that "can emerge through this form of defamiliarizing the human" (p. 125).
3 See www.acmheconference.org/wp-content/uploads/2018_ACMHE_program-web.pdf.

4 Kimmerer (2015: 47).

5 Kimmerer (2015).

6 Kimmerer (2015).

7 Arguably, we simply can't experience the world the way an insect, animal or tree does, so we can *never* achieve an emic perspective. But we might entertain the possibility of doing so and so open ourselves to new understandings of forests and trees. This may be generative for theorizing, as Eduardo Kohn (2013) has modeled boldly with his proposal for an "anthropology beyond the human." It may also help us to temper our own arrogance in assuming that we *can* understand forests, or any other complex system, in its full complexity, from the perspective of all participants.

8 Carolyn Frank (1999) offers a thoughtful guide for teachers who want to look at their own classrooms in new ways. She writes that her goal was to help teachers who were "adept at reading the patterns of classrooms as students because of their many years of schooling," to "hold off reading classroom patterns from their personal perspectives until they could see classroom patterns from the perspective of all of the members of the classroom" – not an easy feat at all.

9 I have been inspired in using Go Pros by the work of my colleague Ananda Marin (2019), especially for considering how bodies orient in learning environments.

10 Lofland and Lofland (1995). See endnote #5.

11 Nancy Scheper-Hughes (1993: 28) refers to the pre-reflexive turn assumption of ethnographers as an "invisible and permeable screen through which pure data, 'facts,' could be objectively filtered and recorded," allowing the traditional ethnographer to exaggerate "his" claims to an authoritative science of "man" and of human nature."

12 There are many important conversations about ethics in field relationships. See for example Paris and Winn's (2017) edited volume on *Humanizing Pedagogies*, Michelle Fine's (2017) *Just research in contentious times*, Wendy Luttrell's (forthcoming) contemplation of "pragmatic reflexivity" and Margaret LeCompte's (2010) history of the treatment of human subjects and ethical issues in ethnographic research. See also considerations of the ethics of revelations made in autoethnographic research (Bochner and Ellis, 2016) and considerations of how to exit as well as enter the field (Ariana Mangual Figueroa, 2017).

13 Thorne (1993).

14 Daysi Diaz-Strong, Maria Luna-Duarte, Christina Gómez and Erica R. Meiners, in a chapter in Django Paris and Maisha Winn's (2017) edited volume on humanizing methodologies, provide a refreshing view of the value of such closeness. So too do the other authors in this volume.

15 Scheper-Hughes (1993).

16 Rosaldo (2004).

17 Crawford (1996: 169).

18 As another example see Down et al.'s (2006) exploration of their own emotional dissonance in fieldwork – uncomfortable feelings that forced them to engage in identity work in order to understand their reactions to others.

19 In *Never in anger: Portrait of an Eskimo family* and *Inuit morality play: The emotional education of a three-year old*, Jeanne Briggs actively used her own feelings, as they arose in the field, and the *contrast* between her own responses and those of her participants, to bridge the self-other divide in order not just to "see" in new ways but to *feel* in new ways. Hers is an ethnography of emotional life, one that she builds from examining her own emotional ignorance relative to the feelings of the families she lived among.

20 Ruth Behar's (1997) *The vulnerable observer: Anthropology that breaks your heart* is a collection of essays that weave together such deeply personal and emotional experiences as the death of Behar's grandfather with the study of aging in a Spanish village. Behar's (2003) earlier groundbreaking work, *Translated woman: Crossing the border with Esperanza's story*, intertwined her experiences as a young assistant professor and her narration of the life of a Mexican indigenous woman.

21 "Studying up" refers to the study of groups who are empowered in the larger society and/ or that have more social power than the ethnographer does. In 1972 the anthropologist

Laura Nader (1972) argued for the importance to democracy of studying those with political power. Yet very few ethnographers have taken up the call, precisely perhaps because relations of power make it harder to access privileged social worlds. See also Priyadharshini (2003), Hamann (2003) and Emihovich (1999).

22 Scheper-Hughes (1993).
23 Tara Brach (2013: 131) refers to the "trance" of making others unreal: "Real humans feel hope and fear; their motives and moods are complex and shifting; their bodies keep changing. In contrast, 'unreal others' are two-dimensional. It's fairly easy to recognize our stereotypes – prostitute, crack addict, politician, movie star, dictator. Less obvious is how our insecurities and attachments affect our capacity to accurately 'take in' our colleagues, friends and family."
24 In Rodriguez (2010).
25 Thorne (1993).
26 Hochschild (2016) suggests that these reactions may be rooted in our own childhood experiences, such that it is harder to feel empathy with those whom we assume to have had different childhood experiences than we.
27 Brach (2013: 210).
28 Brach (2013: 131).
29 Goldberg (1986: 53).
30 Ellis and Patti (2014). Chris Patti (2019), in "Sharing a big kettle of soup: Compassionate listening with a Holocaust survivor," elaborates on the deeply personal relationship he cultivated with a Holocaust survivor as the man (Sal) approached death. He takes us into the conversations they had, revealing both conversational, comfortable, light-hearted exchanges – reminiscent of the "pláticas" described by Fierros and Delgado Bernal (2016) in their work in Latinx communities – and their more tearful and vulnerable exchanges, as Sal shared his life wisdom: "Life, even after the Holocaust, even with all I've seen, is about *learning to love one and another and love ourselves* – and to learn to *really listen to each other*."
31 Phoenix (2013). See also Phoenix and Brannon (2014).
32 See Oxhandler (2017).
33 There are countless "how to" books on meditation. One that provides solid grounding in diverse traditions from both Eastern and Western approaches is David Fontana's (1999) *The meditation handbook: A practical guide to eastern and western meditation techniques*. There are also many websites and Apps that offer free, guided meditations of different styles. Many are oriented around a particular approach or person, and many are designed to "sell" something to you. I like Tara Brach's free (donations accepted), thematic, guided meditations aimed at expanding awareness of psychological processes: www.tarabrach.com.
34 See Kristeller and Johnson (2005). I have adapted this form of meditation from my practice within the Vipassana tradition at Insight LA: https://insightla.org/.

References

Behar, R. (1997). *The vulnerable observer: Anthropology that breaks your heart*. Boston: Beacon Press.

Behar, R. (2003). *Translated woman: Crossing the border with Esperanza's story*. Boston: Beacon Press.

Bochner, A. and Ellis, C. (2016). *Evocative ethnography: Writing lives and telling stories*. New York: Routledge.

Brach, T. (2013). *True refuge: Finding peace and freedom in your own awakened heart*. New York: Bantam Books.

Briggs, J. L. (1970). *Never in anger: Portrait of an Eskimo family*. Cambridge, MA: Harvard University Press.

Briggs, J. L. (1998). *Inuit morality play: The emotional education of a three-year-old.* New Haven: Yale University Press.

Crawford, L. (1996). Personal ethnography. *Communications Monographs*, 63 (2), 158–170.

Diaz-Strong, D., Luna-Duarte, M., Gómez, C. and Meiners, E. R. (2017). Too close to the work: There is nothing right now. In Paris, D. and Winn, M. (eds.), *Humanizing research: Decolonizing qualitative inquiry with youth and communities.* New York: Sage Publications.

Down, S., Garrety, K. and Badham, R. (2006). Fear and loathing in the field: Emotional dissonance and identity work in ethnographic research. *Management*, 3 (9), 95–115.

Ellis, C. and Patti, C. (2014). With heart: Compassionate interviewing and storytelling with Holocaust survivors. *Storytelling, Self and Society*, 10 (1), 93–118.

Emihovich, C. (1999). Studying schools, studying ourselves: Ethnographic perspectives on educational reform. *Anthropology and Education Quarterly*, 304 (4), 477–483.

Fine, M. (2017). *Just research in contentious times.* New York: Teachers College Press.

Fierros, C. O. and Delgado Bernal, D. (2016). Vamos a platicar: The contours of plática as Chicana/Latina feminist methodology. *Chicana/Latina Studies: The Journal of Mujeres Activas en Letras y Cambio Social*, 15 (2), 98–121.

Fontana, D. (1999). *The meditation handbook: A practical guide to eastern and western meditation techniques.* London: Watkins Press.

Frank, C. (1999). *With ethnographic eyes: A teacher's guide to classroom observation.* New Hampshire: Heinemann.

Hamann, E. T. (2003). Imagining the future of the Anthropology of education if we take Laura Nader seriously. *Anthropology and Education Quarterly*, 34 (4), 438–449.

Hochschild, A. (2016). *Strangers in their own land: Anger and mourning on the American right.* New York: The New Press.

Kimmerer, R. W. (2015). *Braiding sweetgrass: Indigenous wisdom, scientific knowledge, and the teachings of plants.* Minneapolis, MN: Milkweed Editions.

Kohn, E. (2013). *How forests think: Toward an anthropology beyond the human.* Berkeley, CA: University of California Press.

Kristeller, J. L. and Johnson, T. (2005). Cultivating loving kindness: A two stage model of the effects of meditation on empathy, compassion, and altruism. *Journal of Religion and Science*, 40 (2), 391–408.

Lawrence-Lightfoot, S. (2012). *Exit: The endings that set us free.* New York: Farrar, Straus & Giroux.

Lofland. J. and Lofland, L. H. (1995). *Analyzing social settings: A guide to qualitative observation and analysis (3rd edition).* Davis, CA: University of California Press.

Luttrell, W. (2005). "Good enough" methods for ethnographic research. *Harvard Educational Review*, 70 (4), 499–523.

Luttrell, W. (forthcoming). Reflexive ethnography. In *Oxford research encyclopedia of education and communities.* New York: Sage Publications.

Mangual Figueroa, A. (2017). La carta de responsabilidad/The problem of departure. In Paris, D. and Winn, M. (eds.), *Humanizing research: Decolonizing qualitative inquiry with youth. Humanizing research: Decolonizing qualitative inquiry with youth and communities.* Thousand Oaks, CA: Sage Publications.

Marin, A. (2019). Seeing together: The ecological knowledge of Indigenous families in Chicago urban forest walks. In García-Sánchez, I. M. and Orellana, M. F. (eds.), *Language and social practices in communities and schools: Bridging learning for students from non-dominant groups.* New York: Routledge.

Nader, L. (1972). Up the anthropologist: Perspectives gained from studying up. In Hymes, D. (ed.), *Reinventing anthropology* (pp. 284–311). New York: Pantheon Press.

Oxhandler, H. (2017). Namaste theory: A quantitative grounded theory on religion and spirituality in mental health treatment. *Religions*, 8 (9), 168.

Paris, D. and Winn, M. (eds.). (2017). *Humanizing research: Decolonizing qualitative inquiry with youth and communities*. Thousand Oaks, CA: Sage Publications.

Patti, C. (2019). Sharing 'a big kettle of soup': Compassionate listening with a Holocaust survivor. In High, S. (ed.), *Beyond testimony and trauma: Oral history in the aftermath of mass violence*. Vancouver: University of British Columbia Press.

Phoenix, A. (2013). Analyzing narrative contexts. In Andrews, M., Squire, C. and Tamboukou, M. (eds.), *Doing narrative research* (2nd edition, pp. 72–87). Thousand Oaks, CA: Sage Publications.

Phoenix, A. and Brannon, J. (2014). Researching family practices in everyday life: Methodological reflections from two studies. *International Journal of Social Research Methodology*, 17 (1), 11–26.

Priyadharshini, E. (2003). Coming unstuck: Thinking otherwise about 'studying up'. *Anthropology and Education Quarterly*, 34 (4), 420–437.

Rodriguez, R. (2010). *Amoxtli-the Xcodex*. Austin, TX: Eagle Feather Research Institute.

Rosaldo, R. (2004). Grief and a Headhunter's Rage. In *Death, mourning, and burial: A cross-cultural reader* (pp. 167–178). Hoboken, NJ: John Wiley & Sons, Inc., 2018.

Scheper-Hughes, N. (1996). *Death without weeping: The violence of everyday life in Brazil*. Berkeley, CA: University of California Press.

Thorne, B. (1993). *Gender play: Boys and girls in school*. New Brunswick, NJ: Rutgers University Press.

Tuck, E. and Yang, W. (2017). R-words: Refusing research. In Paris, D. and Winn, M. (eds.), *Humanizing research: Decolonizing qualitative inquiry with youth and communities*. Thousand Oaks, CA: Sage Publications.

Interlude III
TRYING TO DO THINGS DIFFERENTLY

I tried following my own advice for doing things differently (see Chapter Two) and for seeing more fully, using all my senses, by returning to the same city street I had attempted to describe in my first field notes back in 1995. This time, I was on foot. I centered myself before entering the space and sat on a public bench, dictating into a voice recorder what I smelled, tasted, heard, felt, thought and noticed. I will spare readers the details of my chattering mind in the notes I wrote up from this recording but share some reflections on what I learned.

Certainly, I saw, heard, felt, sensed, smelled and tasted much more than I did in my first foray into this community by car in 1995. Unlike in my attempt to describe the rain forest (in the previous Interlude), it felt relatively easy to name those things. (Naming smells wasn't very easy, however, and when I had my eyes closed, I felt much more challenged than when I could rely on my dominant sense of sight.) The forest hadn't sorted itself for me into nameable, discreet things. But in the city, my Western-trained analytical mind couldn't *stop* organizing what I saw into categories. I described people, vehicles and people. In my effort to use all my senses, I found myself *separating* them: describing first what I smelled, then what I heard, tasted, felt and saw — with occasional interruptions by my chattering mind making comparisons, offering interpretative commentary or voicing worries and fears.

Registering "like things" seemed to be my default way of recording rich detail. Perhaps it helped me to do that, but arguably, it interfered with seeing relationships among things, such as how people moved in relation to each other and to the land.[1] It may also have inhibited me from noticing things that didn't fit into dominant categories, such as the pigeons that I now presume were there, the (sparse) trees planted along the sidewalk, ground coverings or the sky. In writing up elaborated notes, I realized how little I remembered beyond what I noted in those initial, recorded "jottings." I kept trying to draw myself back in to my mind's eye, to conjure up more details, but those moments in time have become frozen into the photos my brain took of them, and I can't see what is just beyond the frame, in the background or out of focus: all the things I didn't fully grasp when I was there.

The details that I did capture are instructive: they show me what my unconscious mind considered salient. For example, when I took in people moving past me, I usually grasped some details of their clothing, how they were moving, what they were carrying or what they were doing as they walked – but rarely all those things. I described most in categorical terms, either by (presumed) age, gender, race\ethnicity or social positions (businessmen, students, homeless), but again, rarely *all* of those things. I wonder now about when and why I either marked or invisibilized particular aspects of people's (presumed) identities. In describing several people as homeless, I did not make note of just what led me to this assumption about their relationship to homes. By seeing them so immediately as "homeless," what other aspects of their beings did I miss?

Becoming more conscious of both what and how I sensed the world – when trying actively to do things differently! – was humbling. Contrasting my attempts to describe more and less familiar spaces (the city and the rain forest) helped me to more fully recognize the limitations of this human instrument that I am. We may know, intellectually, that our prior experiences, assumptions, interests, values, likes, dislikes, senses of safety and trust – and so many more things that often get reduced to mere labels as our "positionalities" – all shape what and how we see the world. But we may not fully grasp just how much they do so, especially working with the powerful yet limited technology of words. Periodically engaging in exercises like this may help us stay humble, and honest.

Note

1 Thanks to my colleague Ananda Marin for helping me to think in new ways about how we can analyze the world while keeping such relationships intact. See Chapter Five.

4

BEING THERE AGAIN, NOW

Writing up field notes

'We have lived; our moments are important. This is what it is to be a writer: to be the carrier of details that make up history.'

(Natalie Goldberg[1])

You've finished a long day in the field. You have jottings about what you saw and heard; perhaps you supplemented this with a voice memo that you recorded before heading home. You trust that these have captured some of the vivid details that you might otherwise forget. You know the maxim: "Never sleep on your field notes." You recognize that you should write up expanded fieldnotes before you start filling your mind with other things. But you are tired, and the last thing you want to do is sit in front of a computer and write out your notes.

Writing elaborated, detailed, extended and typed field notes may feel burdensome at times, as I anticipated in the preamble to field notes presented in Chapter Two. It's mental labor and can be physically exhausting as well: my back and neck ache after a day of writing. Even my fingers often hurt! (Of course, this pain is nothing like back-breaking physical labor, and I recognize the privilege I have to be my own task master.) It may be tempting to just dash off a quick story about a field day and consider it done.

Sometimes, that may be enough – coupled with jottings, video or photo images, handwritten notes and/or voice recordings from the field. But writing out extended notes can be an important part of the ethnographic process. In this chapter I consider how a mindful approach to writing up field notes can help us to see more, reflect on our seeing and, hopefully, find pleasure in the work.

Why extended notes?

The page guidelines that we provided to undergraduates in my class (see Chapter Three) were mostly to impress upon students the idea of unpacking what we see in close detail. Virtually no students filled two to three single-spaced pages of description of their first impressions of the site. Nor did I in my first notes. While I am certain that there is enough in any setting to meet that goal, it can be hard to remember that much detail. Nor are we likely to be willing to engage in what may feel like a very tedious act of recording things that seem transparent or obvious. To activist scholars, this may seem like a waste of time that could be better spent *doing* things in the world. I have sometimes wondered: if I have only so much time, where should I direct my energy?

But writing out details is important, for all the reasons I have already suggested. This preserves things that will easily be lost as each day gets glossed in our memories. The notes are a step away from the lived experience, and they always involve our interpretations of field experiences. The closer we are to the experiences themselves, the less we will have moved into our own stories about what we experienced. And the more we summarize and gloss over detail, the further we move away from the "raw material" of those stories and into the stories we have accumulated through our lives.

Perhaps even more importantly, writing out the details of our time in the field makes visible to *us* what we thought, or now think, is important, interesting, surprising, noteworthy or normal. In this sense, our field notes are both data about the field and data about our perceptions of the field, while in the field and while reflecting on it. We can work with our notes productively – enhancing the reflective practices that are so important in ethnography – by treating them both as primary data and as data about our own mind processes. What did we notice? What did we not? This involves being mindful of our own minds and aware of our own awareness.

A mindful approach can help us to see better, and more, through the act of writing. Rather than trying just to "get through" the notes, we re-immerse ourselves in the field experience through our mind's eye. We may be able to see things we didn't initially realize that we saw, by peering around the corners or pulling up the rugs from our conscious minds.

At the same time, being aware of our own thoughts and feelings *as we write* may help us to take more pleasure in the act of writing. We can choose to feel more consciously and to reframe the nature of the task. When the act of writing starts to feel burdensome to me, I remind myself that the opportunity to write is really a gift. Writing is my art form. It's a craft. I *get* to sit and write. I like to believe that my words will matter: that they will make a small contribution toward a better world. As I write, I imagine I am sculpting something beautiful to put out into the world. This time is a gift. Not something just to get through.

The joy of writing field notes

How can we take joy in the hard work of writing?

I hope readers will indulge me as I take on a conversational tone in this chapter, speaking in the familial "you" and imagine myself talking to you. One way to make our writing more pleasurable is to make it less isolating, to experience it as relational. A child in my study of immigrant children language brokering once wrote, in a journal entry in which she depicted herself translating for her mom: "How I feel about translating is excited, because it feels like I'm talking to someone." With this, María seemed to acknowledge the pleasure that literacy practices can evoke when they serve to connect us to others. I take inspiration from María when I say, "How I feel about writing about field note writing is excited, because it feels like I am talking to young researchers who are entering into this work, and perhaps I have a few things that could be useful to share!"

Getting started

What if you approached the task with excitement and anticipation? You are going to get to revisit this day in your life. You'll be creating a record of experiences to preserve into your future, to look back on when these days all blur into memories of a past long gone. (Of course, you will also look at them before you get much older, and you will *use* them for your work.) What if you didn't think of this as something you have to "get done"? Could you find ways to *enjoy* this re-experiencing of a day in your life? The quote by Natalie Goldberg at the start of this chapter comes from a book about the craft of creative writing that I will reference repeatedly, adapting her sage advice to the particular craft of writing ethnographic field notes.

It may help to create an environment for your writing. We set the stage for other rituals in our lives; why not for our work? Light a candle. Read a poem or other inspirational writing about writing. Surround yourself with words or images that comfort, uplift, encourage and inspire you. Above my desk I have a painting of a character who appeared in a dream; I see her as my muse, encouraging me to be more daring than I would otherwise be.

Now, see if you can settle your mind, using the meditative practices described thus far in this book or others you have adopted. Or perhaps, settle your body first, because your mind will follow. Try anchoring yourself in your physical body, wherever you are in the world. Feel the ground beneath your feet. Stretch your arms, wiggle your fingers and circle your neck. Get your head into your body, and connect your body to the world around you. Take in where you are.

I wrote these words while waiting for my car to be repaired, sitting in a sunny spot in a nearby taco restaurant. The walls were bright yellow. Two ceiling fans churned, sending a light breeze through the otherwise comfortably warm room. Brightly colored papel picado hung from the ceiling. Sounds included quiet chatter in both English and Spanish, laughter from the women at the far end, the hum of a refrigerator, the sound of dishes being stacked in the kitchen. The sunshine poured through the glass window and was absorbed into my skin.

When you are ready, settle into a chair. What does the chair feel like? I shift to the present tense to describe to you this moment in time (though I added this intro much later, standing at my home desk, listening to rain):

My chair feels quite hard, but oddly grounding. My feet touch firmly on the floor. The edges of the laptop cut into my wrists. I feel annoyed with the ergonomically incorrect design of this little machine that I spend so much time in front of. My mind starts to wander, wondering if I should go home and work there. I try to rein my mind back in. Then I pause. Why this language of mastery, domination and control that I use to refer to my relationship with my own mind? What if I followed my mind's lead rather than thinking that I need to be in control? And just who is that "I" anyhow?

Massaging these words much later, on that rainy winter day, I return to imagining future audiences reading this. (Or really, not "audiences" at all – but real, live people: some people I know personally and many I don't but can imagine sitting in a library somewhere, or at a desk, highlighter in hand, or curled up on their sofa, or sitting in a seminar with other students of ethnography, debating the value of these words.) Somehow, this makes me feel less lonely in the solo work of writing and more willing to engage. I have chosen to invoke these presently-absent-future-readers overtly, and inviting them (you) into the conversation shapes both what I say and how I feel about writing. Writing as if I am talking to readers makes the writing so much more pleasant and doable:

Join me as I open up a file. What do you see on your screen? I see bits of dust and smudges on mine, as well as a calming picture of me with my kids, looking out on the ocean. What does the air around you feel like? How is the quality of light in the room? What do you hear, smell, see and feel?

Be present in the act of writing

As you begin to write, what do you notice about your hands as they stroke the keyboard? Asking myself that question as I wrote the first draft of these words, I suddenly experienced the rhythm of the pecking, the click-clack noise of the keys responding to the pressure of my fingers. I embraced the musicality of the activity, and experienced a newfound delight in writing. I noticed that I had to type the *k* on my keyboard extra hard, as it seemed to be sticking, and that changed my rhythm, adding a bit of syncopation.

And what enters your mind? I get a sudden urge to check my e-mail, to read what my friends had posted on Facebook, to play a round of solitaire scrabble. A mindful approach helped me to notice these urges without actually indulging them. I kept dancing with my keyboard, listening to the click-clack of the keys and surprising myself by the way the letters sprang into life on my screen. Things began to flow, and I stopped worrying about *what* I had to say; I decided to follow my mind rather than "rein" it in. This was a first draft. I could revise it later. That approach is really *perfect* for field note writing; it's exactly what such experts as Emerson, Fretz and Shaw[2] suggest: just let words pour out of you, without censoring or editing them at all. This will keep you closer to the raw experience than any polished writing could ever do. When our editor/monitor voice kicks in, we cut off the flow.

Did you jot anything down or voice-record any notes when you were in the field? These can also help you move past any writer's block you experience as you start to unpack your thoughts. Just listen, write out the things you already described when they were fresh and see what else comes to mind to expand your notes.

If the physical act of writing feels burdensome, you might experiment with dictation software. Your computer may help you make a record of your own notes. Just remember, it can't think for you or be mindful with you; and for me, there is something about the physical act of moving my fingers on the keyboard, in symphony with my mind, that seems important. I feel more disconnected from my own thoughts when I dictate rather than type them out. But perhaps that is because I have spent so many years working this way. Sometimes my fingers feel like an extension of my mind, so closely linked that I can't fully think without writing.

Just start

Don't think too much about what you will write. Start with whatever comes to mind. Natalie Goldberg again offers:

> First thoughts have tremendous energy. It is the way the mind first flashes on something. The internal censor usually squelches them, so we live in the realm of second and third thoughts, thoughts on thought, twice and three times removed from the direct connection of the first fresh flash.

She explains, with a perspective fueled by her own explorations of Zen practices: "First thoughts are also unencumbered by ego, by that mechanism in us that tries to be in control, tries to prove the world is permanent and solid, enduring and logical."[3]

What might we take from Goldberg's ideas for the writing of *field notes* and the kind of writing that ethnographers and social scientists do? Field notes are our first attempt at trying to understand our field sites and put our thoughts into words. All kinds of fears may rear their head as we put pen to paper. These fears fundamentally ride on ego: our worries that we will not be "good enough" academics, that we will not have something interesting or important or profound to say, that we will be judged for the words we put on paper or the things we don't say.[4]

Because theory is so prized in academia, we may find our ego-minds drawn toward *theorizing* about our field sites. Abstractions may feel more familiar and comforting to our academic selves. This is what I did in my first notes on my post-doctoral study. (See Chapter Two.) But when we strip away our anxieties and stay with what we *experienced*, giving up the reins of control and not forcing what we saw into the theories we have read (which is different than using theory as a tool for seeing[5]), all kinds of fresh ideas may emerge. We may be surprised at where our attention goes and what it leads us to understand. Surprises – the fresh ideas that emerge from raw experience – are the crown jewel of ethnography.

Natalie Goldberg likens writing to meditation, in that many thoughts and feelings may arise as one sits on a meditation cushion or on a chair in front of a computer screen. She counsels:

> You must be a great warrior when you contact first thoughts and write from them. Especially at the beginning you may feel great emotions and energy that will sweep you away, but don't stop writing. You continue to use your pen and record the details of your life (field) and penetrate into the heart of them.[6]

So pick up a pen, or a stylus, or open your keyboard, and write whatever you recall, whatever flows out of you about this day you spent in the field.

Be there again

To write field notes, you need to go *back* to what you experienced a few hours ago. You must move into your mind's eye and try to "be there" (somewhere other than where you are right now, settled in your chair) again. Doesn't this violate the "be here, now" advice that I have been advocating in this book? But perhaps there are ways both to "be here, now" and to "be there, again" – present in the past, as you re-immerse yourself in your field experience by means of your notes, while staying aware of the note-writing experience as well.

For sure, you will be "in your head" to a great degree, reliving the movie of your experiences. Your jottings will help you, but they are just words on a page (or recorded in a digital file). Your need to re-immerse yourself in the field in your mind's eye, to remember not just what was said or what you or others did, not just the details you managed to jot down, but the look and feel and smell and taste and sound of the experience. *Be there, again.* Try to capture the scene in ways that will invite your readers to be there with you as well should you decide to borrow excerpts from these notes for your finished product.

Goldberg could be writing about ethnographers, not fiction writers, as she describes the curious way that writers examine lives that other people just live. But as a result, writers – and ethnographers – get to live twice:

> They go along with their regular life, are as fast as anyone in the grocery store, crossing the street, getting dressed for work in the morning. But there's another part of them that they have been training. The one that lives everything a second time. That sits down and sees their life again and goes over it. Looks at texture and details.[7]

So rather than seeing fieldnotes as a burden, perhaps you can enjoy the fact that you get to live twice!

Resist the press of time

In writing up field notes, there is a tendency to convert the rich pastiche of images, actions, sights and sounds into an easy chronological narration of events: first this happened, then this, then this. A day in the field may get reported as a neat story with a clear beginning, middle and end, told from our own ethnocentric perspective. A mindful approach reminds the ethnographer not just to "be here, now" while observing but to "be there, again" when writing up the notes. Resisting the chronological drive to narrate "what happened" can help us to see patterns and processes as they unfold, rather than in fixed and stagnant ways.

As we re-immerse ourselves and write up our notes, we need to resist the forward press of time. This means not worrying about the time it takes to write them. Turn your attention away from the ticking clock. Forget about where else you want to be or what you need to do when you finish. It also means resisting the press of time in your narration of past events. It's easy to fall into the trap of chronologizing your notes, telling a rapid-fire, sequential story about your activities in the field: "I entered the field, did this, saw that, experienced this, wondered that and then I left." You may want to rush through that neat narrative just to get the notes done. But what if you just stayed with the experience of the first thing you did or saw, exploring it from different angles? Or what if you skipped around, detailing different scenes without having to "get through them" in order to get on to the next, and the next, and be done? While events may flow together in a narrative in your mind, and one thing may seem to have led to another in some kind of causal way, it's also possible that you observed disparate events that are only tied together by the fact that you observed them. What would happen if you unpacked them in reverse or mixed up the chronological order? Would that better allow you to "be there" in the scene, without trying to get to the next one?

Dash words upon the page

When we try to get every word "just right" in writing, we can block the flow of thoughts. In contrast, when we "dash words upon the page,"[8] we free ourselves a bit from our inner critic. Spelling, punctuation and grammar aren't important. No one will be grading our notes or even reading them directly. The content is what matters, and too much attention to form will get in the way of preserving the content. It can be liberating to write without self-correcting.

I find it challenging *not* to correct my own typos in my field notes. I wish I could let them be, because the act of deleting and repeating pulls my mind in the wrong direction: away from the momentum of the field, and its raw "suchness," and into an editorial, analytical and narrative mode. Even punctuation contributes to turning experiences into stories, with pauses and fits and starts. I wish I could truly engage in run-on-thinking-writing, not surveilled by the grammar and spelling police in my brain, but I have been so thoroughly shaped by school notions of "correct writing" that it seems impossible to free my mind of these chains. I wonder what more I could see if I did.

Once again, I quote Goldberg, who points out the following:

> Our language is usually locked into a sentence syntax of subject/verb/direct-object. There is a subject acting on an object. "I see the dog" – with this sentence structure, "I" is the center of the universe. We forget in our language that while "I" looks at "the dog," "the dog" is simultaneously looking at us.[9]

She states that in Japanese, subject and object are set in an exchange or inter-action, more like "I dog seeing." I have been arguing throughout this book that fieldwork is always, inevitably done from the "I" of the observer,[10] but what would it mean to set ourselves in closer proximity to and relationship with the objects of our viewing?

Write from different perspectives

Even if we could work with a non-dualistic grammar, our field notes are almost certainly written from our perspectives: we record what we saw, felt, noticed, thought, wondered, observed and did. But we can still try to consider: how might our participants describe the same events? How might they *see* the things we saw? Consider their physicality: what would they see from their physical positions, based on their size and height and the direction of their gaze? And consider as well their social locations. We can't know what they thought or felt or even what they observed. But trying to put ourselves in their shoes may help us to see our own write-ups in new ways.[11]

Work with photos and images

Did you take any photos while in the field? These can make your job of descrip-tion easier, though you still have the hard task of putting images into words. Field notes should *supplement* photos, or vice versa. Photos – and even video – can't capture the feel, smell or taste of the experiences. They don't record your thoughts. But they can free up your brain from having to conjure details; you can focus on other dimensions of the experience. They also freeze moments so you can see the details. What was that on the table? Who exactly was in the group that gathered? Who was standing next to whom? What were they wearing? How did they hold their arms? Direct their gazes? Writing from photos makes it easier to record all the details. You may also find pleasure in painting a photo with words.

Choose a few scenes to enrich

One of the hallmarks of ethnography is to write *rich* descriptions. (I will address the second hallmark – *thick* descriptions – in Chapter Five.) As I have emphasized, we can't record everything we see. We also really don't need to describe *everything*. But you can choose a few scenes to hone in on and capture in magnificent detail. This material may be very useful in your final representations. It will also help you to see more richly and evocatively.

Rich descriptions are vivid. A table is not just a table. It could be an oblong table made of dark mahogany wood, standing on thick, tapered legs, with nicks and scratches on the top, dressed with a lacy white table runner, a blue-and-white ceramic vase of purple begonias set on top. Or perhaps it is a square plastic table top on foldable metal legs, covered with a pink checked table cloth. Details matter; these convey something about the history these tables hold, their aesthetics and their use. But even these descriptions leave out so much. And what about human beings in interaction with each other? Description does not just mean a long string of adjectives attached to still-life objects; description is packed into the details of actions as well.

Beyond describing people, places and things, ethnography involves detailing actions, activities and relationships. Here, I will underscore what most ethnographic guides stress: show; don't tell.[12] Stay close to the details. Use the approaches I laid out in the last chapter to slow your mind down, and ask yourself what you are really seeing (rather than making assumptions about what you think you see). Howard Becker suggests that "careful description of details, unfiltered by our ideas and theories, produces observations that, not fitting those categories, require us to create new ideas and categories into which they can be fitted without forcing."[13]

Watch the details work for you

In a fiction writer's workshop I attended led by six novelists, writer Pam Houston[14] advised:

> Keep it tactile, close, detailed, real. Let the details do their work. They know more than you. The details are full of power. This is the way to let the subconscious mind into the process. Write them down just as they are. Don't try to interpret.

This is good advice for ethnographic field note writing as well. It is through details that we may, later, recognize things that our unconscious minds understood better than our conscious ones. Detailing how two people stood as they spoke with each other – where their gaze was directed, how their jaws were set, where they placed their hands, whether they slumped or stood erect, the lilt in their voices, the spaces between their words – we may intuit a great deal about their relationship. You may surface new understandings for yourself in the process of writing. If such thoughts – interpretations – enter your mind, you can write them down, in what is typically considered an "observer comment" or some kind of bracketed way of recording your thoughts about fieldwork. Just don't lose touch with the details. Return to the scene as soon as you finish bracketing your comments, and let the details do more work.

For example, one student in my fieldwork class wrote about the air quality he perceived in the community on his first trip from the west side of Los Angeles (where the air may indeed be cleaner, as it is closer to the ocean) to the fieldwork site near downtown Los Angeles. In his first notes, Paul (a pseudonym) wrote: "I noticed the quality of the air; whether it was dust, or something else, something kept blowing into my eyes. I had to stop each time to take off my glasses and blink it out." In his second set of notes, he commented:

> [T]he somewhat poor quality of the air when I stepped onto campus – something with a granular feel kept getting into my eyes as I walked to the MPR. I wondered if it was dust because I couldn't think of what else it might be.

In the body of these notes, Paul seemed generally uncomfortable in the field setting. He wasn't sure what to do or say to the kids. Unlike other students, he commuted alone to the field site, and he hadn't yet made many connections with his peers.

By his third set of notes, Paul seemed to relax a bit more. He knew more kids, and his peers, by name. He was starting to "get along" with participants. Here, he wrote again about the air quality:

> I noticed, in contrast with the last two weeks, that the air felt clean and there was little wind; the last two times something kept blowing in my eyes and caused them noticeable irritation. I assumed it was dust in the air.

While indeed the wind may have affected the air quality in the first two weeks, and while indeed what Paul felt might have been dust in his eyes, it's also possible that his field notes reveal an unconscious process at work. When the research team discussed Paul's notes, we wondered if Paul's changing sense of comfort in this context was symbolized by his concern about air quality. There may be many ways our unconscious minds try to talk to us; we can notice what we notice – the details – and consider what it might mean.

Seeing ourselves seeing others: revisiting our notes

As I have argued, the words we choose may clue us in to our own assumptions. After dashing our words on the page, we can step back and attend to our word choices. This allows us both to stay close to our initial thoughts and feelings *and* to be more conscious, aware and mindful of what becomes evident to us through the writing. This is reflectivity in action: we need to see ourselves seeing others and reflect on our selves as we reflect the world.

This year, instead of asking my undergraduate apprentices in ethnography to write open-ended field notes, I experimented with giving them a little more focus.

My aim was to facilitate processes of reflection and stimulate greater self-awareness. After writing out their first impressions of the community and the school, I asked them to step back and revisit their notes, asking themselves what assumptions they made. I invited them to review their writing to "add additional detail where you glossed things over or made assumptions." I also encouraged them to try to see the school from different perspectives. Finally, they were to reflect on what they learned or *un*learned from writing.

Students varied in what they reflected on, but most became more aware of assumptions they had made: about the school (based on where it was located or what they thought on their way to the site), about the kids (what they would be like, what race/ethnicities would be represented there and what they would or would not know) and about their own roles in the program and how children would view or treat them. Some recognized their absorption with their own perspectives and the challenge of seeing how others see and experience the world. They also noticed some things they hadn't initially noticed, because they had normalized them. For example, Mario, who was bilingual, realized he hadn't noted, and now couldn't recall, whether things were said in Spanish or English. They recognized where they had glossed over detail. Several noticed that their initial anxiety or fears (e.g., that the kids would be "rowdy" or that they wouldn't know what to do) were unrealized.

Karina was quite explicit in the assumptions she had made about the school; this reflection helped her to see how she had internalized negative stereotypes about a community that she identified with:

> By how the neighborhood looked, I assumed that the school was going to be one of the worse schools in the country. I assumed that the teachers and staff at the school would be incompetent[,] which would result in the students not being that smart and not respecting the adults. However, the kids were great and very smart. They are probably smarter than students in more affluent communities. I feel bad for assuming . . . that the students there are not as smart as students in wealthy communities. In a way, I was doing what Rogoff talks about in her TedTalk, without realizing it[.] I was thinking that because the majority of the students could be children of Hispanic immigrants, that they were not going to be as smart as children from nonimmigrant backgrounds. I, myself am an immigrant, but still, I do not know why I was assuming these things about the people in this neighborhood. It could be because of the various [things] I've read about this in school. . . . It could be that as an adult, I focus on things that children do not notice, such as how dirty, or poor something looks. Writing this made me think about myself when I was a kid in El Salvador, while I was attending school[.] I loved my school, my school was perfect, [and] it was not until I grew up and moved to the United States that I started to see the flaws. For example, for lunch they would only give us rice and we had to take our own plate because the school did not have any, and to this day, I still think about how happy I was in that

school[;] I do not remember if I was ever hungry or anything like that[.] I just remember how much I loved going to that school.

Ebony noted assumptions she had made about her peers' feelings:

As I read over my fieldnotes I noticed that I made many assumptions about the ways others may have felt. I generally try to rationalize people's behavior so that I can better understand them and give them the benefit of the doubt. What I mean by this is I don't automatically assume someone is trying to harm me or be hurtful with their actions or words. By rationalizing their behavior, however, I also make assumptions about other people's feelings. I noticed this when I was describing my classmates. I assumed that most of them felt confused, anxious or nervous about their first day of B-Club. I assumed this mostly because these are the ways I felt on my first day, but I did not consider people like Mario who said, "I work with kids regularly, so this is all exciting." I began offering him advice on easing his stress and anxiety before even considering that he may not be stressed. He may be happy! With all of this it made me reflect further on the assumptions I have on the newcomers and the belief that "I know it all." I definitely do not want to come off this way because I am still learning how to add to our community of learners. I do not want to make assumptions and generalizations that will ultimately make me miss other important ideas in class. I don't want to miss the gorilla in the room!

Vincent reflected on assumptions he had made about children's knowledge and skills:

Lu asked me if she could wear one of the cameras, when I told her that she needed to wait because I still needed to figure out how [to] operate it and put it on, she responded "[O]h don't worry, yo ya se como se pone and how to use it. Ya me lo e puesto antes, just give it to me and I can show you como se hace." (OC: *I assumed that because Lucia was so young, she had no idea how to operate or wear the Go Pro camera. In retrospect, I feel like I was trying to assert an authority as one of the adults in the room making assumptions as to what the kids knew, needed, or wanted. I have learned that next time I can ask the children "[D]o you know how to use this?" and "[C]an you show me how to use it?"*)

One student, Louis, felt he hadn't made any assumptions. He explained that he had been consciously cultivating the stance of "make no assumptions" for years. But even Louis gained some insights into how he saw the world – what he noticed and where his attention went – by re-reading his own write-up:

In terms of assumptions I don't think I made any. I don't come into spaces with an idea of how it will be, that's living in the future which takes away from the now. I try to enter spaces not assuming or expecting anything. Expectation is the root of all heartache and assumptions distract from surprises and wonders. When I enter a space, I'm simply there to experience whatever it is that I will experience. This carefree philosophy of mind was developed sometime in high school and I carry it with me to this day. The only assumption I think I made was that the children would be smaller than me. That was it. I know it sounds a bit strange, but through years of experience I've learned that assumptions are a waste of my time and energy.

As I review my writing, I realize how many times I spoke of excitement and energy. . . . Coming into the space from the viewpoint of an older student is what I think brought me such envy at the excitement and energy levels of the kids. . . . Thorne's notions about the viewpoint I bring in as an adult makes me realize that I am bringing experiences into the space I'm entering. These experiences haven't been had by the children, for they will endure their own sets of experiences throughout their life . . .

What struck me in reading students' reflections was the fact that they were all quite different. There is not a single formula of correctness about how to deepen and expand our ways of seeing in the world. We may focus on how we project our feelings onto others; how we gloss over detail; how we see from particular angles and not others; how our positionalities shape what we contemplate on and how we see it; and how our prior experiences influence what we see, or how the literature does so.

We can try to do it all – but perhaps that will lead us to second-guess ourselves into a place of paralysis. Paralysis is not useful to our work as researchers or social change agents. But *expanding* our ways of thinking is. We can *both* write from our unique angles of vision, without second-guessing ourselves – *and*, after writing, to revisit our ideas and ask ourselves gently how we might see things differently, or more.[15]

BOX 4.1 CLUES TO OUR VIEWS OF OTHERS

Taking up the ideas about seeing beyond categories, and more deeply, from Chapters One and Three, consider who you have constructed as an "unreal other." Who you have not seen fully or whom you have not seen at all?

The categorical labels can give us clues to our views. When do you see people as individuals, and when as members of a group? What groups do you see them in? What aspects of their identity are made salient, obscured, marginalized or denied by those labels? For example, do you describe ten-to-fifteen-year-old humans as children? Young people? Students? Boys and girls? Particular kinds of boys and girls, based on race/ethnicity, gender, personalities, institutional identifiers, behaviors, activities and interests?

Our grammar both reveals and conceals a great deal, providing clues to whom we see as "other" and how we see the world. We can train ourselves to analyze the grammar of our thinking. We can also learn to rewrite it.

Pronouns reveal real or presumed relationships between people, and the relationship between self and others is a critical one for ethnographers to attune to. We might consider who, or what, do we name as "it" or "them," versus "you," "I" or "we"? Pronouns also suggest who we assume to be a group – a plural "you" or "them."

I became more aware of this as I wrote this book and caught myself many times in this manuscript referring to readers as "you," only to realize that I really could – and should – include myself in the address. In the previous paragraph, for example, I initially confronted the reader with what some might perceive as confrontational words, "Who are *you* willing, or not willing to see? (emphasis added). Checking myself, I revised my use of pronouns to include myself in that challenge. Who are you, I, we, willing or not willing to see? Am I able to see my readers as "like me," and me "like they"? I also did a search for the times I used the word "other" and considered what I meant when I referred to any group of "other" people. Sometimes the word "other" seemed apt – a loose marker for "other people" – but other times it seemed to serve a distancing function that kept me from seeing those "others" more fully.

Nouns – labels – are not always clear-cut "things." The labels we use to describe groups of people also may reveal to us what we presume are the meaningful groups in any given setting and what their unifying features are. What are we assuming, and missing, when we refer to a group as "students," "teachers," "the elderly" and "kids?" In classrooms, we may see young people as "students" – not as young *people* at all. In a park, we may see those same people as "kids." On the schoolyard – given that schools heavily mark gender – we might see kids as groups of "girls and boys." As we explored in Chapter Three, various within-group distinctions (age, ethnicity/race, school affiliations, size etc.) may be more or less salient, depending on where we are, what we are focused on, how larger cultural and ideological forces shape our thinking and more. In that chapter we saw how we all can so easily see forests, not trees, much less the varieties of leaves on different kinds of trees. When we see categories, we miss variation, nuance, complexity and detail.

Adjectives are also rarely "just" descriptive. They are subtly valanced. This is true even for ones that may seem like mere "facts." Is the dress the teacher is wearing "red" or "scarlet"? Not only are there subtle qualitative differences between these terms, there are different associations with each. Scarlet is bold. To me, it connotes the scarlet letter.

Often, the words we choose imply a comparison even if we don't realize it. We may think a setting is "loud," "busy," "quiet" or "calm." But is this just our perception? Is it one that everyone in that context might ascribe to? What implicit or explicit points of comparison frame our judgments? What value judgments are we bringing to bear, or what assumptions about what this space "should" or could otherwise be like?

The verbs we choose also convey subtle shades of meaning and presuppositions. For example, we found that many undergraduates described kids in our club "grabbing" things. "Grabbing" seems quite different from "taking." We asked, "Why this use of the word 'grab'?" It seemed to be something the undergrads saw *kids* doing, not their peers. We considered the assumptions that lay underneath this word choice: did this belie a belief that children should wait to be given things, rather than take them for themselves?

Implicit points of comparison are also often revealed by the words we used to *connect* our ideas. By noticing where we used words like "but" versus "and," we (can) reveal for ourselves what we saw as normative, correct, important, subsidiary, disputable, unquestionable and/or true. "The kids were running around, but seemed happy" may suggest that kids shouldn't be happy running around, or they shouldn't be running around, or someone should notice them running around and reprimand them, so they won't be happy. "Actually the principal seemed nice" suggests that the author presumes principals, or this principal, not to be so. The "actually" signals surprise. Little words can reveal how our unconscious mind interprets what we see.

Our beliefs about causes and effects, or the causal sequence of events, (a) revealed through our use of words like 'because,' 'therefore,' and 'then.' The tiny words that connect(ed) our ideas suggested where and how we connect(ed) with others, and align(ed) ourselves. They (can) also illuminate places where we disagreed or misaligned.

Revisit your fieldnotes with these considerations in mind. Rather than edit your notes, add commentary. This mindful approach keeps you honest while you learn to rewrite the grammar of your thinking.

Add to your notes

Some guides to fieldwork treat the documentation process as a simple, two-step endeavor: First you record jottings, taken in the field or soon after leaving, as an attempt to fix your memory and stay as close as possible to the "truth" of what you heard and saw. Then, as soon as possible after leaving the field, you are expected to write up "complete," fleshed-out notes that convert the jottings into extended prose and capture all the details you can possibly remember. And then you are done, until you revisit your field notes to code in the analytical stage of the work.

But what about thoughts that arise, and things that you remember, in between the field and the write-up or after you think you are done? Recollections may bubble up when you least expect it, triggered by something you hear, see, smell or remember. You may realize and say, "I forgot to write that out!" Details may further surface when you get away from your thinking mind – even perhaps presenting themselves to you in your dreams. You may wake up one morning with new recollections and new insights into your fieldwork.

By all means, add to your notes any time. Just keep yourself honest. Don't change what you initially wrote or even add details into the original text without marking it as a later addition. You can write addenda, or alternative, additional notes, and reflect on the changes. You could even rewrite a scene from your field experience, from scratch, seeing what new details surface in this second telling. This may force you to reconcile what could even appear as "alternative facts" – things you remember quite differently than you did the first time around.

But have compassion for yourself. Writing field notes is hard work. Writing the world in all its detail and complexity onto words on paper is an *impossible* task. Being a mindful ethnographer doesn't mean being a perfect one – just one who strives to be thoughtful and aware – and who is kind with herself as with the "others" she represents.

The *pain* of writing field notes

Before concluding this chapter, I want to temper my suggestion that writing field notes can always be a joy. How joyful they are may depend greatly on what we are writing about. For me, writing about the kids of B-Club brings immense pleasure: just thinking about the ways they move so fluidly into and through the activities of our play-based program and seeing their smiles in my mind's eye make me happy. But there have been painful moments in our club: in the lives of these children and families, in undergraduates' lives and in our own. If we are really present with participants, we will feel their pain, not just their joy.

Many ethnographies document tremendous pain and hardships. I cannot imagine that Nancy Scheper-Hughes felt much joy when writing notes for her weighty tome, *Death without weeping: The violence of everyday life in Brazil.*[16] Feeling deeply allowed her to write a compassionate portrait of how Brazilians deal with death and violence, and in so doing she brings the reader into an empathic stance vis-á-vis people whose lives are very different from their own.

Jason De León notes the way his own emotions became numbed by the regularity of death, violence and suffering in his ethnography of border crossing (*The land of open graves: Living and dying on the migrant trail*):

> It all started to blur together. Disturbing images lost their edge. As an observer, you grow accustomed to seeing strangers cry at the drop of a hat. Tears no longer had the impact they once did. Tragic stories repeatedly told under the strain of a cracking voice transformed into well-worn hymns that lost their provenience and became difficult to seriate. I fought sensory overload so as not to lose sight of the big picture or the brutal details. I tried to write it all down so that I could alter connect the observed realities to larger structural forces.[17]

Or at least, he says, this is what he told himself when he had his first encounter with a migrant who had died just an hour before, whose body was now being eaten by flies.

If we align our heads and hearts as we write our field notes, we will feel and think many things. It won't all be pleasant, exciting or joyful. Empathic observation means we can't detach into the safe space of analysis. Our own traumas may get rekindled in the process. Screaming or crying through our field notes might be a more genuine way for recording our thought-feelings. What might open up if we opened the floodgates to our tears?

But connecting deeply and compassionately with the participants in our studies – in *real* relationships – may lead us to much deeper understandings of both others and our selves. We can notice when empathy walls rise up, or tumble down. We can try scaling over them and experience whatever confusions that entails or we can sit with the discomfort that arises when we acknowledge our own limitations.

Could we allow room for whatever we feel, and create room for it on the page, in our hearts, and in our lives?

BOX 4.2 ACTIVITY: REVISITING OUR FIELD SITES IN OUR MINDS

Take a brief moment from your latest field visit. Write out the details that are alive in your mind's eye now. Notice if your mind jumps to the past (comparisons with things you have experienced in other moments or settings) or the future (likely fears or worries about what may lie ahead). Try to bring yourself back into the present as you recall this "present" moment of your past. Try writing as if you are in that moment right now (in the "ethnographic present tense"). Now remind yourself of where you are right now: the floor beneath your feet, the keyboard under your hands, the chair you are sitting on and the temperature of the room . . . and write again about this incident using the past tense. How do these two portraits compare? What do you notice from this attempt to be both present in the here and now, and "there again" in this moment of your past?

BOX 4.3 ACTIVITY: PLAY WITH YOUR FIELD NOTES

Try any of the suggestions I laid out in this chapter: paint a portrait, elaborate a scene, describe a photo or so on. Then try writing a chronological narrative of a fieldwork day. How does it feel to take each approach? Where do you feel most connected to your participants? To your field site? To your own life?

Consider: Where have strong feelings been evoked for you in the field? Take one of these moments and try to go deeper in the feeling.

Consider: What are you not willing to feel? What feelings you may be avoiding? *Whose* feelings are you willing to take up? Whose feelings trigger your own empathy walls?

Notes

1 Goldberg (1986: 44).
2 Emerson et al. (1995) offer many rich examples and suggestions for approaches to field note writing. My suggestions in this chapter are not intended to duplicate or substitute for their important field note primer. My focus is on ways of writing *mindfully.*

   Evocative scenes are especially important for introducing your readers to your field sites, as I discuss further in Chapter Six.
3 Goldberg (1986: 9).
4 Nancy Scheper-Hughes (1993: 28), in calling for "good enough" ethnography (see also Chapter Seven), reminds us that we "cannot rid ourselves of the cultural self we bring with us into the field any more than we can disown the eyes, ears, and skin through which we take in our intuitive perceptions."
5 bell hooks (2017), in *Teaching to transgress*, calls on marginalized people to formulate *new* theory from lived experience. Challenging the theory-practice dualism, she underscores the power of theory for social transformation: "By reinforcing the idea that there is a split between theory and practice or by creating such a split, both groups deny the power of liberatory education for critical consciousness, thereby perpetuating conditions that reinforce our collective exploitation and repression" (2017: 69). This non-dualistic, dynamic and unfolding way of thinking about theory is especially important if our goal is to do *transformative* social research. See also Becker (1993) for thoughts on theory as a "necessary evil" in ethnographic research.
6 Goldberg (1986: 9–10).
7 Goldberg (1986: 48).
8 Emerson et al. (1995: 50). Dashing words on the page means that "notes read like an outpouring, not like polished, publishable excerpts. Knowing that a memorable event fades and gets confused with following ones as time passes, a fieldworker writes using whatever phrasing and organization seems most accessible, convenient and doable at the time. He need not worry about being consistent, and he can shift from one style, one topic or one thought to another as quickly as the fingers can type. In that initial writing, the field researcher concentrates on a remembered scene more than on words and sentences. If the ethnographer focuses too soon on wording, she will produce an "internal editor," distracting her attention from the evoked scene and stopping her outpouring of memory. The goal is to get as much down on paper in as much detail and as quickly as possible, holding off any evaluation and editing until later."
9 Goldberg (1986: 46).
10 Peshkin (1991); Wolf (1992).
11 Anthropologist Margery Wolf (1992), in her *Thrice-told tale: Feminism, postmodernism and ethnographic responsibility*, compares field notes written by several fieldworkers with a fictional story she wrote based on events from the field (and then later represented in a research article). In revisiting her own field notes she found that events that she had turned into a fictional story "began to come back in almost unwelcome detail – sounds, smells, visual images and emotional states." Wolf's book offers fascinating insights into rather considerable differences between notes and finished products of different kinds; she raises questions about perspective and truth – ultimately valuing the retention of "contested meanings" while diverging from postmodern extremists by asserting the importance of making *some* claims to truth – ones that we hold ourselves accountable for.
12 "Show don't tell" is standard advice for ethnographers, as for creative writers. Natalie Goldberg (1986: 68) unpacks what this means: "It means don't tell us about anger (or any of those big words like honesty, truth, hate, love, sorrow, life, justice, etc.): show us what made you angry. We will read it and feel angry. Don't tell readers what to feel. Show them the situation and that feeling will awaken in them."
13 Becker (1998: 85).
14 Hill Collins (2008). The workshop took place at Esalen Retreat Center in Big Sur, California, in the summer of 2017.

15 Patricia Hill Collins (2008) argues for the value of "both/and" rather than "either/or" thinking in her important treatise on black feminist epistemology. Either/or thinking is dualistic. Collins argues for "both/and" thinking as a de-colonizing act.
16 Scheper-Hughes (1993). I think of many excellent ethnographies that bear witness to human suffering in both subtle and overt forms: the experiences of migrants; refugees; and victims of war and acts of exclusion, bullying and marginalization. See, for example, Abu El-Haj (2015), Boehm and Terrio (2019), Bellino (2017), Khosravi (2010), De León (2015), García-Sánchez (2014), Gomberg-Muñoz (2017), Hondagneu-Sotelo (2001), Honwama (2011), González (2006), Heidbrink (2016), Jaffe-Walter (2016), Oliveira (2017) and Spener (2009). (Apologies to the many others I have neglected to list.)
17 De León (2015).

References

Abu El-Haj, T. (2015). *Unsettled belonging: Educating Palestinian youth after 9/11*. Chicago, IL: University of Chicago Press.
Becker, H. (1993). Theory: The necessary evil. In Flinders, D. and Milles, G. (eds.), *Theory and concepts in qualitative research: Perspectives from the field* (pp. 219–229). New York: Teachers College Press.
Becker, H. S. (1998). *Tricks of the trade: How to think about your research while you're doing it*. Chicago: University of Chicago Press.
Bellino, M. (2017). *Youth in postwar Guatemala: Education and civic identity in transition*. New Brunswick, NJ: Rutgers University Press.
Boehm, D. A. and Terrio, S. J. (2019). *Illegal encounters: The effect of detention and deportation on young people*. New York: New York University Press.
De León, J. (2015). *The land of open graves: Living and dying on the migrant trail*. Berkeley, CA: University of California Press.
Emerson, R. M., Fretz, R. I. and Shaw, L. L. (1995). *Writing ethnographic fieldnotes*. Chicago, IL: Chicago University Press.
García-Sánchez, I. (2014). *Language and Muslim immigrant childhoods: The politics of belonging*. New York: Wiley-Blackwell.
Goldberg, N. (2005). *Writing down the bones: Freeing the writer within*. Boston, MA: Shambhala.
Gomberg-Muñoz, R. (2017). *Becoming legal: Immigration law and mixed-status families*. Oxford, UK: Oxford University Press.
González, N. (2006). *I am my language: Discourses of women and children in the borderlands*. Tucson, AZ: University of Arizona Press.
Heidbrink, L. (2016). *Migrant youth, transnational families, and the state: Care and contested interests*. Philadelphia, PA: University of Pennsylvania Press.
Hill Collins, P. (2008). *Black feminist thought: Knowledge, consciousness, and the politics of empowerment*. New York: Routledge.
Hondagneu-Sotelo, P. (2001). *Doméstica: Immigrant workers cleaning and caring in the shadows of affluence*. Berkeley, CA: University of California Press.
Honwama, A. (2011). *Child soldiers in Africa*. Philadelphia, PA: University of Pennsylvania Press.
hooks, B. (2017). *Teaching to transgress: Education as the practice of freedom*. New York: Routledge.
Jaffe-Walter, R. (2016). *Coercive concern: Nationalism, liberalism, and the schooling of Muslim youth*. Stanford, CA: Stanford University Press.
Khosravi, S. (2010). *"Illegal" traveler: An auto-ethnography of borders*. New York: Palgrave MacMillan.

Oliveira, G. (2017). *Motherhood across borders: Immigrants and their children in Mexico and New York.* New York: NYU Press.

Peshkin, A. (1991). *The color of strangers, the color of friends.* Chicago: University of Chicago Press.

Scheper-Hughes, N. (1996). *Death without weeping: The violence of everyday life in Brazil.* Berkeley, CA: University of California Press.

Spener, D. (2009). *Clandestine crossings: Migrants and coyotes on the Texas-Mexico border.* Ithaca, NY: Cornell University Press.

Wolf, M. (1992). *A thrice told tale: Feminism, postmodernism and ethnographic responsibility.* Stanford: Stanford University Press.

Interlude IV

PAUSE

Before beginning the next chapter:

Pause.
Breathe.
Take in the white space on this page.
Let. It. Settle.

5

ANALYSIS

Let it settle itself

No thought, no reflection, no analysis, no cultivation, no intention: Let it settle itself.
(Tilopa)[1]

Suspending judgment, or putting a pause between what we see and what we think about what we see, is key for minimizing the unconscious imposition of one's own biases. This is the disposition that mindfulness practices help us to cultivate. Thus far I have discussed many ways to hold our assumptions, values, beliefs, thoughts and experiences in check as we step into new field sites and then participate actively in them – noticing and attending to these things but continuously bringing ourselves back to sensorial details and embodied experiences, rather than playing follow-the-leader to our thinking-thinking-thinking minds.

Yet at some point, all ethnographers are called on to have something to say about what we have witnessed. Analysis is central to all research, and readers will expect us not just to describe what we see with rich detail but to tell us what those practices mean. Indeed, the hallmark of ethnography is "rich, *thick* description," and "thickness" is achieved by using rich details analytically – placing them in their context and eliciting their potential meanings.[2] I consider different ways of balancing description and analysis in the final re-presentations of our work in Chapter Six; in this chapter I focus on the analytical process that will lead us to those re-presentations.

Unsettling ourselves

In my office, I have a card with the quote by the Indian philosopher Tilopa that introduces this chapter. I've placed the card on a shelf in front of a row of books

FIGURE 5.1 Tilopa card

about data analysis, enjoying the contradiction that this sets up. What would it mean to let our data settle itself? What happens when we move to a place of *no* reflection or analysis? Doesn't this run counter to everything we learn about research methods?

Some readers may be unsettled by this idea. Like me, you may have relied on well-honed analytic capacities to achieve school success. Having interesting ideas about my field site makes me feel like a real ethnographer. Or at least, it may mask my feelings of incompetence, even to myself. Using these experiences to spin theory makes me feel like a true scholar. By bringing a critical eye to the work, my activist self is reassured that I am not just studying the world but contributing to changing it. I also enjoy reading other people's interesting ideas. I sometimes feel a kind of heady "rush" when I read an especially insightful and critical analysis of the social world.[3]

I have tended to believe that these insights come from working really hard, with our minds, to connect the world of ideas to what we see and experience in the world. But what about vice versa? Could we let the world speak to the theories we have read – through our experiences in that world? And what about filtering them through our hearts – not just our minds – or seeing what bubbles up when we turn off our thinking-thinking-thinking minds and tune into intuitive processes?

Suspending thought, words and analyses – and letting things settle – does several things. First, it can open the way for intuitive understandings to emerge. Many things are there to be read in our field sites but not seen because of the mental formations we impose. Suspending top-down analyses allows more room for unexpected findings – the hallmark surprises of good ethnography – to emerge.

In turn, this pause may help us detach a little from our own strongly held ideas, making more space for divergent ways of reading and understanding the world within our work. In doing this, more profoundly transformative possibilities may be revealed. These may move us beyond *both* hegemonic, established, dominant or traditional viewpoints *and* mere reactions to them. More profoundly transformative approaches may include *both* our standpoints *and* those of the "others" we study. They may help us reach past the many dualities in which we so often get ensnared.

Letting things settle before "working" the material can also calm and center us, allowing our more authentic selves to emerge. In the press to publish or perish, scholars may be reluctant to slow anything down. But we may be surprised at how much better our work can be, and how much more easily it can flow, when we don't try to make it happen.

Beyond dualities, categories and taxonomies

I've always been a list-maker. I create endless to-do lists – all of the things that I plan to do today, tomorrow, this week and next year. I use lists analytically as well.[4] Perhaps for that reason, I have found James P. Spradley's taxonomic approach to domain analyses[5] helpful. Following Spradley's model, I made charts of the various domains of child language brokers' translation work (educational, social, financial, commercial etc.[6]); the genres that youth encountered when reading, writing and speaking for others; and more. These lists made me feel like I had accomplished something: I could tell the world, "Look at all the things kids do! See the variety of texts they work with! Recognize the importance of their work!" There is something empowering about making visible things that were not necessarily transparent before. It gave me a sense of control over my data.

It was when I faced cancer – the life event that most propelled me into meditation and new ways of living – that I began to realize that my illusions of control were just that: illusions. I came to see that list-making can be a crutch, a way of making me *feel* more in control than I am. It helped me to *avoid* other ways of understanding and experiencing my life – especially messy, chaotic, confusing, surprising, destabilizing and frightening things.

The lesson I offer to readers is this: For sure, create taxonomies, code your notes, look for patterns and identify categories. Bound and organize your thinking in a way that it gives you a sense of control over the messy realities you are trying to name in your work. These may be useful to you and to your readers. They may be helpful to the world, as they make visible things that were not visible before. Then, recognize the limitations in that ordering, and don't get overly attached to your own taxonomies. Continuously ask yourself what does not fit easily into the boxes you have created. What do these analytical categories illuminate . . . and what do they obscure? In particular, what might be difficult, uncomfortable or messy to consider? Contemplative practices may help you find ways to look at those more chaotic thoughts and feelings and see where they lead you.

In the remainder of this chapter, I suggest some non-dualistic, heart-centered, mindful approaches to letting data settle, unsettle and resettle. This is deliberately a short chapter. I do not intend it as a comprehensive guide to all forms of ethnographic or qualitative data analyses. There are many other books with tips on what to do with your data.[7] Many will counsel you to be rigorous, detailed, conscientious and disciplined, to work hard and bring precise methodological tools that you can clearly articulate to readers. There is a place for such work, and articulating our processes is very important. But my focus here is on surfacing other ways. I write with my younger, list-making, anxious self in mind: suggesting other possibilities, and encouraging ways of working with both our heads and our hearts.

Slow it down

The pressure to publish in academia may push us to race through our data analyses. My first advice for allowing more other ways of thinking to emerge is as follows: Slow it down. Step back. Sit with your data. Feel it. Listen more deeply. We miss a great deal when we rush pell-mell forward.[8] It's especially easy to lose touch with our hearts.

Ann Phoenix is a social psychologist[9] who does oral history work that involves listening closely both to what people say and to what they don't. I worked with Ann while on sabbatical in 2009, and learned from her approach to analysis. Sitting with Ann and four other researchers at a long table, we looked at the first page of a transcript from one of Ann's interviews. We began with the first *word*, blocking the rest of the words in that sentence and on that page. We speculated about what we thought the person would say next. Slowly, we uncovered the first line, word by word. We read, pondered, noticed our assumptions and predictions and, very often, were surprised. Proceeding line by line, it took several hours to work through one page of the text.

What we were doing was slowing down our minds enough so we could check our assumptions about what we thought people were saying, where they were going and what they meant. This is very different from simply reading through a transcript, listening for key themes and leaping to "code" what we hear. We would have missed so much subtext. There were all the things that people didn't quite say but seemed to hint at. Often what's not said is as important as what is, and this too became more evident, when we contrasted what we assumed people might say with what they actually did.

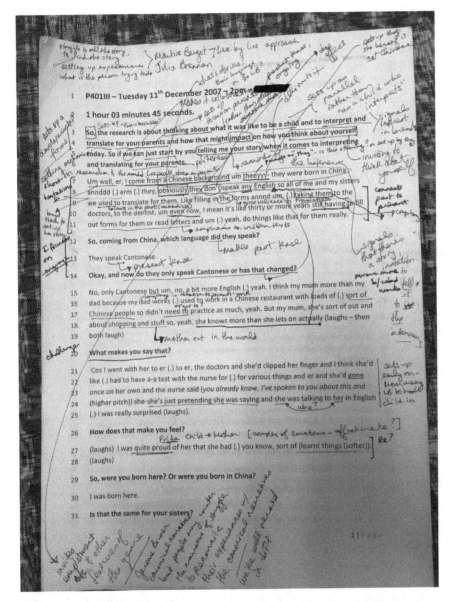

FIGURE 5.2   Analysis of transcript

Listen, and listen again

Slowing down our reading of transcripts is a way of listening more deeply to what our participants are saying. (Slowing down our reading of our field notes is a way of listening more deeply to our *selves*.) If you have audio-recordings, you can listen to actual voices *as* you read your transcripts. Or listen with your eyes shut before looking at the printed words. What comes across in the timbre of the voices? Where do people hesitate, stumble, speed up or pause? Some of this may be captured on the page, if you did a close transcription of every um and pause. But all the transcription conventions of the world can't capture everything that is conveyed in spoken words. If your interviews were videotaped, even better still! You can listen and *watch* for subtle body cues that convey meanings that lie under the words people choose. You can notice body language, facial expressions, tightening or relaxing of the body and the direction of the gaze.

Listen with your heart

Most importantly, what are you listening for? Confirmation of your own ideas and theories, connections to things you have read, or that other people have said, or divergences from them? We need to suspend our egos, not filtering *others'* words through *our* ideas. Are we tempted to entrap people in their own words in a "got you" kind of way that makes for a clever, critical analysis – but not a kind one? What about listening to the *people* – to what they seem to be trying to say, which may or may not be what comes across in their words? What are they trying to communicate to you across the self-other divide that gets heightened when you step into the roles of researcher and the researched? Could you lean in a little closer and listen with your heart as well as your ears?

Awaken unconscious processes

The year I faced cancer, I had multiple decisions to make. I pored over medical journals, reaching for a meta-analysis that would tell me what to do in a case like mine – what one doctor told me was "the most unusual case he had ever seen." My oncologists offered me statistics about survival rates based on different treatment options. My economist cousin suggested that I create a Boolean analysis of my options. My daughter suggested I read the stars.

The advice that seemed most useful combined these divergent approaches. My surgeon advised that these were decisions I should make with both my head and my heart. She knew that research, data and information were important but that all the information in the world couldn't predict my own future, much less determine the path I wanted to take toward it.

Applying this to data analysis, those, like me, who are so well trained in logo-rational processes may benefit from approaches that artists more typically take. These methods may help us move away from right-brain processes and into more intuitive ones. They help us balance our heads with our hearts.[10]

Pay attention to your dreams

When you feel stuck, you can try the things I have suggested in this book: step away from the screen, go for a walk, meditate . . . or take a nap. Try inviting your psyche to show you a way past your impasse. Be open to what it may say and how it may communicate the ideas, as they will often not be obvious. Pay attention to the unusual elements of your dreams: the bizarre or absurd, the things that seem strange.

Eduardo Kohn worked with dreams to develop his pathbreaking, provocative ethnography of the "more than human" in the Amazonian jungle: his own dreams, and those of his participants, which included both the people and animals in the village.[11] He wrote: "Dreams came to occupy a great deal of my ethnographic attention." Defending their place in empirical research, he further stated:

> Dreams too are part of the empirical, and they are a kind of real. They grow out of and work on the world, and learning to be attuned to their special logics and their fragile forms of efficacy helps reveal something about the world beyond the human.[12]

For the purpose of mindful approaches to analysis – my focus in this chapter – the important point is that dreams work at an unconscious and symbolic level, not through a direct one-to-one correspondence between words and ideas. This helps to get us out of our thinking-thinking-thinking, logocentric mind. As Kohn notes, "[I]mages can work on us if we would let them."[13]

However, we don't have to go into a deep dream state to tap into associative chains of thoughts. When we move into meditative states, our thoughts are still quite alive and active, but they are less regulated or tightly controlled as they are when our neo-cortex is in charge. Thus we can watch our mind at work, noticing how one thought leads to another. Where in that chain of thoughts do your fieldwork concerns present themselves? What associations do you make therein?

Draw, doodle, dance

Pick up a blank sheet of paper. Pull out a set of colored pencils or pens . . . bright colors . . . sharp new tips . . . Feel the anticipation that you might have felt as a child with a new set of markers or a new box of crayons.[14] Research suggests that colored pens matter for children in school – they write in more vivid and colorful language when they have access to different kinds of pens.[15] While researchers may not be using stubby number 2 pencils on recycled paper as so many children are required to do in school, do we consider brightening or enlivening our analyses by using different materials? Materials matter, as post-humanists remind us; our thinking is shaped by the technology that we can access. Try getting away from your keyboards and utilizing other technologies for moving thoughts from or through your mind to the page.

If you don't know what to draw, just pick up a color that calls to you, and scribble. You may unleash unconscious processes. Or at least, you may unleash some pent-up energy, stress or nervousness that may settle you enough to work more mindfully with your own thought processes.

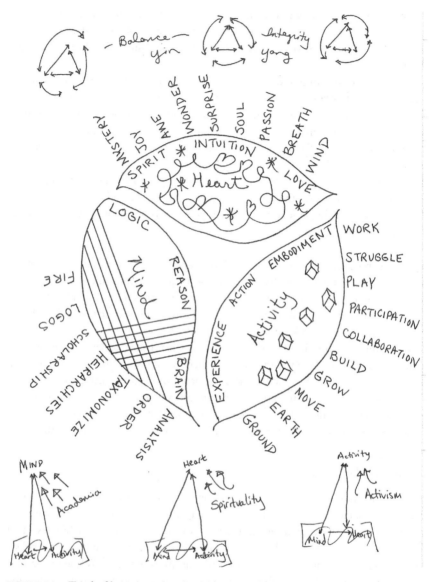

FIGURE 5.3   Triad of heart, mind and activity

In your fieldwork jottings, or later when you are writing up your notes, or developing your analyses, see what happens when you move away from words, especially words that are neatly ordered into lists or sentences and narrative reports on sequences of events. Point a pen at a blank sheet of paper and see what flows from it besides words as you contemplate your research study. Where on the page do you make your first marks? Does this tell you anything about what might lay at the center or in the margins of your work? Here's an illustration I made to help me think about this book (in black and white, due to printing constraints).

As a compromise between working with the left and right sides of your brain, you might retreat to the comfort of words on this paper, but don't try to order them on the page. Just scribble out whatever words come to mind about your fieldwork, and place them wherever you feel inspired. What clusters with what? Draw lines, boxes, stars and shapes around the words. How do these words feel to you?

And how might you get your whole body involved in the process? Do you like to dance? Try moving your whole body in an interpretation of a day in the field. This approach, I will admit, feels hard to me. I almost deleted this section. I imagined some readers laughing at the idea of an interpretive fieldwork dance. This reaction in turn forced me to face just how much I have learned to separate my body from my mind and to believe that "real" analysis happens only in our heads. But really, we might laugh at the ludicrousness of thinking we can understand human interactions only through words on a page or even through videotaped images. My colleague Ananda Marin, who studies embodied learning,[16] suggests the irony of thinking that researchers can understand the learning that happens through movement by sitting and observing movement on videotape. She incorporates movement into analytical work.

Sing the harmonies of your data

What might a focus on structure and elements keep us from *feeling* or sensing-intuiting-perceiving in other ways? Robin Wall Kimmerer reflects on guiding her biology students to analyze vegetation in a field excursion, as a newly minted professor: mapping vegetation, soils and temperatures; plotting data on graphs; identifying phenological patterns; and recording the sights and sounds of the forest in facts and figures in field notebooks. At the end of the trip she reflected,

> I had given them so much information, all the patterns and processes laid on so thick as to obscure the most important truth. I missed my chance, leading them down every path save the one that matters most. How will people ever care for the fate of moss spiders if we don't teach students to recognize and respond to the world as a gift? I'd told them all about how it works and nothing of what it meant.[17]

Kimmerer describes listening to her students singing in harmony as they walked the final trail at the end of the trip and realizing that "it wasn't naming the source of wonder that mattered, it was wonder itself." And that in the end, she wasn't her students' real teacher, the earth was: "All we need as students is mindfulness. . . . My job was just to lead them into presence and ready them to hear."

Sitting with our data, we can lead ourselves into presence: readying ourselves to hear what is there to be heard in the world. What truths might we reveal if we attuned our own hearts to our data and sung their harmonies aloud?

Settling, unsettling, re-settling

Mindful approaches to analysis may benefit from *unsettling* our data as much as allowing them to settle. We can move through iterative processes of letting things settle, seeing what bubbles up, working those ideas up analytically, letting the analyses settle and then unsettling them again in some way. We can play with developing a thesis, considering its antithesis, and letting it merge into some kind of synthesis, in a dialectical Hegelian[18] analytical dance.

Seeing others seeing us: member checking

One way to potentially unsettle our ideas is to ask our participants to respond to them. "Member checking" is an important, if underutilized, methodological approach. This involves sharing what we have written with the people we have written about. For researchers who are sincerely committed to working with and past self-other dualisms, and keeping a careful check on their own biases, member checking is imperative. But often such checking, if done at all, is very limited. We give polished papers to a few participants and ask their permission to publish the words. How many will feel they really can object to our portraits, or suggest different ones? How many will *want* to work through our thinking?

Instead, we might sit with our participants and read the relevant sections of our papers with or to them. Or watch them read, noticing their reactions. Where do they stiffen, pause, look up and look away? We can invite their commentary as they read. I discuss this further in the next chapter.

Not all participants will be invested in our words or willing to plod through them. Some may think researchers are rather silly. I recall sharing a power point presentation with María, a then-ten-year-old language broker; she said, "That's a lot of words!" She did not seem too interested in reading through them with me. She wanted to go outside and play.

If we aren't able to share our analyses and representations with participants, can we imagine that we are? Try reading aloud your descriptions of participants and picture them listening. How do you think they will feel?[19]

Tell the story of your analytical dance

Whatever processes you engaged in, document what you did so you can tell the story of your analytical dance when you write up your results. Knowing what you did, more or less in what order, in what ways, will allow you to make visible to others how you came to the conclusions you reached. Tell it as a story, and insert yourself into it: "I began by looking at x . . . [and] I noticed y. I decided to do q.

I went back and asked myself *z* about *w*. . . ." Allow yourself dead ends: "I did all of these things, and then realized I wanted to take a different approach." Be honest with yourself and your readers about your process, including about your own hesitations and confusions. Too often we present final "truths" to the world without admitting the messy processes behind those truths and our imperfect claims on them.

BOX 5.1 ACTIVITY: POST-FIELD ANALYTICAL MEMO/ MEDITATION

Try meditating after a long day in the field. Close your eyes, anchor yourself in your body and settle your mind. Sit quietly, following whatever approach to meditation you choose – though, for the purpose of this activity, I suggest that it not be a guided one. Let your thoughts move where they will. Notice them. Notice the chains of connections between them. What experiences, events, conversations, activities or images from your field site appear? How are they connected? What is their feeling tone? Don't *analyze* your thoughts; just notice them. After a time, open your eyes, reconnect to the world and take up a pen and paper or your voice recorder. Jot down what you recall from this meditative chain of thoughts or record it. Your "mind chatter" may prove useful to your fieldwork, helping you attend to things your unconscious mind took in that your conscious mind did not. The feelings you had about these events are important; some may hold much more energy than others. These are the ones to look more closely into. What are your emotions trying to tell you?

Notes

1 See Chos-kyi-blo-gros, M., Torricelli, F., Sans-rgyas-bstan-dar and Cayley, V. (1995).
2 See Geertz (1988). Geertz nicely unpacks the interpretive processes of ethnography, which aims not to strip context but to *use* context to get at meanings.
3 When my children were young, they sometimes complained, "Mom, can't we just watch the movie? Do we have to critically analyze *everything*?" Seeing myself through my children's eyes helped me to realize how much I have privileged my mind. It has been a long process of rebalancing: knowing when to turn my mind on and when (and how) to turn it off.
4 I've also used list-making to criticize myself. When I was in seventh grade, I made lists of all the things that I believed were wrong with me. One was titled, "My sins against God and man," another "My faults." I wonder now about writing more generous, kind, compassionate lists. So often we are asked to name our limitations as researchers as well: all the things we did imperfectly. How would it feel to write a list of all your research *strengths* (if only for yourself)? Or better yet, a truly balanced, compassionate view of both your strengths and challenges?

5 Spradley (1979).
6 See Orellana et al. (2003a, 2003b).
7 Readers might find Lofland and Lofland's (1995) comprehensive *Analyzing social settings: A Guide to qualitative observation and analysis* more practical. Glaser and Strauss' (2000) well-grounded approach to grounded theory is an important foundation. Howard Becker's (1998) *Tricks of the trade: How to think about your research while doing it* offers some helpful ways of breaking out of the boxes of your own thinking. For a comprehensive overview of more traditional ways of analyzing qualitative data, see Miles and Huberman (2017). Bhattacharya (2017) provides another comprehensive overview of different approaches, attending to how these are informed by different conceptual lenses. Venus E. Evans-Winter (2019) offers a black feminist, de-colonizing approach to qualitative data analysis that includes suggestions for rituals for caring for head, heart and body, drawing from experiences of being black women and daughters. Tahiwai-Smith (2012) offers more on de-colonizing methods. Sally Galman (2017) crafted a clever, graphic novel that makes ethnographic analysis fun. For other helpful guides, especially for educational ethnographers, see Carspecken (1995), Chamaz (2014); LeCompte (2010), Rockwell (2009) and Wolcott (1994). I note a proliferation of new books about using computer software for qualitative data analysis; searching on Amazon for "qualitative data analyses," these are what first pop up. Qualitative data analysis software can offer ease of managing and sorting through large corpuses of data and are especially useful for working with similar kinds of data, such as interviews. In my own view, however, there is no substitute for sitting with our fieldnotes, interview transcript and artifacts: reading and re-reading, viewing and re-viewing, listening and re-listening to them.
8 This flies in the face of the advice given to young scholars, but I think we will do our best work when we take time to do it well. And quality matters, even in this publish or perish world.
9 Phoenix (2013).
10 Many great thinkers, including Albert Einstein (e.g., in Wilber, 2001), have shared how they work with both intuitive and rational-scientific processes. Gregory Bateson (1972: 75), in his explication of his own "habits of thoughts," argues that "advances of science come from a combination of loose and strict thinking." While he anchors this thinking strongly in data – which he considers "the only reliable source of information, and from them the scientist must start" (p. xvii) – he admits to having combined "mystical thinking" and "a vague mystical feeling about the pervading unity of the phenomena of the world" (p. 74).
11 Animals' dreams, you may ask? Kohn (2013) attended to how people interpreted the dreaming states of animals, part of his ethnographic attention to the relations between humans and other kinds of beings.
12 Kohn (2013: 13). Kohn builds on a psychoanalytical (Freudian more than Jungian) approach to dream analysis, noting that Freud's contribution was "to develop ways to become more aware of these iconic associative chains of thoughts . . . and then, by observing them, to learn something about the inner forests these thoughts explore as they resonate through the psyche." See Person et al. (2013) for Freud's ideas about *day*dreaming, fantasy and the creative process. I am more intrigued by C. G. Jung's approach to dream work than Freud's, because Jung expanded beyond explorations of the *individual* unconscious to consider how we tap into the *collective* unconscious through archetypal and metaphorical thinking. There is much that we know that lives beneath the surface of our conscious minds; tapping into that through dream analysis can enrich our social science analyses and deepen our understandings of our own motives for our work. See Freud (2010) and Jung (1963). See Chodorow (1997) for a compilation of Jung's writing on "active imagination," which involves working with dreams and other ways of tapping into unconscious processes for both healing and creative stimulation. See Aizenstat (2011) for a unique, neo-Jungian approach to examining archetypal elements in dreams and to "animating" them in order to see what our unconsciousness is trying to speak to in our

everyday lives. (A "dream-tending" workshop at Pacifica Graduate University introduced me to these ideas.) Epel (1994) presents twenty-six writers' approaches to working with dreams in their own creative processes.

13 Kohn (2013: 14).
14 Cameron's (2016) now classic guide for artists, *The artist's way*, may be useful for ethnographers as well. For a depth psychological approach to access deep reservoirs of creativity, see Quibell et al. (2019).
15 Schiller (2012).
16 Marin (2019).
17 Kimmerer (2015: 221).
18 Hegel (2015), as discussed in the introduction.
19 I almost wrote, "How do you think you would feel?" This is a typical question that adults ask in trying to cultivate empathy in youth. But empathy is not really about imagining that other people are us and focusing on what *we* would feel. Deep empathy involves stepping out of our own identities to try to experience what *others* feel. Our own feelings can provide hints, clues and possibilities, but other people have different histories of experiences in the world. Striving to understand how others will experience our words means taking those histories into account. What might seem inoffensive to us could be felt very differently by others. See Hanson (2009) for a Buddhist-inspired, neuro-science-informed practical guide to cultivating empathy by keeping attention on others. See Zaki (2019) for a summary of social psychological research suggesting that empathy can indeed be actively cultivated. See Hollan (2012), Maibom (2017) and Hollan and Throop (2014) for ethnographic approaches to *studying* empathy in diverse cultural groups.

References

Aizenstat, S. (2011). *Dream tending: Awakening to the healing power of dreams*. New Orleans, LA: Spring Journal, Inc.

Bateson, G. (1972). *Steps to an ecology of mind: A revolutionary approach to man's understanding of himself*. New York: Ballentine Books.

Bhattacharya, K. (2017). *Fundamentals of qualitative research*. New York: Routledge.

Becker, H. S. (1998). *Tricks of the trade: How to think about your research while you're doing it*. Chicago: University of Chicago Press.

Cameron, J. (2016). *The artist's way*. London, England: Penguin.

Carspecken, P. (1995). *Critical ethnography in educational research: A theoretical and practical guide*. New York: Routledge.

Charmaz, K. (2014). *Constructing grounded theory*. Thousand Oaks: Sage Publications.

Chodorow, J. (ed.). (1997). *Encountering Jung on active imagination*. Princeton, NJ: Princeton University Press.

Chos-kyi-blo-gros, M., Torricelli, F., San s-rgyas-bstan-dar and Cayley, V. (1995). *The life of the Maha siddha Tilopa*. Dharamsala, India: Library of Tibetan Works and Archives.

Emerson, R. (2001). *Contemporary field research: Perspectives and formulations: 2nd edition*. Long Grove, IL: Waveland Press, Inc.

Epel, N. (1994). *Writers dreaming: 26 writers talk about their dreams*. New York: Carol Southern Books.

Evans-Winter, V. E. (2019). *Black feminism in qualitative inquiry: A mosaic for writing our daughter's body*. New York: Routledge.

Freud, S. (2010). *The interpretation of dreams* (J. Strachey, trans. and ed.). New York: Basic Books.

Galman, S. (2017). *The good, the bad and the data*. New York: Routledge.

Geertz, C. (1981). Thick description: Toward an interpretive theory of culture. In Emerson, R. M. (ed.), *Contemporary field research.* (pp. 37–59). Prospect Heights, IL: Waveland Press.

Glaser, B. and Strauss, A. (2000). *The discovery of grounded theory: Strategies for qualitative research.* New York: Routledge.

Hanson, R. and Mendius, R. (2009). *Buddha's brain: The practical neuroscience of happiness, love and wisdom.* Oakland, CA: New Harbinger Publications.

Hegel, G. W. F. (2015). *Hegel's philosophy of mind.* UK: Andesite Press.

Hollan, D. (2012). Emerging issues in the cross-cultural study of empathy. *Emotion Review,* 4 (1), 70–78.

Hollan, D. and Throop, J. (2014). *The anthropology of empathy: Experiencing the lives of others in pacific societies.* New York: Berghahn Books.

Jung, C. G. (1963). *Memories, dreams, reflections.* New York: Vintage.

Kimmerer, R. W. (2015). *Braiding sweetgrass: Indigenous wisdom, scientific knowledge and the teachings of plants.* Minneapolis, MN: Milkweed Editions.

Kohn, E. (2013). *How forests think: Toward an anthropology beyond the human.* Berkeley, CA: University of California Press.

LeCompte, M. (2010). *Designing and conducting ethnographic research.* RLA Press.

Lofland. J. and Lofland, L. H. (1995). *Analyzing social settings: A guide to qualitative observation and analysis (4th edition).* Davis, CA: University of California Press.

Maibom, H. L. (eds.). (2017). *The Routledge handbook of philosophy of empathy.* Oxford, UK: Oxford University Press and New York: Routledge.

Marin, A. (2019). Seeing together: The ecological knowledge of Indigenous families in Chicago urban forest walks. In García-Sánchez, I. M. and Orellana, M. F. (eds.), *Language and social practices in communities and schools: Bridging learning for students from non-dominant groups.* New York: Routledge.

Miles, M. B. and Huberman, A. M. (2017). *Qualitative data analysis: A methods sourcebook.* Thousand Oaks: SAGE.

Orellana, M. F., Dorner, L. and Pulido, L. (2003a). Accessing assets: Immigrant youth as family interpreters. *Social Problems,* 50 (5), 505–524.

Orellana, M. F., Reynolds, J., Dorner, L. and Meza, M. (2003b). In other words: Translating or 'para-phrasing' as a family literacy practice in immigrant households. *The Reading Research Quarterly,* 38 (1), 12–34.

Person, E. S., Fonagy, P. and Figueira, S. A. (2013). *On Freud's creative writers and day-dreaming.* New York: Routledge.

Phoenix, A. (2013). Analyzing narrative contexts. In Andrews, M., Squire, C. and Tamboukou, M. (eds.). *Doing narrative research* (2nd edition, pp. 72–87). Thousand Oaks, CA: Sage Publications.

Quibell, D. A., Selig, J. L. and Slattery, D. P. (2019). *Deep creativity: Seven ways to spark creative spirit: Inspirations and invitations for writers, artists, and other creative minds.* Boston, MA: Shambhala Press.

Rockwell, E. (2009). *La experiencia etnográfica: Historia y cultura en los procesos educativos.* Buenos Aires, Argentina: Editorial Paidós.

Schiller, P. B. (2012). *Start smart: Building brain power in the early years.* Lewisville, NC: Gryphon House, Inc.

Smith, L. T. (2012). *Decolonizing methodologies: Research and indigenous peoples.* London: Zed Books.

Spradley, J. P. (1979). *The ethnographic interview.* New York: Holt, Rinehart and Winston.

Stetsenko, A. (2019). *The transformative mind: Expanding Vygotsky's approach to development and education.* New York: Cambridge University Press.

Wilber, K. (2001). *Quantum questions: Mystical writings of the world's great physicists.* Boston, MA: Shambhala.

Wolcott, H. (1994). *Transforming qualitative data: Description, analysis and interpretation.* Thousand Oaks: Sage Publications.

Zaki, J. (2019). *The war for kindness: Building empathy in a fractured world.* New York: Crown Publishing.

Interlude V
ON THE WRITING OF THIS BOOK

In developing this book, I tried to immerse myself mindfully in the process of writing. Allowing the time ideas needed to develop, I cycled through the chapters, returning whenever I felt beckoned (by something I read, a conversation I had, and sometimes by my dreams) back to a section I thought I had finished, rather than rushing toward a premature conclusion. I tried to experience the writing as a sculptor might: kneading wet blobs of clay into form, chiseling, shaping, making nips and tucks, and sometimes starting over. I took inspiration from Dr. Seuss: "The writer who breeds more words than he needs is making a chore for the reader who reads."[1] A file with "cuts" grew to several hundred pages.

Striving to write concisely usually pushes me to cut redundancy. But in writing about mindfulness, I have come to see the value of spiraling, recycling and revisiting core constructs. Reading on Buddhism and mindfulness, and listening to Dharma talks, rarely do I acquire new "information." More often, I am presented with ideas that I've heard many times before, in slightly different forms. But hearing them again, and again, and again, in similar but somewhat different ways, helps to anchor them more deeply, bringing new insights and deeper understandings. It also deepens the *unlearning* of ideas that were inculcated through many years of school, where our minds were trained to disconnect from both heart and activity.[2] I am reminded of things that I am coming to know, or already kind of "know," but often forget, or don't grasp fully. This helps to keep me from slipping back into old ways of thinking and instead continuously trying to embrace fresh approaches to thinking-feeling-doing.

As I wrote, I also noticed where my mind wandered. Sometimes I let it go, and watched where it took me, rather than tethering it back to the work at hand. These meanderings often led me to interesting places. Other times, I brought myself back to the ideas I was working out, in a similar way as I "return to the breath" when my mind meanders while meditating. As much as I could, I took pleasure in the physical act of writing as well as its intellectual and social aspects: noticing how my fingers felt as they struck the keyboard, how my eyes locked on the words as they popped up on the screen. Doing this, the familiar act of typing became strange. I found the curvature of letters strangely pleasing, as I played with different fonts.

At times I found myself forgetting my own advice about immersing myself in the process with pleasure. I would stare at the screen, peck out a few words, delete them, then try again, my frustration growing. Old voices in my head clamored louder and louder. Any joy I had felt in writing slipped away. I wanted to abandon the entire project.

Stepping away from the screen, I would immerse myself in nature, quieting the verbal side of my brain. Often, there, ideas would bubble up, like a fountain from within, with no need to coax or cajole, to "rein in" or force into alignment. Sometimes I would pull out my voice recorder and let it flow. There was still a great deal of work to do later, to smooth things out and fine-tune the wording. But that felt less like the taming of a wild bull, and more like sculpting.

I did the best I could to be fully present in the physical, aesthetic, social, cultural, situated and intellectual act of writing this book. As much as possible, I found pleasure in the process, knowing that I was writing these words at a singular moment in my life and that this moment, like all others, would pass. I tried to trust the process, accepting that the book would be done when I felt it was ready to put out in the world, and that whatever timeline I might imagine was just an idea. The process felt personally transformative.[3] All I can hope is that some small seeds of these ideas may be transformative for others as well.

Notes

1 Seuss, T. G. Found on https://writerswrite.co.za/dr-seuss-on-writing/.
2 See Kleinsasser (2000) on writing to unlearn.
3 I recognize that such wisdom is not easy to embrace when you feel that you are racing the tenure clock. But as I tell my students, what are we really racing toward? Would we say about our lives what we say about our work: "Can't wait to be done!" This *is* our life, and to some extent, we chose it. See endnote #2 in Chapter Seven.

References

Kleinsasser, A. M. (2000). Researchers, reflexivity and good data: Writing to unlearn. *Theory into Practice*, 39 (3), 155–162.

6

RE-PRESENTATIONS

"Maybe you had a single tear rolling down your cheek, or maybe you were crying for days afterward. Touching and powerful stories hit you in the most inexplicable, unexpected, and undeniably human ways . . . Commuovere (Italian, verb): To be moved in a heartwarming way, usually relating to a story that moved you to tears. . ."

From Lost in translation: An illustrated compendium of
untranslatable words from around the world[1]

When we sit down to write the final re-presentations of our ethnographic journeys, we are faced with the task of taking the rich pastiche of sights, sounds, images and feelings that were evoked in the field setting, then "reduced" into field notes and filtered through our analyses, in order to re-present our field experiences in words for readers to imbibe. Words can *never* do justice to the complexities of what we have seen, experienced, touched and felt. Words are not things themselves; at best, they can only point toward our experiences and those of the people we re-present. This is very important to remember but so easy to forget. We get invested in the stories that we tell about what we have seen and experienced, and we want to write them into enduring truths upon the page.

One of the hallmarks of ethnography is "rich description," and the sensorial, awareful approaches I have suggested in this book should facilitate the gathering of sensorial detail that can help us paint vivid scenes on the page. But in the final write-up, we are much further away, in both time and space, from our immersion in the field. What words will we fix in ink, as the definitive, final re-presentations of our research?

In this chapter I address issues that arise in the write-up of our ethnographic stories. I suggest ways of approaching our re-presentations mindfully, consciously and compassionately. I share guidelines that I have developed over the years and strive to uphold. I raise questions for you to consider for your own socially and personally transformative research.

Bringing readers into presence

Our fieldwork is finished, and we have left the field. But we want to bring readers back into some kind of "presence" with us in our work, as we create scenes on the page – ones that may stay with readers long after reading them. That is the beauty of artistically composed ethnography: it makes a set of people, a village, school, home or street corner into something share-able and rememberable.

At the same time, we need to remember that what it really does is preserve *the author's* portrait of those people or that village, school, home or street corner. In what follows, I suggest narrative approaches that help us to be honest in offering these as *our* re-presentations – and as portraits that were painted at a particular moment in time, from particular angles of vision. This includes reflecting on how *emotionally* honest we can or want to be, about the feelings that were invoked for us in the field site (when our rational minds did not squash them) and the emotional truths[2] we want to invite our readers to *feel* as well as to think about.

To be or to have been? Dilemmas of the ethnographic presence

Mindful research calls for the power of presence, but the power of the present *tense* can be abused.[3] While the only real time we can ever experience is that which is happening right now, the events of the world, and in our field sites, are continuously changing, and the present that we write about is already the past. New events transpire. The people we write about grow older by the minute. They, and their cultural contexts, change. They learn, evolve and adjust their beliefs, values, practices and behaviors. Writing about our field sites in the present tense can lead readers – and ourselves – to a false sense of fixity about social and cultural processes that are continuously in flux.

One way of reminding readers not to get too comfortable with the past-as-presence is to write about ourselves in the act of writing up the past. We can introduce ethnographic vignettes with explicit statements from the chair of the writer and intersperse our analysis with commentary. Ruth Behar illustrates this evocatively in her ethnographic essays in the *Vulnerable observer*,[4] moving fluidly between her own present musings about her own life and memories from fieldwork. This interweaving of personal and political presence engenders new insights into the phenomena she was studying (e.g., death, aging and changes in community cultural life). In an essay reflecting on an earlier ethnographic project, she notes:

> I dedicated my book, *The presence of the past in a Spanish village*, which focused on the traditions and memories of those who were structurally in a grandparent relation to me, to my own grandparents. While my own motives were not

altogether clear to me at the time, with hindsight I have come to realize that my quest to understand "the presence of the past" in Santa María was but another link in the parallel question to recover my own, and my family's past.[5]

Later in the same piece, Behar takes the reader further into the presence of her ongoing life, after the death of her grandfather. She writes: "Postscript, 1989. I can no longer declare ignorance of death in my family. As I revise this chapter one more time, I realize, profoundly, how the texts of our lives, like those of our ethnographic subjects, do not sit still.[6]

Such commentary invites readers into our re-presentations, while reminding them that they *are* re-presentations. We are writing about moments in time that are not fixed and frozen. These moments will continuously recede into the distant past, and many things can and will change. Indeed, pointing toward the possibility of change is one way that our ethnographic work can become transformative. We can show readers how things are in the world, now – from our understandings, based on our immersion in the work – while also imagining, and helping others to imagine, how they might be otherwise.

Reflect on our positionality

Behar was a pioneer in the "reflexive turn" in anthropology. Her first book, *Translated woman: Crossing the border with Esperanza's story,*[7] broke new ground by reflecting deeply on her representation of the main character in her ethnography: Esperanza, an indigenous Mexican woman. Behar also wove into her story reflections on her own positionality as a junior scholar, striving to get tenure, proving herself as an anthropologist and developing Esperanza's story toward that end. She struggled with concerns about appropriation: Who gets to translate whose lives? And what gets lost in the translation? She identified both differences and commonalities between her own experiences crossing borders, and those of Esperanza, complicating the us/them dichotomy and using her own thoughts and feelings to try to understand Esperanza's – as well as to recognize the limits on her own understanding.

Thirty years later, it is standard practice for us as researchers to examine our "positionalities": who we are in relation to the people in our field sites. As discussed in Chapter One, this is an important move away from speaking from the seemingly omniscient yet unaccountably absent presence of the observer that predominated in early anthropological work. Our histories of experiences in the world, ethnic/racial, cultural and social positionings, life stages, political leanings, values, beliefs, hopes, dreams, wishes, fears, wonderings, thoughts, worries, expectations, curiosities and imaginings – all shape what and how we see. We can never escape our own positionalities. No matter how reflective and reflexive we strive to be.

Being as honest as we can about how all these things shape what and how we see, we temper the authoritative renderings we may wish to offer. Doing this owns the fact that we are the instruments of our ethnographies. We remind readers that they might want to be a little cautious about the stories they will read.

Often, ethnographers acknowledge their positionality in a fleeting, confessional way, at the start of the book, or in an appendix, and then move on to assert their perspectives anyway. A not uncommon proclamation is that we don't believe our positionality really impacted what we "found," because we were able to hold our positions properly in check. Or that it only affected it in limited ways. We may take up the voice of a reassuring narrator, suggesting that we are aware of just how our experiences shaped what we saw and that we have it all under control.

But if we take seriously the idea that we can always, only, ever understand the world through the instruments of our being, then our findings were necessarily shaped in profound and pervasive ways by our presence in the field. We should be as reflective and honest as we can about who we are and both what and how we have come to the understandings we offer, based on the work we have done and the evidence we have gathered, and the ways we have filtered it through our accumulated life experiences. But we should not presume – to ourselves or to our readers – that we can necessarily *know* how our positionalities shape our research, much less control it.

The practice of briefly turning the mirror on one's self and then turning it away may lead readers to forget that what we read is necessarily always partial and from a particular standpoint, even if the author has taken careful measures to minimize her power. We need other ways to temper the authorial voice. Naming our positionality should be more than a symbolic, confessional gesture, done up front and then forgotten. Moreover, we can use the light that we shine on ourselves to illuminate something bigger than ourselves, and bigger also than the "others" we hope to reveal.

Remind readers of our role as narrators

Increasingly, many ethnographers insert themselves into their writing in explicit and purposeful ways, reminding their readers continuously of the "I" of the observer[8] throughout the text. We make sure readers know that the report they are reading was written from a particular perspective, at a particular place and time, by assuming an explicit stance as narrators in the write-up.

This ongoing narration of the field worker's experience makes for richer and more engaging stories even as it serves ethical purposes. In Michelle Bellino's *Youth in postwar Guatemala: Education and civic identity in transition*,[9] for example, we travel with the author to visit four high schools in Guatemala to see how they discuss atrocities and human rights violations committed during the war. This involved movement across different classed and racialized spaces and political ideologies. We see how Bellino was received in and integrated into each site, as well as how she experienced these spaces and the people, their histories and interactions.[10]

The question we as ethnographers need to grapple – or play – with as we place ourselves in our stories is just how much and in what ways. How marked or visible was our presence to others in the actual fieldwork – and how marked or visible do we choose to make it in our write-up? Do we foreground or background ourselves? How often should we remind readers that we were there? How do we keep the focus on our participants – not "naval gazing"[11] – while revealing ourselves? In the balancing of self and other, where do we begin and end?

Often, I have begun my first drafts of ethnographic writing with my own story: how I came into the field, what I brought with me and what my thoughts were as I began the work. This seems the only honest way I can begin. However, it has not always been the place I chose to begin my *re-presentations*. After writing these beginnings, I stepped back – literally and figuratively – and considered other ways to commence.[12]

This is a question that even auto-ethnographers think about, as we use our life experiences to illuminate something bigger than ourselves. Auto-ethnography is not just about looking in the mirror; it is about refracting our views both inward and outward as we use the relationship between the self and the world to understand the world and ourselves. It is about placing ourselves in our ethnographies in order to tell richer, fuller and more stories, rather than "sneak[ing] ourselves in as minor characters."[13] As Arthur Bochner and Carolyn Ellis note, it holds us to a "higher standard of vulnerability."[14]

How much, and what aspects of your social positions, psychological make-up, life histories and experiences will you choose to reveal?

Use rhetorical structures to "step up" and "step back"

Rhetorical structures can help us both to "step up" – insert ourselves into the stories – and "step back" – not take over the stories. Gabrielle Oliveira uses interludes[15] as a way to bring readers into her fieldwork and to separate the theory-building that she does in the main chapters of her book (*Motherhood across Borders: Immigrants and their children in Mexico and New York*) from more descriptive narrations of her fieldwork. The interludes follow Oliveira's progress in the field as she met new families and family members and proceeded with her research. The interludes serve to punctuate her progress in the field, while reminding readers that families' lives were unfolding in time as well.

Ariana Mangual Figueroa[16] also uses interludes to bring the reader more directly along with her into her fieldwork – specifically, into the *liminal* spaces in her study of young immigrant children in New York City classrooms – and she examines their experiences of identity, belonging and safety as they walk in the city, visit a museum and go to recess, lunch and the restroom. As a linguistic ethnographer, Mangual Figueroa is intent on *hearing* these young people as they express themselves in different ways in these diverse physical spaces. We hear with her as we listen to the girls' talk, recorded through wearable microphones. In these interludes, Mangual Figueroa is not part of the story at all; the girls are having their own conversations, though they are aware that she will listen to their tapes, and Mangual Figueroa is careful to remind readers of her absent-presence as well as the privilege we have of listening in to the girls' conversations.

Inspired by Mangual Figueroa and Oliveira, in this book I moved some of "me" into interludes, some into endnotes and some into boxes set aside from the main story line. Much more ended up in the trash bin of my computer. Writing it out was an important part of the process; so was letting some of it go.

Probe the relationship between "our" and "their" stories

Our ethnographies are never just about the people we write about; we are always part of the stories we tell, even if we do not call them auto-ethnographies. But they are also not just, or centrally, about us. It is the understanding that emerges through the encounter between our selves and others that offers possibilities for working with dualisms in order to understand a larger whole.

Some researchers have found creative ways to weave together their own views and those of their participants. Wendy Luttrell's ethnography of teen mothers-to-be in a school for pregnant girls involved inviting the girls to represent themselves, with images. She worked with the girls to create collages to represent their lives and talked with them about their meanings. The collages allowed the girls to express themselves in different ways than in interviews; thus, these served as a methodological and analytical tool as well. In the final re-presentation, in book form, the girls' collages have a strong presence. They are included in full color, glossy images.[17,18]

The connections between our research interests and our lives are sometimes obvious, and sometimes less so. Nancy Scheper-Hughes began her 600-page tome on child death in Brazil with a brief vignette about childhood memories of growing up at the foot of the Domino Sugar Refining factory in Brooklyn, New York. In introducing her fieldwork in a sugar-farming community in Brazil, she wrote:

> This book takes me full circle from childhood to midlife, for it is, I think, no coincidence that my anthropology finally brought me "home" to Northern Brazil and to those verdant but cloying fields of sugarcane . . . to work with people who invariably describe themselves as having grown up "at the foot" of the cane. Foot of the factory, foot of the cane, we are all implicated (as workers and consumers) in the vicious sugar cycle and in the *miséria morta*, deadly misery, it leaves in its wake. As a child of the Williamsburg Eastern European (later Puerto Rican) slum, I was marked by the image of the Sugar House, and in writing about the cane cutters and their families of Bom Jesus da Mata, I am also trying to reach out and touch the fading images of those sugar workers I knew as a child and whose faces I remember . . .[19]

We may not be aware of such connections when we begin. Sometimes we will be brought full circle through our work, to new understandings of our own lives. This is one of the ways in which research can illuminate "me-search."[20] Elsie Rockwell, in a Spanish language treatise ethnography,[21] argues that the ethnographic experience should transform the ethnographer herself:

If one does not experience a profound transformation in ways of perceiving, interpreting, and understanding the place one has studied, the long labor of field work and qualitative analysis makes no sense. The ethnographer does not go into the field to confirm what she already believes, but to construct new ways of seeing both the familiar and the strange.

Generative tensions

Personal and social transformation

The kind of ethnography I am advocating for, at the juncture of mind, heart and experience, may lead to the personal transformation of the ethnographer. Simultaneously, ethnography can – and in my view, *should* – point toward transformative understandings of the social world as well.

As ethnographers we invariably enter the field with certain assumptions about how the world works. These perspectives have been built over our life spans. Our conceptual frameworks and the literature may lead us there as well. This may help us see things that are not transparent to everyone. It may also orient us to see what we already knew or assumed to be true. We may be eager to expose those "truths" to the world. But if we end up arguing for things we already knew when we began, what has our work added? If we merely "prove" things we already knew or believed before conducting research, we haven't allowed the ethnographic process to work through us, opening us to surprises, transforming us personally and leading to new insights for social transformation.

I have discussed various binaries throughout this book. There is one more I would like to consider now: the opposition between "hegemonic," dominant, mainstream or "traditional" approaches to research, which focus on documenting the world as it is, and "critical," deconstructivist or counter-hegemonic analysis of those social realities. Like other dualities, the tug-of-war between these sometimes seem to tear apart. Are we in the "critical" camp or the "mainstream"? Are we working with dominant ideologies or counter-hegemonic ones?

Note that these pose as dualities. What about a third possibility: one that combines attention to documenting the world as it is, with a critical eye, but merges these two (rather than counter-posing them) in order to imagine the world as it could be? This asks us to see spaces for possibility of something new that could emerge. Profoundly new ways of seeing may be exactly what the world needs to move forward in surprising, unprecedented and transformative ways.

The power and danger of the authoritative voice

Graduate students entering into academia often struggle with taking up authoritative voices in their writing. For some of us, those struggles continue long into our years in the practice. Who are we to stake claims about what we know about the world? Why should readers believe what we set forth? How can we assert our voices into the symphony – or cacophony – of academia, in ways that are heard, and that contribute something, without overstating our truth claims?

Ruth Behar names her own struggles with taking up an authoritative voice; this may resound for many readers, as it does for me:

> Authorship is a privilege to which many of us are not born, but arrive at, often clumsily, often painfully, often through a process of self-betrayal and denial; they don't say that authorship is a privilege constituted by the gender, sociohistorical background, and class origins, or lately, class diasporas, of the anthropologist doing the writing. . . . Those whose nationality, racial, ethnic, or class position make them uneasy insiders in the academic world often feel as if they are donning and removing masks in trying to form a bridge between the homes they left and the new locations of privileged class identity they now occupy.[22]

On the one hand, we run the danger of over-compensating for our fears of inadequacy and asserting claims we cannot adequately back up. This includes falling into the trap of telling more than showing: making authoritative statements rather than leading our readers to understanding. On the other hand, there is the risk of paralysis: we may be locked by imposter syndrome into fear of saying anything at all.

A self-compassionate and mindful approach helps us first to be aware of these tensions. We can notice when our tender egos are in the driver seat, leading us to inflate the value of our work, or the converse: stoking fears that we will be found out to be fraudulent, insufficient or imperfect. (And indeed, we most certainly will be imperfect, by some measure.) When do we feel either inflated or deflated about our words and ideas? Perhaps, we can notice with compassion for ourselves and extend that compassion to others when we read seemingly self-congratulatory, or self-deprecating, or just imperfect or incomplete texts.

Doing your best to set both fears and high hopes aside (or just giving a nod to them when they rear their heads), you might sit quietly and ask yourself, "What do I have to offer to the world from my fieldwork?" Deciding what you want to say, based on what you can say, with your data, and what you *want* to say, based on your moral and ethical commitments, is different from what you think you *should* say, wish you could argue, what others may want you to report, the stories they might expect you to tell or what the literature or some conceptual framework might corral you toward. But if we can cut through all the voices that tell us what we think we "should" or shouldn't say, our own voices may ring true. As Susan Tiber Ghen wrote, in a book about Jungian-inspired writing, "When we write from our authentic self, there is a vibration and clarity in our words."[23]

Beyond egos toward ethos

We can also become more aware of what we do when worries arise. Does fear of rejection, ridicule, critique and judgment make us hide under a bushel? When the

critical voices in our own heads start chattering, do we freeze? Panic? Throw ourselves into a word frenzy, hiding our clearest ideas behind a convoluted academic
voice?[24] When my own self-disparaging mind chatter started – many times as I
wrote this book – I found myself running back to the literature, thinking I needed
to read one more article or book.[25] Given the vast territory of literature I touch
on in this book, much of which has *not* been my main area of academic expertise,
this is a process that could have continued for the rest of my life, ensuring that this
book would never see the light of day.

I also found myself turning to others: tell me if this is okay? For sure, getting
feedback on our writing is imperative. Writing is never really a solitary activity;
we are always in some way in dialogue with our readers, so inviting others overtly
into the conversation can be enriching. Readers can often point to things we can't
see in our own work. This book benefited immensely from having the eyes of
trusted colleagues and friends on it. I have also come to deeply appreciate the practice in academia of *anonymous* peer review, because anonymity may allow people
to say things that they wouldn't dare to say directly. I want *honest* feedback, to
give me perspectives on my work that I can't see so readily myself. Friends might
be reluctant to say what they really think. Or they may know us so well that they
hear our words differently than strangers do. They may read more generously than
will readers who don't know us.

But even people who basically agree with our ideas will likely want us to do
many different things with our words, and not all the advice we get will serve us.
Ultimately, I had to decide what I was able and willing to do with the suggestions
I received. Turning away from external recognitions – "likes" from our friends
as well as the rewards that academia bestows upon us, in the form of acceptances,
"revise-and-resubmits," awards,[26] reviews and accolades – and tuning in to our
own inner compasses can help us to withstand the critiques that will inevitably be
mixed in with any praise and decide for ourselves what we want to say, how and
in what ways.

The stories we tell will never be just our own, or come only from a place of
ego, if we have done our ethnographic work well. Ralph Cintrón writes:

> [T]he modern ethnographer is now largely defined as one who lives with
> others over a long period of time, and this definition acknowledges that the
> process of coming to know a people – hence, the right to make a knowl-
> edge claim – is deeply entwined with the creation of ethos, an ethos that is
> acceptable to the Other. One's credibility or character is created during min-
> iscule moments of interaction, each moment interpreted consciously or not
> so consciously by others. Within this corpus of interactions, interpretations,
> and reinterpretations, the organic shaping of an ethnographer's ethos occurs.
> Obviously, such shaping takes time, and the apparent shape of the ethnog-
> rapher's ethos will tell the Other, who is also always establishing his or her
> ethos, what to share and what not to share from the otherwise secreted com-
> munity. . . . My central claim, then: The persuasiveness of the ethnographic

knowledge claim is constituted through and through, both in the moments of fieldwork and the moments of the final text, by ethos.[27]

Cintrón goes on to link ethos to logos: our re-presentations of ethnography in words on a page. If we want to move beyond our egos, we need to consider both what we want to share and how we can appropriately share the ethos that we cultivated through fieldwork, and honor the ethos of the "Other" through logos. What do we have to say that is true not just to our own truths but to the truths that others unveiled to us? What might these people consider *helpful* to share with the larger world?

Balance of description and theory, head and heart

Readers will likely want different things from a book. Some will want more theory, some more description, some more summary and some more detail. Sharing our words with diverse readers can help us gage where we landed on the balance of those things, but we will never please everyone. This is one of the decisions you will need to make: how to balance theory and description.

However, perhaps "balance" isn't the right word here. Ethnography is about *blending* theory and description, or weaving them together: using theory to thicken description, and description to deepen and extend the theory. I would suggest that the balance to seek, in order to do this, is that of head and heart. Some ethnographies spin off into a very heady space, and while they may convey a great deal of information, or do a great deal of theorizing work, they don't move me in the same way as do ethnographies in which the ethnographer stayed much more closely connected to their own lived, emotional, cognitive and embodied experience in the field. The power of ethnography is that it is built on that physical, emotional, psychological and cognitive immersion. Ethnographies, like all great stories, may lead readers to an experience of "commuovere" (as in the opening quote). If we just want to provide information, why not write a different kind of report?[28]

When we write about difficult and even terrible things, as many ethnographers have done – death at the border, child death, the separation of children from their parents under draconian immigration policies, life in war zones and other ways in which humans suffer – what responsibility do we have to telling not just the "factual" truth of our encounters but their emotional truth as well? How can we keep that emotional truth alive when we retreat from the field and into our analyses, taking readers (and ourselves) further away from these direct human encounters?

Artistic, scholarly, moral and ethical commitments

Our final re-presentations are not just artistic and scholarly endeavors; they are deeply moral and ethical ones. Taking seriously the Buddhist challenge that lies at the heart of the triad of heart, mind and activity, we might ask these questions:

What is our responsibility in bearing witness to the lives of others? What will readers understand of the world and what might they do with that understanding as a result of reading our words?

Scheper-Hughes notes that ethnography is

> always a highly subjective, partial, and fragmentary – but also deeply felt and personal – record of human lives based on eyewitness and testimony. The act of witnessing is what lends our work its moral (at times its almost theological) character. So-called participant observation has a way of drawing the ethnographer into spaces of human life where she or he might really prefer not to go at all and once there doesn't know how to go about getting out except through writing, which draws others there as well, making them party to the act of witnessing.[29]

Implicitly, I think Scheper-Hughes was naming the work of ethnography as a triad of heart, mind and experience/action, because being witness morally compels us to act, if only to share what we have witnessed, bringing greater awareness of the pain of others to the world.

If you aim to do the kind of transformative social research I am advocating, what might you say that is true (grounded in data), helpful and a real contribution to the world? We can't say everything we might want to – nor, arguably, from a moral and ethical standpoint, should we. We may need to think carefully about how we represent both the "heroes" and the "villains" in our stories (as well as to reconsider this facile duality). The method of "portraiture," established by Sara Lawrence-Lightfoot,[30] involves a search for "goodness." Michelle Bellino unpacks this:

> not a call for gratuitous praise but a reminder of the power of researching and representing human lives and the responsibility to document complex realities without slipping into critiques that highlight what is flawed, broken or damaged at the expense of what is healthy or strong.[31]

Imagine your ideas reaching out from your field site, sifted through your mind, passing from your hands into a computer and being transformed into print or little bytes that will then travel across mountains, oceans, cities and walls, to show up on other people's computer screens or on paper held in their hands and from there into their heads – and perhaps also their hearts. What words can you offer that could move people to take action, to promote the kind of social change you hope to see in the world?

The power and limitation of words

Logos – words – are the tool of our trade. In writing up ethnographies, we read and listen to countless words that others have spoken and written and craft many more words of our own. As a language scholar, writer, activist and teacher, I have had great faith in words: in their power to bridge between people, open up new understandings, convey information, connect with others, heal wounds and express beauty. They can be tools to imagine new possibilities and bring them into being. At the same time, I have come to see that their power is double-edged: they can be used to hurt or inspire, cut down or build up, divide or unite, animate or repress. They can speak some kind of truth and illuminate that which is in darkness or distort, confuse, misrepresent and obscure. And sometimes, they may just waste time, energy and paper.

In academia, the press to "publish or perish" can lead to the production of a great deal of verbiage. How many of those words are really memorable or useful for transforming the world? What would we write if we were not just trying to secure tenure or a degree but being fully intentional about how our words can contribute to what we want to bring about? Are we in touch with both our minds and our hearts, as we bring these together in the activity of writing, producing texts that will take on lives of their own? What do we want those texts to do?

Of course, we can't really know how our words will be taken up or what they will be used to do. We don't have control over how they will be received, whatever our aims might be. Even with their tremendous potential power for good or evil, words are imperfect tools. Being mindful of the words we use will never mean that we will get them all "just right" – exactly as we might intend or hope our readers will understand. We can make our word choices quite mindfully and still have them "bruised or misunderstood," as Audre Lorde[32] wrote. We can think we are very clear and miss something that may lie underneath our own consciousness. All we can do is be as conscious as we can.

Listen through others' ears

Having trusted colleagues and friends read our words is one way to see beneath their surface. It can be helpful to have people who are both close to your fieldwork and quite distant from it respond to our re-presentations. What do they take from our descriptions? What more do they want to know? Where do they have an emotional response: to a word, an idea, or something they feel is missing? I sometimes ask readers just to highlight words they had any reaction to at all, without retreating to their heads to try to explain their reactions to me. I can then revisit my word choices, hearing them better through the ears of my readers.

Some of the best ears for our write-ups, in terms of holding us accountable for the truth and kindness of our representations, are those of our participants. Who better to respond to our re-presentations than the people we are assuming the power to represent? Can we find ways to speak whatever truth we feel compelled to name, but do so in ways that our participants will also find true, and fair? Is there anyone you would *not* want to read your re-presentation? Why?

If you can't or don't want to share your actual words with your participants – and there could be many reasons why this might be difficult to do – you can, at least, imagine yourself reading to them. When I imagine that I am the teachers I write about, or the students, or parents, I hear my own words in new ways. I see how the subtle word choices that I discussed in Chapter Four can reveal my own stance vis-á-vis these participants. Small adjustments may convey the same points in more compassionate and connecting ways. This is challenging when writing "critical" analyses of power relations, but I think we can name power processes while still being kind to those we might want to critique or who might not like to hear what we have to say.

When you really have things you *want* to say from your fieldwork, that speak to some larger truths about the world, and that you think-feel are important to share – both helpful and truthful – you may begin to find your own, unique and appropriately authoritative voice. You can temper your claims to absolute truth while still offering your own perspective, your own summary of many hours in the field and your own re-voicing of other people's lived experiences as a gift to the world.

BOX 6.1 ACTIVITY: INVITE YOUR INFORMANTS INTO YOUR RE-PRESENTATIONS

Imagine yourself sitting in a room with some of your key informants. Picture each of them in turn, looking at you. Look into their eyes, and try to see into their hearts as well. Invite them to listen to you as you share with them some of your representations. Read aloud from your drafts, and imagine them listening to you. How do you imagine they will respond?

BOX 6.2 ACTIVITY: WRITING PROMPTS

Thomas Larson,[33] writing about the genre of memoire, offers a list of lies that memoirists often commit. I suggest several from his list that might be extended to ethnographers, especially auto-ethnographers, and those of us who aim to be honest about our participation in the field: "the 'white lie, or leaving stuff out'; the 'lie of emotional evasion,' or not writing about things one is truly ashamed of; the 'lie of the re-created self,' or making one's self look good by emphasizing the right events that will bring out the writer's better behavior."

Write freely to this prompt: What "lies" have you told about your fieldwork? What are you holding back on, out of fears, uncertainties or insecurity? What emotional truths may you be withholding? What would it feel like to write them into your story? Try writing an interlude that reveals some of your feelings to yourself.

Notes

1 Sanders (2014).
2 A distinction between truth and "emotional truth" has been made by memoirists, who struggle with the unreliability of human memory as they narrate the details of their lives (for which they did not, most likely, write fieldnotes!). Some writers opt for "emotional truth" – i.e., a story that feels true to the emotions experienced in a given situation. I'm using emotional truth in that sense but also asking about truth in terms of honesty. Holding back on our emotions is, arguably, a way of being untrue to them, akin to the "lies" that Larson (2007) names. See also Barrington (1997), Karr (2016), Kephart (2013) and Murdock (2003).
3 Kris Gutierrez and Barbara Rogoff (2003) discuss the ways in which the use of the "ethnographic present" tense can reinforce essentialized notions of cultural practices.
4 Behar (1996).
5 Behar (1996: 78).
6 Behar (1996: 86).
7 Behar (1996).
8 Peshkin (1991).
9 Bellino (2017).
10 Bellino (personal communication, June 2019) took on the challenges of listening fully to people who hold different political ideologies, including ones that differ from her own.
11 See Luttrell (2003).
12 For example, when I wrote the introduction to my book about the after-school program I have worked in in Los Angeles for the last ten years, I started by explaining my own prior experiences as a teacher and an activist in this community. I then moved to introduce some of the kids. A friend said, "Why don't you start with the kids" (Gracias Ericka). So I flipped the order: I started with a portrait of the kids and then backed into my story of coming into this work with them. It was important for me to know where I was starting from, but it is not necessary for readers to start there.
13 Bochner and Ellis (2016: 26).
14 Bochner and Ellis (2016: 55).
15 I was inspired by both Oliveira (2017) and Mangual Figueroa (forthcoming) in organizing this book with interludes as well. The interludes seemed to invite a more personal stance and narrative style.
16 This work will appear in a forthcoming book (Mangual Figueroa, under review).
17 Luttrell (2003) doesn't claim that the images speak for themselves; she includes her analyses that emerged from conversations with the girls, but she notes that she tried not to privilege her interpretations over the girls' direct representations.
18 All ethnographers gather far more raw material than we can ever do justice to, but as Lisa Dorner (personal communication, July 12, 2019) reminded me when she read this passage, we can always re-visit, re-think and re-work this material into new re-presentations, coming to new insights as we do.
19 Scheper-Hughes (1993: xi–xii).
20 Ty-Ron Douglas (2017) distinguishes research (as external investigations of what is known), me-search (inward interrogations "of who I am at the core") and "we-search" (focused on what is needed by those whom we aim to serve).
21 Rockwell (2009).
22 Behar (1993: 338).
23 Ghen (2018).
24 My father did not go to college. In his later years, he began writing a column for his church newsletter. I would read his essays and struggle to understand what he really wanted to say. He seemed to be trying too hard to be erudite. Initially, I felt critical. Slowly, I came to recognize this as a voice of over-compensation likely due to imposter syndrome – and to hear more compassionately that voice when it arises in my own and others' writing as well.

25 Howard Becker (2007) writes about being "terrorized by the literature" – a paralyzing fear that many young scholars feel (as well as older scholars like myself, because it is perhaps even harder to keep up on the current literature once the demands of our work take over; the graduate school "luxury" of time to read is something to be treasured – but it's hard to treasure if we feel terrorized).

26 Academia has entered into a new era that I sometimes call the "awards culture." I understand the importance of recognizing good work and the political need to support young scholars in securing their place in this business. Awards can do both those things. But whose work gets rewarded, and whose does not? Does the drive to write things that others will "like" delimit what we are willing to say?

27 Cintrón (1997: 3–4).

28 Jason De Leon (2015) struggled with his representations of death at the border in *The Land of open graves: Living and dying on the migrant trail*. He admits to a flattening of his own affect, in which "disturbing images lost their edge," because "as an observer, you grow accustomed to seeing strangers cry at the drop of a hat. Tears no longer had the impact they once did." He writes that he "fought sensory overload so as not to lose sight of the big picture or the brutal details," trying to write down everything so that he could later connect the observed realities to larger structural forces" – trying to convince himself that that is what he must do, as an ethnographer/witness of these terrible things.

29 Scheper-Hughes (1993: xii).

30 Lawrence-Lightfoot (1997, 1983).

31 Bellino (personal communication, June 2019).

32 I've been inspired by Audre Lorde (2007) to be bolder than I might be otherwise. She wrote that what is most important to us "must be spoken, made verbal and shared, even at the risk of having it bruised or misunderstood." Consider Brené Brown's (2017) popular, research-based lessons on the power of vulnerability and "the courage to stand alone" and take bold stances.

33 Larson (2007).

References

Barrington, J. (1997). *Writing the memoire: From truth to art.* Portland, OR: The Eighth Mountain Press.

Becker, H. (2007). *Writing for social scientists: How to start and finish your thesis, book or article,* 2nd edition. Chicago, IL: University of Chicago Press.

Behar, R. (1993). *Translated woman: Crossing the border with Esperanza's story.* Boston: Beacon Press.

Behar, R. (1996). *The vulnerable observer: Anthropology that breaks your heart.* Boston: Beacon Press.

Bellino, M. (2017). *Youth in postwar Guatemala: Education and civic identity in transition.* New Brunswick, NJ: Rutgers University Press.

Bochner, A. and Ellis, C. (2016). *Evocative ethnography: Writing lives and telling stories.* New York: Routledge.

Brown, B. (2017). *Braving the wilderness: The quest for true belonging and the courage to stand alone.* New York: Random House.

Cintrón, R. (1997). *Angel's town: Chero ways, gang life, and rhetorics of the everyday.* Boston, MA: Beacon Press.

De León, J. (2015). *The land of open graves: Living and dying on the migrant trail.* Berkeley, CA: University of California Press.

Douglas, T.-R. (2017). My reasonable response: Activating research, meSearch, and WeSearch to build systems of healing. *Critical Education,* 8 (2), 21–30.

Ghen, S. T. (2018). *Writing toward wholeness: Lessons inspired by C. G. Jung.* Asheville, NC: Chiron Publications.

Gutierrez, K. and Rogoff, B. (2003). Cultural ways of learning: Enduring traits or repertoires of practice. *Educational Researcher,* 32 (5), 19–25.

Karr, M. (2016). *The art of memoire.* New York: Harper Perennial.

Kephart, B. (2013). *Handling the truth: On the writing of memoire.* New York: Gotham Books.

Larson, T. (2007). *The memoir and the memoirist: Reading and writing personal narrative.* Athens, OH: Swallow Press and Ohio University Press.

Lawrence-Lightfoot, S. (1983). *The good high school: Portraits of character and culture.* New York: Basic Books.

Lawrence-Lightfoot, S. (1997). *Art and science of portraiture.* Hoboken, NJ: John Wiley & Sons.

Lorde, A. (2007). *Sister outsider: Essays and speeches.* Berkeley, CA: Crossing Press.

Luttrell, W. (2003). *Pregnant bodies, fertile minds.* New York: Routledge.

Mangual Figueroa, A. (under review).

Murdock, M. (2003). *Unreliable truth: On memoire and memory.* New York: Seal Press.

Oliveira, G. (2017). *Motherhood across borders: Immigrants and their children in Mexico and New York.* New York: New York University Press.

Peshkin, A. (1991). *The color of strangers, the color of friends.* Chicago: University of Chicago Press.

Rockwell, E. (2009). *La experiencia etnográfica: Historia y cultura en los procesos educativos.* Buenos Aires: Paidós.

Scheper-Hughes, N. (1996). *Death without weeping: The violence of everyday life in Brazil.* Berkeley, CA: University of California Press.

Sanders, E. F. (2014). *Lost in translation: An illustrated compendium of untranslatable words from around the world.* New York: Ten Speed Press.

Walkerine, V. (1997). *Daddy's little girl: Young girls and popular culture.* Cambridge, MA: Harvard University Press.

Interlude VI

MEDITATIONS ON WRITING

Connecting mind, heart and earth

Locating myself in particular moments and spaces when these words were first put together, and later revised, helped me to experience the power of place for writing. Planting my feet on the earth (or the floor above that earth), I thought about those who had moved through this geospatial, metaphysical and intellectual space before me. I share from a voice recording as I prepared to write this final chapter:

> I'm seated on a wooden stump, about twelve inches high – one of a dozen or so lined up on the top of a hill above the Deer Park Monastery in Escondido, California.[1] I'm participating in a retreat at this Buddhist center, which was founded by the Vietnamese monk Thich Naht Hahn, who took as his life mission the work of bringing an engaged form of Buddhism to the West. A half dozen other lay retreatants and I are living as the monks and nuns do: following a schedule of walking, sitting, working and eating meditation. All around the center are signs reminding us to be present wherever we are. Today is designated "lazy day" and we are free to do whatever we like. I took myself on a hike up to this lookout in this early morning hour, bringing along my trusty voice recorder, and I was inspired to dictate these musings.
>
> The mist shrouds the ocean off in the distance. There are birds calling. I know there are blue jays, woodpeckers and humming birds, because I have seen them, but I can't distinguish their calls, and I don't see any right now. Except for the birds, what feels most palpable here is the silence: like a blanket, covering me and the hills around. The colors are muted, shades of green, punctuated by orange, yellow, green, blue-painted cabins down below. The chaparral is quite dry and I think about climate change and the work we did yesterday to clear the dry brush near the roads, as a fire prevention strategy.
>
> I sit here, my feet planted on the ground, looking out at the hillside, wondering about the irony of thinking about this book rather than being fully present in the here and now. It seems I am retreating to my head when I should be in my body, in my senses, in the Now. Or is this very idea – that when we think we are somehow disconnected from our bodies and from the earth around us when we write – a product of Cartesian dualism? I plant my

feet more firmly and realize I can be in both my head and my body simultaneously and that that connection may actually fuel what I want to say.

I had just finished reading a slim book about writing by Robert Yagelski, called *Writing as a way of being: Writing instruction, nonduality and the crisis of sustainability.*[2] This book revolutionized my thinking for this last chapter and gave me a whole new way of understanding the work that I do as a writer. It helped me see that I don't need to apologize to my mindful self for spending time writing. Nor do I need to see writing as a retreat "into my head" and away from the world at all. Influenced by Yagelski, as I sat on that hilltop, I further mused:

> Perhaps, in dictating these words – and later when I will write them up – I can actually connect *more*, rather than less deeply with the world around me and with beings who populate it than I would if I tried to shut down my thinking mind. My senses are vehicles for taking *in* the world, but my words – both spoken and written – are vehicles for *connecting* inner and outer worlds. I can be both in my body and my senses and in my mind simultaneously. This scene that I imbibe all around me will become part of my book; I will carry it with me in my mind's eye and in some sense, impressed upon the cells of my body, when I go and sit at my computer and peck out these words. For sure, it will be transmuted and transformed as it passes from experience into these spoken words, and it will further mutate as it moves into words on the page, through an editing process, and into publication, before reaching readers who did not sit with me on this morning, looking out, experiencing this juncture of the space-time continuum with me. But you have experienced other moments of wonder, spirit and connection to the earth, and I hope you can connect those experiences to these words to grasp a little more of what I am trying to say – and bring that into your own work as well.

I encountered Yagelski's book late in the process of writing this one. It was like meeting a friend. A kindred spirit. An inspiring muse. My academic scholar mind first worried: perhaps Yagelski or people who have read his work will think I have copied him – because so much of what I have already written resonates so deeply with what he wrote there. The same could be said of other authors as well, I'm sure.

Then I stopped and laughed to myself. How silly we academics are, thinking ideas are the unique property of individuals rather than instruments for changing the world. When I identified principally as an activist, I was happy when I found others who thought like me and said the things I said. Together, this made the messages we delivered louder. Wouldn't it be fabulous if the world were flooded with the values we believe in?

I recognize that this is complicated in academia, where individuals stand to benefit from the ownership of ideas, originality matters and ego reins.[3] Giving credit where credit can be important to counter especially histories of appropriation, the politics of citations (in which the rich get richer, as those with greater visibility become more visible – and not surprisingly, those people are disproportionately white, male and from the global, English-speaking north). Part of our work should involve a conscientious effort to bring neglected, muted and silenced voices to the table and into dialogue. But we can *connect* our ideas with those of others, giving them more visibility even as we build a larger, shared vision together.

When this book is finished, Routledge Publishing Company will own the rights to the copyedited final version. I will "own" (in some odd sense of ownership) the particular ways I chose to put these ideas into words on these pages. But I can't claim these ideas are uniquely "mine." I have tried as best I could to locate my ideas within larger histories, putting them together in my own way while still honoring the ideas of others. My aim has been to bring together voices and perspectives that are not often in the same conversations, thus helping to spread their reach, and then to offer them to the world, in the hope that the conversation will continue and grow.

Treating our writing as a gift shifts our attention in some important ways. Sometimes the gifts we receive are not the ones we hoped for or expected, but if we accept them with open hearts, we may find something useful or surprising in them. The task for the gift-giver is to prepare the gifts with love and care and then *let them go.*

Notes

1 https://deerparkmonastery.org/plan-a-visit/?gclid=CjwKCAjw2qHsBRAGEiwAMb PoDMsXNs5ZLkZq16bV3T3nJ1uFnvKa5Y0uX42-q2Co_BuJ2xORUSeoDRoCkuk QAvD_BwE.
2 Yagelski (2011).
3 See Patel (2014) for an anti-colonialist critique of publishing property rights.

References

Patel, L. (2014). Countering coloniality in educational research: From ownership to answerability. *Educational Studies: A Journal of the American Educational Studies Association*, 50 (4), 355–377.

Yagelski, R. (2011). *Writing as a way of being: Writing instruction, nonduality, and the crisis of sustainability.* New York, NY: Hampton Press.

7

LETTING GO

"Letting go gives us freedom, and freedom is the only condition for happiness. If, in our heart, we still cling to anything — anger, anxiety, or possessions — we cannot be free."
Thich Naht Hanh[1]

One of the most important adages of Buddhism is captured in the words, "Let it go." Let go of our attachment to things and ideas. Let go of expectations, hurts and worries. When we hang on to thoughts, feelings, concepts and mental formations, we suffer. This is not a letting-go with *resignation* or resentment. It's not about letting go of doing what we can do to reduce suffering, address injustices and make the world a better place. It's about knowing that we have done or are doing what we can do, the best we can. It's about letting go of the things that may actually hold us back from doing better, different or more transformative work.

In this chapter I consider what we have to be willing to let go of, to let be, to set free, as we loosen our words from the chains to our computers and our minds and put our ideas out in the world. I share the things I am trying to let go of as I finish this book. I recognize that it is much easier to say these things from a secure position with tenure. But I hope young researchers will still find something of value in these words, and perhaps some support for your own tenure cases, as well as for choices you make about how to contribute to the world as you live out your lives.

Letting go of completion

As the deadline(s) I had established with my publisher approached, I became keenly aware of the press to produce in academia – the "publish or perish" maxim that haunts most young researchers. I asked myself what underlies this fear of perishing, since we all, ultimately, do perish at the end of our lives. What are we racing toward or running from? What if I actually did die before I published this book?

Arguably, doing and producing more, more and more can be a way of avoiding acknowledgment of the deadlines we will all meet one day, at the end of our lives.[2] I tried to embrace the possibility that this book might never see the light of day – or that I might not be there to see it be published – and write it anyway. Why? Because I *wanted* to, because something compelled me, because I felt I had something to say. But I also tried to slow my press to reach some elusive finish line[3] and let go of the idea of absolute completion.

I certainly don't have a definitive final word for all of the epistemological questions I have raised in this book. I can't tell you how to write your own ethnography: how to balance description and analysis; how to bring your readers into the story while reminding them that it is a story; how to hold responsibility for your narration while recognizing that it is only one way that a story could be told; and how to proffer some kind of truth while accepting that it will always, inevitably, be partial. I can't resolve the paradoxes I have named or offer the perfect balance of head, heart and activity. I can't tie this package up with a neat, pretty bow.

Instead, I hope that the questions themselves and the illustrations I have offered will help you to find your own way through the forest, as it were – or whatever part of the forest you are wandering in right now. I hope that I have sparked some conversations you can have with yourself and with others and that these ideas will lead you somewhere interesting and be useful for your own journey in academia and in life – just as the many, many words of other people have led me here. I am sure that my own ideas will continue to develop as I read more texts, talk with more people, hear the reactions that others have to my words, meditate more, engage in social action and live a little longer on the planet.

Eduardo Kohn writes about lineages of signs that extend into the future such that "each instantiation will interpret the previous one in a way that can, in turn, be interpreted by a future one."[4] And so it is with writing; indeed, academic writing demands that we connect our thoughts to others' in self-conscious and explicit ways. These interconnections build ideas and, hopefully, allow them to grow and change. For Kohn, thoughts are living. Just like biological creatures, their progeny may or may not survive into the future; "ideas may or may not be taken up in the thinking of a future reader"[5] of this book. I can only hope they will – not in proscriptive or constraining ways, but in generative ones – just as Kohn's words were so inspirational for me.

Letting go of perfection

I worked on this book long and hard, in fits and starts over a three-year period, filling my nights, weekends and summer breaks with countless hours of writing, editing, reading and re-writing. I grappled – and danced, or played[6] – with both the ideas and the words I used to express them. This process could have gone on ad infinitum: writing more or fewer words, adding more citations, deleting redundancy, soliciting more feedback, moving sections around, tightening, fine-tuning, tweaking and chiseling. I could have added more caveats and conditions to sharpen points, deepen my own understanding and, perhaps, ward off some critique. I knew I would eventually have to decide when my time and energy would be better redirected to other things, and either hand this manuscript over to a publisher or file it away in a dark corner of my computer. (In this "publish or perish" world we should always remember that publishing is our *choice*. If you are reading this you will know which choice I made.) My aim is for the sweet spot of "good enough"[7] – good enough to share with others, good enough to be of some value in the world. Not perfect.

Letting go of worries

I have not always practiced what I preach in this book, and in writing it, a new form of "imposter syndrome" presented itself. Who was I to proclaim an approach to "mindful research" that I am relatively new to and that really doesn't come easily to me? I know that I have much to learn and that my own journey continues. It has deepened through the writing of this book.

Periodically, as I wrote, I worried about how it would be received. What would my scholar friends think about this turn I've taken in my academic work? Would my activist friends see me as having gone "too soft"? I worried a little less about the opinions of spiritual practitioners; they may merely raise their eyebrows at the obsession that academics seem to have with trying to fix everything in just the right words.

Letting go of expectations

If I'm honest, I'll admit that I hope people will *like* what I wrote. Thus, part of my "letting go" is to accept that some will like what I have to say and some won't,[8] and the flip side of letting go of worries is to let go of expectations as well. Readers will have their own reactions based on their own journeys in research and in life. Some may find the words they need for their own work; others may return to these ideas at a later time. For some they may not resonate or feel useful at all. Could I allow that just to be and still offer my grain of sand and hope that it will be useful to some people in some way? We might think of our writing as a gift that others can accept, or not, as they choose.

Letting go of ego

When we stop worrying so much about what we will have to say at the end of the day, or the year, or how others will judge our findings, we create room for curiosity, interest, pleasure and even joy in our work. We may wonder, imagine and delight in what we find as we see the world with fresh eyes. We may discover things that help us live more fully – engaging more completely in the activities of our chosen profession, rather than focusing all our attention on future goals, hoped-for outcomes and elusive end products.

Mindfulness practices can help calm the anxieties that inevitably arise as we try to make our way and stake our place in the business of academia. We may still *feel* some degree of stress or pressure about our work, but we can get better at noticing those anxieties and accepting them as part of the process. Simply acknowledging them can help them to have less power over us. All of this can soften the egoic force of academic work. In a business that builds altars to the human ego, we will likely never transcend our egos entirely, but we can recognize when they take center stage, driving our actions and feelings. We can distance our work as best we can from an anxiety-inducing sense of ownership and fears of judgment. We can also notice what new understandings emerge when we loosen our tight grasp on truth claims we have invested in, and keep open a sense of wondering.

Letting go of the field

The hardest thing that we may need to let go of at some point is our field site, and the relations we established therein. Unless you have an ongoing space for engaged field work and community-based social action – as I am happy to have had in Los Angeles for the last eleven years[9] – you may, at some point, have to say goodbye to your study participants, and move on. Even in my site there are goodbyes that happen every year, as members of our club age out of the program and members of our research team move through the hoops of their school careers. Our site continues, with some sustained membership, but there is also considerable turnover. Some relationships run their course and need to be let go.

The important thing to remember is that these *are* relationships and they should be let go – or continued in new form – with thought and care. Ariana Mangual Figueroa[10] was the first scholar I know of to have put focused attention not just on how we enter field sites but on how we exit them. How will you exit yours? Will you leave some of your re-presentations behind, in some form? What will you take in your heart, and what do you hope to leave in the hearts of the people you met?

BOX 7.1 ACTIVITY: PRACTICING GRATITUDE

Make a list of all the gifts you received from your fieldwork experience. Write a thank you letter to your participants. Tell them what you learned from them, what you appreciate about them and what you are grateful for.

Make another list of the things you want to let go of as you wrap up your fieldwork. Fear? Worry? Anxiety? Regrets? Counterbalance this with reflections on what you hope to take with you, and put out into the world.

BOX 7.2 ACTIVITY: CONTINUING THE JOURNEY

Now that you have reached the end of this book (whether or not you took a direct or a more circuitous and punctuated path through this book), take a minute to sit with your thoughts. What thoughts and feelings have surfaced for you? What do you want to explore more? What will you bring from these ideas into your own work? What might you leave behind?

Notes

1 Naht Hahn (1997).
2 *The Tibetan book of the dead* and, its more modernized counterpart, *The Tibetan book of living and dying* (Rinpoche et al, 2012) offer a profound meditation on life as preparation for the one deadline that will someday meet us all. Lyall Crawford (2009: 159) offers another kind of meditation on death in an auto-ethnographic text, detailing how as a young man he witnessed a friend be eaten by crocodiles: "watching a young and vital person suddenly cease to exist snapped me into a different and more encompassed order of living." He elaborates: "The conviction that 'now is all there is' brings a certain slant to the ethnographic process. It engenders a certain kind of mindfulness. It makes the doing and writing and performing of ethnography a particular path for waking up and preparing for death" (p. 161).

　　When we recognized our inevitable, shared fate as living beings – our common vulnerability – we may better rise above the things that divide us. We come to see how tiny we are in the grand scheme of things and how so many of the things that we fear and worry about are not so important. (And even if they *are*, worrying about them doesn't keep them from happening.)

3 I recognize that this may feel jarring to young scholars, who receive very different messages in the academy. The growing movement for "Slow Scholarship" may provide some ammunition for arguments to tenure committees about the importance of slowing down in order to do *better* scholarly work – and help the academy resist neoliberal pressures of production. See Berg and Seeber (2016), Bergland (2018), Harland et al. (2015), Hartman and Darab (2012), Mountz et al. (2015), and Stewart and Valian (2018). See also *The inclusive academy* (2018) for consideration of how a focus on fast productivity especially hurts women and scholars of color. These arguments are particularly important in a time when much attention is going to the popular notion of "grit" (Duckworth, 2016) – with the implication that those who don't make it just weren't resilient or "gritty" enough. There is extensive debate about the construct of grit; see Credé et al. (2017), Chandra (2016) and Love (2019) for some critiques.

4 Kohn (2013: 77).
5 Kohn (2013: 77).
6 Writing this made me realize how much academia, and politics, pulls me toward the language of "struggle." Indeed, there are many struggles in life, and recognizing them can help us know where we want to put our energy. But more and more I'm convinced that there are other ways to think about this energy work: as dance, play, engagement with the world, as being animated from within and motivated by love, not tension or resistance. See also Box 5A. I am trying to self-consciously choose language that is more uplifting and embracing. I often slip.
7 I connect here with several inspiring women who call for "good enough-ness" in our work:

　　Nancy Scheper-Hughes (1993: 28), who, tired of postmodernist critiques (I might add, the many other kinds of critiques that academics seem so good at), wrote: "Given the perilous times in which we and our subjects live, I am inclined toward a compromise that calls for the practice of a 'good enough' ethnography." Acknowledging the limitations of her viewpoint, she offered, "Nonetheless, like every other master artisan (and I dare say that at our best we are this), we struggle to do the best we can with the limited resources we have at hand – our ability to listen and observe carefully, empathically, and compassionately."

Wendy Luttrell (2003), in an article titled "Good enough methods for ethnographic research," echoes this, noting that we need to be vulnerable enough to defend against our own fantasy of being the perfectly self-conscious, reflexive researcher. (See also Luttrell's, 2019, review of reflexive qualitative research in the Oxford Research Encyclopedia of Education.)

The third inspiration is my performance-artist daughter, Elisa Noemí, who has long played with the initials of her full inherited name, Elisa Noemí Orellana Faulstich, trying to see herself as "good ENOF" – or just ENOF – not punished by the impossible standards of perfection of the world. With training in clowning techniques, she embraces mistakes as a way of revealing our imperfect human nature, allowing us to take ourselves a little less seriously, laugh at our shortcomings and perhaps let others off the hook as well.

8   My brother Robert listened to me talk through many dilemmas as I wrote this book, trying to take on thorny issues as clearly as I could. "If everyone likes it, you've failed," he told me. "And you can quote me on that." These ideas are by their very nature unsettling, not safe, easy or free of controversy (as is life).

9   *Immigrant children in transcultural spaces: Language, learning and love* (Orellana, 2016) reports on the first six years of this program. The program is part of a larger network of community-university partnerships, UC-Links, with programs that have been sustained against odds over many years, after first being established by Mike Cole in San Diego in the 1990s. (See Cole and the Distributed Literacy Curriculum, 2006; see Vasquez (2002) and Flores et al. (2014) for reports from other long-standing sites. For more information about the UC-Links networks, see https://uclinks.berkeley.edu/.)

10 Mangual Figueroa (2017).

References

Berg, M. and Seeber, B. K. (2016). *The slow professor: Challenging the culture of speed in the academy.* Toronto, Ontario: University of Toronto Press.

Bergland, B. (2018). The incompatibility of neoliberal university structures and interdisciplinary knowledge: A feminist slow scholarship critique. *Educational Philosophy and Theory,* 50 (11), 1031–1036.

Chandra, R. (2016). Grit: Is it Baloney? *Psychology Today.* Retrieved from www.psychology-today.com/us/blog/the-pacific-heart/201606/grit-is-it-baloney.

Cole, M., Vasquez, O. and Distributive Literacy Consortium. (2006). *The fifth dimension: An after-school program built on diversity.* New York: Russell Sage Foundation.

Crawford, L. (2009). Personal ethnography. *Communications Monographs,* 63 (2), 158–170.

Credé, M., Tynan, M. C. and Harms, P. D. (2017). Much ado about grit: A meta-analytic synthesis of the grit literature. *Journal of Personality and Social Psychology,* 113 (3), 492.

Duckworth, A. (2016). *Grit: The power of passion and perseverance.* New York: Scribner.

Flores, B. B., Vásquez, O. A. and Clark, E. R. (2014). *Transworld pedagogy: Reimagining la clase mágica.* Lanham, MD: Lexington Books.

Harland, T., McLean, A., Wass, R., Miller, E. and Sim, K. N. (2015). An assessment arms race and its fallout: High-stakes grading and the case for slow scholarship. *Assessment & Evaluation in Higher Education,* 40 (4), 528–541.

Hartman, Y. and Darab, S. (2012). A call for slow scholarship: A case study on the intensification of academic life and its implications for pedagogy. *Review of Education, Pedagogy, and Cultural Studies*, 34 (1–2), 49–60.

Kohn, E. (2013). *How forests think: Toward an anthropology beyond the human.* Berkeley, CA: University of California Press.

Love, B. L. (2019). *We want to do more than survive: Abolitionist teaching and the pursuit of American freedom.* Boston, MA: Beacon Press.

Luttrell, W. (2010). *Qualitative educational research: Readings in reflexive methodology and transformative practice.* New York: Routledge.

Mangual Figueroa, A. (2017). Speech or silence: Undocumented students' decisions to disclose or disguise their citizenship status in school. *American Educational Research Journal*, 54 (3), 485–523.

Mountz, A., Bonds, A., Mansfield, B., Loyd, J., Hyndman, J., Walton-Roberts, M. and Curran, W. (2015). For slow scholarship: A feminist politics of resistance through collective action in the neoliberal university. *ACME: An International E-Journal for Critical Geographies*, 14 (4).

Naht Hahn, T. (1997). *Stepping into freedom: An introduction to Buddhist monastic teaching.* Berkeley, CA: Parallax Press.

Orellana, M. F. (2016). *Immigrant children in transcultural spaces: Language, learning and love.* New York: Routledge.

Patel, L. (2014). Countering coloniality in educational research: From ownership to answerability. *Educational Studies: A Journal of the American Educational Studies Association*, 50 (4), 355–377.

Rinpoche, S. (2012). *Tibetan book of living and dying: The spiritual classic and international bestseller.* San Francisco: Harper.

Rinpoche, S., Gaffney, P. (Ed.), Harvey, A. (Ed.) The Tibetan book of living and dying. London: Rider Books.

Scheper-Hughes, N. (1996). *Death without weeping: The violence of everyday life in Brazil.* Berkeley, CA: University of California Press.

Stewart, A. J. and Valian, V. (2018). *An inclusive academy: Achieving diversity and excellence.* Cambridge: The MIT Press.

Vasquez, O. (2002). *La clase mágica: Imagining optimal possibilities in a bilingual community of learners.* New York: Routledge.

INDEX

Note: Page numbers in *italics* indicate figures.

academia: analytical mind and 4; awards
    culture in 156n26; dualistic thinking and
    30–31; generative tensions and 11–12;
    mindfulness and 4; publish or perish
    culture 153, 161, 165n3; slow scholarship
    in 165n3; thought-feeling approach in
    66–67
acceptance 94–95
activism 11, 12, 15–16
activist 4. 5, 7, 11, 12, 13, 18, 54, 57, 77, 95,
    105, 126, 153, 155n, 159, 163
activities: Continuing the journey 165;
    Doing things differently 67–69; Inviting
    informants into re-presentations 154;
    Letting your mind settle 19; Making the
    strange familiar 70; "Metta" meditation
    for ethnographers 96–97; Pause 41;
    Playing with your field notes 120; Post-
    field analytical memo/meditation 135;
    Practicing gratitude 164; Revisiting our
    field sites in our minds 120; Writing
    prompts 154
alternative facts 27
analysis: dance/movement and 133; data
    128–130; doodling/drawing and
    131–132, *132*, 133; dreams and 130–131,
    136n12; listening and 129–130; listening
    with heart 130; singing the harmonies of
    data in 133–134; slowing it down 128,
    129; taxonomic approach to 127–128;
    telling the story of 134–135; unconscious

processes and 130; unsettling data 134;
    unsettling ourselves 125–127, 134
analytical mind 4, 47–49, 70
anthropology: beyond the human 97n2,
    98n7; colonialist history of 28–29;
    insider/outsider positionalities in
    42n13; reflexive turn in 88, 144; *see also*
    ethnography
audience 14–15
authoritative voice 148–149, 154
auto-ethnography 2, 20n2, 50–52, 146, 154
axiology 40

Becker, Howard 63, 112
Behar, Ruth 88, 98n20, 143–144, 149
Being Ethnographic (Madden) 28
Bellino, Michelle 145, 152
Bentz, Valerie Malhotra 2, 28, 38, 40–41
Blackhawk, N. 31
Bochner, Arthur 146
Bone Black (hooks) 22n35
Botelho, Maria José 81
Brach, Tara 6–7, 93, 99n23
Braiding Sweetgrass (Kimmerer) 42n21, 83
Brayboy, B. M. J. 31
Briggs, Jeanne 98n19
Buber, Martin 78
Buddhism 7–8, 19, 21n14, 38, 41, 158, 161

cancelling 40, 43n43
Cartesian thinking 30–31, 158